The Money Mirror

*How Money Reflects Women's
Dreams, Fears, and Desires*

Annette Lieberman
& Vicki Lindner

ALLWORTH PRESS

Published by Allworth Press
an imprint of Allworth Communications, Inc.
10 East 23rd Street, New York, NY 10010

Cover design by Douglas Design Associates, New York, NY

Book design by Sharp Des!gns, Holt, MI

ISBN: 1-880559-41-2

Library of Congress Catalog Card Number: 96-83239

To our parents

Dorothy and Irving Lieberman

and

Mary and Victor Lindner

*who made it possible for us
to become the kind of women
we wanted to be*

Acknowledgments

We would like to thank Neil Shandalow, economist and financial adviser, who gave knowledge, inspiration, and support to this project; writer Jacqueline Thompson, who knew about money and steered us to much of the biographical material we used in this book; Berenice Hoffman, literary agent; Tad Crawford, who conceived the Allworth Press edition; Ellen Gorman Forbes and Martha Niebanck, who organized and hosted our suburban and Massachusetts money-awareness groups, respectively. Most of all, we would like to thank the 123 women who participated in our money study, particularly those who agreed to be interviewed. Without them, this book would not exist. We are especially grateful to the women in our New York money awareness groups, who met over a period of a year and gave themselves, body and soul, to the emotionally trying subject of money. We can only hope these generous women took away a portion of the knowledge that they offered us.

Table of Contents

Introduction

T his is a book for women who want to connect the meaning of money to their inner lives.

We are not going to tell our readers how to earn higher salaries. Instead, we will help them examine the personal fears and social pressures that hold them back from deciding how much money they want and need. We will not give specifics of different retirement plans, or explain the difference between a stock and a bond. Instead, we will explore the deeply rooted reservations that have kept women away from the hundreds of finance books already in libraries and on bookstore shelves. We will tell our readers why they spend too much, save too much, and fear becoming homeless bag ladies in their old age. We will describe the way ambitious women confuse their emotions with financial issues when they negotiate with employers, or with important people in their personal lives.

Most important, we will show our readers how to define and discover their true financial identities by looking at the messages about women and money that they have gotten from their culture over time, and the way those messages were transmitted by their families and internalized. We will reveal how the "money myths" we inherited in childhood plague our relationships with intimate partners, friends, and family members, and keep us from living happy, healthy financial lives.

We believe that when women look into their money mirrors—at the reasons for their financial behavior—they take the first step toward positive change.

We are not writing for the highly successful women (too few) who seem to "have it all"; nor are we writing for the women (too many) clinging to the poverty line. We are addressing women like ourselves—college-educated, middle-class professionals who have achieved, or want to achieve, significant career goals, but who are also struggling with personal, domestic, and work-related issues. These are the women who, like ourselves, could be doing better with money and who could use knowledge about their relationship with money to enhance their lives.

Many books have been written exploring the psychological background of other problems that afflict millions of women (love relationships and obesity, for example); ours was the first to investigate the emotional and social origins of our problems with money and to describe them in detail.

How did we come to write such a book? In the mid-eighties, Annette Lieberman, a New York psychotherapist who specializes in the psychology of women, began to notice a change in the issues that preoccupied the female patients in her clinical practice. Money began to enter her sessions with them in ways it never had before, and she observed an increasing concern with financial issues. Patients who were earning adequate (or less-than-adequate) salaries worried that emotional blocks were preventing them from making as much as their capabilities indicated they could. Some noted money troubled their relationships. Others reported irrational or compulsive spending patterns and disturbing feelings of guilt and greed in relation to money. Money was involved in fears about the future, even for women with high earnings.

Sometimes, Lieberman felt, the money issue was conspicuous because it wasn't there. Women who were living alone did not seem to recognize that taking care of themselves had a financial, as well as an emotional, component. Some, balancing on a precarious financial edge, refrained from exploring money issues and continued to dwell on problems with men. All seemed to lack the vocabulary to talk about their important financial lives. The time, Lieberman thought, was exactly right for a new kind of book, one that would provide a major breakthrough in our understanding of the emotional relationship between women and money.

Economist John Kenneth Galbraith has said, "There is nothing about money that cannot be understood by the person of reasonable curiosity, diligence and intelligence."[1] What prevents intelligent women from understanding, or wanting to understand, money? What are the fears and confusions that beset women when they earn, negotiate, invest, and manage money, and where do they come from? How do women relate to money in a modern world, where it is not only possible, but necessary, for them to be financially successful? These were the questions we asked and set out to answer.

The Money Study

We began our study of the relationship between women and money with a preconceived, and, as it turned out, inappropriate goal. In the money-hungry eighties, we wanted to tell women how to eliminate the emotional blocks that were standing between them and large amounts of money. We hoped to whip out our book in a couple of months and become gadzillionaires ourselves! We believed, like many women, that there was a "magical" attitude about money-making that certain people—mainly males—had. We thought we could discover this "money secret" and disseminate it. As we considered and researched the traditional role money has played in women's lives, talked to other women, and examined our own money issues, however, we realized it was more important to uncover the real meaning of money to women than to tell them how to make "magical megabucks." We began to realize that making a lot of money was not the answer to women's complex web of challenging external and internal difficulties. We rapidly altered our original plan: We wanted to tell women about the role money played, not only in their financial well-being, but in their inner lives.

We began our money study, then, with a simple hypothesis: Women held different perceptions of their relationship to money than men did. We set out to elicit subjective information that would expand and define this hypothesis, and that could be interpreted from a clinical perspective. We wanted to see if we could associate women's feelings about money with new theories explaining female psychological development. Unlike other researchers, we were not interested in obtaining quantifiable "yes" or "no" answers to questions like, "Do you balance your checkbook?" or in producing statistical generalizations. If it is true that three out of ten women review their finances once a week, as one study of women's financial behavior enthusiastically proclaimed, what about the remaining seven? Why weren't all ten taking care of themselves financially?

With questions like this in mind, we designed a study that would give us information about how women used money to express anxieties and joys, or to adapt to stressful personal events, and how their financial behavior reflected their upbringing and the social and economic changes that have dramatically altered women's roles since the middle of the twentieth century.

First, we asked participants to fill out a questionnaire, which we later expanded to include seventy-five questions. Although some questions asked for factual information, like the participant's marital status, job description, income, and assets, many asked for essay-type answers. We encouraged the participant to comment on her particular problems with money, and to describe her attitudes toward earning, spending, career goals, and the way money entered into her relationships. (A version of our original questionnaire is included in chapter 10, "Tools for Overcoming Money Phobia.") The participants could refuse to answer any of the questions, provided that they explained why. From the psychotherapeutic perspective, what they didn't say was as important as what they did.

We looked for American-born college-educated women who were "ambitious" (or who derived a sense of self-worth and mastery from professional achievement) to participate in the study. We did not include black women because we felt that their history and culture would put them in a different relationship to money (for example, in 1960, only a third of white women were employed, but half of black women were working), or foreign-born women, for the same reason. We sent the questionnaire to 175 women we knew, and women they recommended, who, in turn, steered us to other willing participants. We tried to get a sampling from a variety of age groups, income brackets, and occupations, and to include married, divorced, and single women. We contacted most participants personally before sending them the questionnaire, and, in some cases, "kept after them" to complete it.

One hundred and twenty-three women filled out the questionnaire. Our participants ranged in age from twenty-four to fifty-two; seventy-two were living in New York City, although the majority of these women had moved to "The Big Apple" from other parts of the country for professional reasons; fifty-two were women from other states on the Eastern seaboard, and from Western, Southern, and Midwestern states. Our participants included a sample from all the occupational categories established by the United States Department of Labor—from film makers to doctors to construction workers. Their salaries ranged from below $20,000 to over $100,000. Although about half of our participants were married or involved in intimate partnerships, only forty-three had children, reflecting, we thought, the trend for ambitious, mostly urban women to have children later, after their careers had been established. (A number of our participants gave birth to or adopted children after the study was concluded.)

From the questionnaires we selected twenty-seven women for two-hour interviews. Since we knew that these participants would provide much material cited in our book, we chose articulate women who had expressed a great deal of personal interest in our subject, and who were highly focused and self-aware (although not always about the role money played in their lives). These women had compelling "voices" and tended to dramatize the money issues, sometimes in unusual ways, that affected large numbers of women.

We also established four money-awareness groups. These were issue-oriented consciousness-raising groups designed to break barriers around the "taboo" topic of money, and help women open up and explore this little-discussed issue with us and with each other. The groups helped women define and compare money problems in order to find solutions by setting personal goals, and gave them a vocabulary for thinking and talking about financial behavior. (The format for the money-awareness group is described in chapter 10, "Tools for Overcoming Money Phobia.") Two of the groups were formed in New York and met monthly or bimonthly for almost a year. We formed another group in Massachusetts and one in a New York suburb. Altogether the groups provided us with thirty-six hours of tape, which we analyzed for our research. A number of the women who joined the money-awareness groups had also filled out the questionnaire and participated in the two-hour personal interview; they offered many hours of their time to investigating their relationship with money and provided a solid "cast of characters" for our book. We are deeply indebted to these intense, interesting, and hard-working women who gave so much of themselves to our project without getting paid.

The questionnaires, personal interviews, and money-awareness groups provided the core of our original research. In the course of the two years we worked on the book, however, we had hundreds of informal conversations with women on the subject of money, which we recorded, too. At parties, on buses and trains, in exercise classes—everywhere we went—all we had to do was mention the title of our book to a woman, and financial confessions and confusions, as well as vital information, would come pouring out.

As we investigated women's relationship with money, then, we found we were also investigating a spectrum of other problems and concerns. For women, to look at money was to look at every confusing facet of their modern identities. Our subject evoked reflections on virtually every topic of interest to women and inspired a wide range of emotions. As we discussed the meaning of money to them, our participants' reactions ran the gamut from laughter to tears. Some women cried when they talked about the money messages they had received from their parents, or about their inability to achieve all they had hoped for professionally. Sometimes we felt like crying as we listened to the sad stories that money inspired. Although money was deeply enmeshed in other problems, when the women in our study made a conscientious effort to separate it out and look at it clearly, they saw many of the other issues that troubled them from a new perspective. Sometimes they saw solutions.

The goal of our research was not to help our participating women solve specific financial problems, but to allow them to establish a new way of talking and thinking about money that they could use as they wished, hopefully, to obtain more power and freedom. Many of the women in our study did become more conscious of the role money played in their lives and thoughts, and would call to tell us about each exciting "new discovery."

Most were able to identify unproductive attitudes toward money that were keeping them from becoming more efficient earners and managers, or that were interfering with their personal relationships. Some were able to take inner knowledge to make external changes in their financial behavior. The changes were not always earthshaking: No one made a fast million after talking with us. However, because even small changes represented alterations in the woman's internal landscape, they gave her important feelings of self-esteem and control, and made her believe she was capable of greater financial accomplishments. Two of our participants became involved in their husbands' businesses. Another was able to see that she had enough money to reduce her teaching hours and pursue her vocation in art. Still another was able to take the first steps toward investing a large hunk of savings. Several became better negotiators. The women who made these changes were surprised to find financial tasks they had regarded as "formidable" easy to accomplish, once they acknowledged the need to do them and examined the emotional blocks that were standing in their way. Said one woman who learned to negotiate with her boyfriend to straighten out "who pays for what":

> Every conversation I had with him was much easier than I thought it would be. I was very anxious about ever talking money with him. And now, we're actively talking about buying a house together. It's premature, because we're both financially insecure at the moment, but we can talk about it. It feels clean, and very easy.

Our hope is that our readers, too, will learn from our book what they need to know to feel "clean and easy" about talking about money—the first step toward developing money awareness, and leading healthier, happier financial lives.

The 1996 Allworth Press Edition

By the middle of the 1990s it became apparent that the women had changed since we had written our book. The "magical" money boom of the eighties was over, and the majority of women we knew had not become high-earning "Superwomen," as that decade's ideal media image suggested they could be. In fact, as more women entered the workforce, high-paying salaries and job equality for women diminished. The women who came to Lieberman in the nineties, and participated in the money awareness workshops she gave in New York and across the country, were still ambitious, and valued professional achievement. Most, she was surprised to learn, harbored the same fears and confusions about money we had identified in the 1980s. Most needed to feel better about money. When they talked about their relationship to money the same anger, sadness, and shame—lots of shame—came pouring out. But nineties women had a new money issue, too: How could they achieve balance between their personal lives and their ongoing lives in the marketplace? They were, Lieberman believed, placing more emphasis on personal fulfillment: creativity, family values, and free time. Whereas the participants in our eighties money study often remained convinced that the real solution to their financial problems was to increase their earning power, women on the tip of the twenty-first century, we feel, are more interested in using the money they do earn to bring harmony and freedom into their lives. We felt that our book, with a more revealing title, new personal stories, statistical updates, and (we admit) a kinder, gentler tone, might be even more appropriate to women now than it was when we wrote it. Hence, this 1996 edition by Allworth Press was born.

Chapter One

The Money Mirror:
A Reflection of Women's
Dreams, Fears, and Desires

The woman speaking below is one of the most revolutionary American women of our time. Like many other psychologically sophisticated, successful, thoroughly modern women, she became aware that money reflected emotional issues—fear, shame, sorrow, and childhood conflicts—that she had not resolved.

> I remember longing to escape the littered, depressing, rat-infested house where I lived alone with my mother; yet I had recreated an upscale, less dramatic version of it in my own apartment with cardboard boxes, stacks of paper, and long absences. I remember worrying as a child about our lack of money and my father's penchant for borrowing it; yet I had saved nothing of what I earned, couldn't resist giving money away, never planned for the future, and often ended up with a familiar feeling of being neglected, deprived and insecure . . . I was turning away from a well of neediness that I feared would swallow me up if I admitted it.[1]

The speaker is feminist leader, author, and founder of *Ms.* magazine, Gloria Steinem.

Why Women Are Afraid of Money

Gloria Steinem is not alone. Women on the edge of the new millennium, who support themselves and their families, spend and invest, are still afraid of money and what it means to them. Some are crippled by anxiety when they contemplate increasing their incomes, saving or spending. Many become deeply uneasy at the thought of negotiating for financial advantages, or discussing the monetary rewards for their ambitious goals. As they avoid confronting their financial images, they restrict their earning potential and jeopardize their future security. Most important, their fear of money—and what it means—prevents them from enjoying money, and using it creatively to enhance their lives.

Money Phobia: The New "Female Complaint"

Our research has revealed that many women think about and relate to money in ways that resemble a clinical phobia—like fear of flying. A phobia, as psychiatrists define it, is an anxiety that attaches itself to a specific object, activity, or situation. This fear, unjustified, or out of proportion to the danger involved, is irrational. Phobic people may be aware of the irrationality of their fear, but they succumb to it anyway, going to great lengths to circumvent the disturbing thing, place, or situation and the terror it inspires: They scrupulously avoid planes and elevators, taking endless train rides or climbing flights of stairs. When they do encounter a phobic situation, they may suffer a "panic attack"—frightening physiological symptoms.

Some phobics deny their fear, or force themselves to deal with it, but they are still afraid. Others may rationalize, saying it is perfectly logical to be afraid of planes and elevators, citing crash and accident statistics. What phobics fear, however, is only a symbol of the real source of their fear, buried in the unconscious mind. In theory, when phobic people uncover the hidden fear, they lose their terror of the substitute situation, and their irrational anxiety melts away.

History and culture give birth to new phobic objects and situations. Before the invention of the elevator, for example, no claustrophobic would fear to ride one. Some phobias affect one sex more than another. Agoraphobia—or panic attacks triggered by being in public places—is a female phobia; 95 percent of agoraphobics are women. As psychiatrist Robert Seidenberg has suggested, agoraphobia symbolizes the dramatic way our view of the role of women in Western culture has changed.[2]

In fifth-century (B.C.) Athens, no respectable married woman was allowed to visit the *agora*, or marketplace, unless she was escorted by a slave or eunuch guard. Married women were locked up at home, under the close watch of servants and vicious dogs. In this way, the Athenian noble was ensured that the heir to his property was truly his son, and not the bastard offspring of a salacious intruder. Prostitutes, the only women who earned any money, were also the only women allowed to go to the *agora*, a public meeting place, and participate in the rich cultural and intellectual life of the time.

What was normal for the average Athenian woman, then, is abnormal as far as we are concerned. Today, women who are afraid to leave their homes and go out in public are considered ill with a crippling psychic disorder—a modern phobia—and undergo psychotherapy and drug treatment.

Money: The New *Agora*

Today's women find themselves in a new relationship to money, and this new relationship has bred new fears. Those of us who have been in the marketplace since we were teenagers, and take money-making careers for granted, tend to forget that only in recent history has our gender begun to earn. Though women have always worked, few worked for pay before the Industrial Revolution, few worked in male-dominated professions before the twentieth century, and almost no woman worked who had the option of being supported by her husband or family.

Whereas a middle-class Victorian woman, schooled according to her era's best standards, undertook paid work as a last resort in desperate financial circumstances, working and getting paid for it is par for the course for today's educated women. Most women want to work, too. To stay home and raise children, while a man provides support—what middle-class women did in the nineteen-fifties, not long ago—is seldom seen as an enviable life plan. About 74 percent of mothers with children—or 22.7 million—were working outside the home in 1992, compared to 26 percent in 1948.[3] And in three out of five American marriages, both husband and wife have jobs.[4] Although women need the money they earn, the majority have told researchers that they would work even if they didn't.[5] The American Dream for women now includes accomplishment, and in our society, accomplishment is symbolized at least partly by dollars. Married or single, young or old, women want to have money they have earned themselves, and this, from a long-range historical perspective, is a revolutionary goal.

Despite ongoing discrimination against women, this desire is being fulfilled. The dramatic increase in the number of women who work has been responsible for a tenfold increase in the gross national product in recent decades. Although the majority of women are still underpaid in sex-segregated jobs, in 1990 women accounted for 44 percent of all economists, up from 14 percent twenty years earlier; for 27 percent of lawyers and judges, from 6 percent; for 38 percent of pharmacists, from 16 percent; for 22 percent of doctors, from 11 percent; and for 30 percent of stockbrokers, from 13 percent. During the same two decades women roughly doubled their proportion among public officials and administrators, bartenders, designers, and advertising or insurance agents.[6]

Although salaries for women have stalled since 1989, today's women are earning more than their mothers would have dreamed possible.[7] Survey after survey has shown that women are optimistic and satisfied with their multiple roles and busy lives. Eighty-seven percent of women polled by Avon Products in 1993 said they believed they could accomplish just about anything they set out to do, and 89 percent were proud of their achievements.[8]

Women's relationship to money, then, like their relationship to the *agora*, has undergone a radical cultural change. Though money is not a place, it comes from the *agora*, an imaginary place where money is earned, traditionally inhabited and controlled by men. In a single century, women have left the safe but confining boundaries of the home and entered this marketplace in droves. Initially they did so to help out at home during depressions and times of personal financial stress, or to keep the economy rolling during major wars. Educated women worked in professions that helped and nurtured others, as social workers, teachers, and nurses. In the sixties, it became acceptable for women to work for personal as well as for economic reasons—to banish the "feminine mystique" and to win self-fulfillment. The next step was the one women took in the eighties: to work for recognition and financial reward, as well as for necessities, and, thanks to inflation and the decline in the value of money, to play an equal and more powerful role in maintaining their families' standard of living.

Another new social phenomenon has changed the significance of women in the marketplace: Because of the prevalence of divorce, and the large number of single women who have not married or re-married, women who never expected to be alone are finding themselves heads of households and sole financial decision makers. Women in their fifties and sixties are staying on the job because they need the money and want to work.[9]

In women's steady progress from home to marketplace, then, earning money for oneself, and the traditional male values money implies—independence, power, and financial reward—is the final frontier.

What should a woman be like? What should she do to survive in a society where women's needs and values are constantly changing? How can she preserve a network of relationships, so important to women, and succeed, in a man's terms, in an economic world? Can she move in on the money-making power traditionally held by men without ending up alone? Will she find a way to balance her emotional needs with professional priorities? Burdened by these questions, ambitious women struggle to integrate their feminine values with the new definition of self they want and need to achieve. Money is one of the important issues that reflect the modern career-oriented woman's uncertainties and fears.

The Money Mirror

Money has a specific value: As a means of exchange, it stands for the worth of goods and services, and for accumulated wealth. In our economy, however, there is no limitation to the amount of money we can desire or get, and our money can increase without us doing any physical labor to make it grow. Unlike food, we cannot eat money, yet we cannot eat—or live—without it. As a result, this important tool has a magical feeling, and a wide variety of emotions can be projected onto it.

For both men and women, money can become a mirror that reflects their fantasies, as well as their struggles to make them come true. Whereas men tend to see money as a reflection of their desire for power and control, for a woman, money can reflect a changing definition of personal fulfillment and social role, the difference between who she has been, is now, and wants to be.

When we looked closely at how women related to the money they earned or wanted to earn we saw that they were using money to express mixed emotions about the home they had come from and the marketplace they had entered. Many handled money in self-destructive or inconsistent ways. Money made some uneasy, so they circumvented it, failing to earn what their capabilities and needs told them they should. The majority had problems negotiating for what they deserved for their goods and services, or with people in their personal lives. They knew they had to make money and spend it, but they refused to think about it, avoiding information that would help them manage or invest effectively. Some had squeamish attitudes about "filthy lucre." Like phobics in stressful situations, they actually experienced "panic attacks" when forced to negotiate, invest, spend, or balance their accounts. Many rationalized their inefficient financial habits, or denied they existed, spending compulsively, investing unwisely, or building protective fortresses with what they earned.

As we studied women's financial attitudes and behavior, it became apparent that their fears fell into seven problematic patterns. To make it easier to discuss these constellations of problems, we gave them names and called them "symptoms." The symptoms of Money Phobia are described briefly below. In the chapters to follow we will analyze each problem and its origins in detail, and look closely at women who suffer from each one.

The Symptoms of Money Phobia

Symptom #1: Money Blindness

The money blind woman closes her eyes to money and thinks of it as vague or unreal. Because she has confused money with other emotional conflicts, she often finds it anxiety-producing to look at all aspects of her financial situation, and may not read financial statements, balance her checkbooks, or know exactly how much she earns and spends. She leaves money management tasks to men she designates as "guide dogs."

Symptom #2: Money Squeamishness

Money squeamish women believe wanting money is "greedy" or "corrupt," and that talking about money is "tacky." Those who persist in thinking that money is not "nice" include Financial Virgins, who associate wanting money with inappropriate visceral desires for food and sex; Weaker Vessels, who believe money will corrupt their life or work; the Genteel Poor, who keep their needs to a minimum; and Money Martyrs, who think it is "morally superior" to be victimized financially. The money squeamish moral attitude harks back to the Victorian concept of the way women should feel about money.

Symptom #3: Money Denying

Money deniers want someone—or something—to take care of them and entertain fantasies that they will be rescued financially. Affected by the mythology of fairy tales, they may associate financial rescue with the vague closure of "living happily ever after," and with the ultimate satisfaction of their emotional needs. They usually spend what they earn, do not take income-producing as seriously as they could, and think making money should be glamorous and exciting. Younger women with this issue may associate financial success with unrealistic career aspirations.

Symptom #4: Money Eluding

Money eluders want to make more money, but are paralyzed by anxieties they have not defined. They do not attach a price tag to their financial fantasies. They also fear finding themselves in a work situation that represents a foreign territory, where they may be exposed to the envy of others and their own lack of perfection will be revealed. Though our sexist society is often at the root of money eluders' issues, they take their inability to earn personally, and may have difficulty balancing their need to make money with other priorities.

Symptom # 5: Money Folly

Money folly victims blow their money or throw it away, as they attempt to solve emotional conflicts by excessive spending. They tend to regard budgeting and saving as punishments instead of useful techniques for taking charge of their financial lives, and sacrifice future security in exchange for immediate gratification.

Symptom # 6: Money Paranoia

Money paranoid women use their money to build "fortresses" that they believe will protect them from an uncertain future and from people who plan to "rip them off" or "suck them dry." They solve emotional dilemmas by maintaining financial control at any cost. They may hoard their money or use it in the wrong way to sabotage themselves and their important relationships.

Symptom #7: Money Confusion

Money confusion strikes when money phobic women negotiate for pay, or for financial advantages in their personal lives. Those with this problem are afraid to separate money from their emotions and may not see that negotiation is a game between adversarial forces. They try to take care of their opponents' needs or expect their opponents to take care of them. They may also personalize money and financial institutions.

Though it makes it easier to talk about fear of money when we break it up into separate problems, the issues women have with money are interrelated and few have only one to overcome. One symptom of Money Phobia, in fact, may be the cause of another. A money squeamish woman, for example, is almost always money eluding, too, and a money denier often overspends—or has money folly.

Women may also suffer from different symptoms at different stages of their lives. A money blind woman, who signs her husband's tax return without reading it, may become money confused when she has to negotiate a divorce settlement. A woman who takes time off from the marketplace when she has a child may become a money eluder when she postpones returning. The symptoms may also have different meanings at different ages. A twenty-four-year-old who fantasizes that a "handsome prince" may rescue her financially has a less serious problem than a forty-year-old who cherishes this dream.

Three Money Phobic Women

The best way to illustrate how the symptoms of Money Phobia interrelate is to look briefly at three women from different generations who suffer from the new "female complaint."

Sally

We first met Sally, twenty-seven, at a New York party. This dark-haired gamin, jiving to a hip-hop beat, hardly resembled our vision of an assistant vice-president of an international bank, earning $50,000 a year—more than her adored father, a Protestant minister, had ever made. Sally spoke enthusiastically about her job which involved representing her bank's services in European capitals and discussed the way the image of women in banking had changed. We looked forward to interviewing this young high-roller to learn how she had achieved an early success and adapted to it emotionally.

By the time our interview took place, however, Sally had become Money Phobic—money squeamish, money blind, money denying and money eluding. She was about to quit her job and was supporting an idealistic anthropologist she had "rescued" from a politically unstable foreign country after knowing him less than a week. They were planning to marry, then head for Bolivia to study Aymara Indians—a trip that would eat up a large chunk of her savings.

After that? Sally hadn't the faintest idea what she or her new husband would be doing for money, or how much money they would need to earn. In a suspiciously short time, she had gone from enjoying her career and the lifestyle she had earned to loathing banking and dismissing the importance of money. "I began to feel my contribution was insignificant and I was selling superfluous services," she said.

Though she had trained for a business career, she now saw her meteoric rise in banking as an accident, and felt that her job required no particular talent or ability. "When I was traveling in Europe I had to pinch myself," she said. "I couldn't believe I was little Sally Boch from Kalispell, Montana, meeting with bank presidents of foreign countries."

Sally told us she was looking for "simplicity." She wanted to return to an "exploratory mode," live on less, and stay in touch with what's "good and beautiful." She was contemplating "creative" careers for which she has no demonstrated ability or training, like photography and writing, and, down the road, settling in the country and having a baby. "It's funny," she told us, "but I've never known what I wanted to be when I grow up. When I talked about this problem with my dad he said, 'Why don't you just be five feet two?'" Sally is not only afraid of money, but of being the kind of woman who is able to earn more than her father. Her exciting new life plan may be emotionally satisfying and politically correct, but does not include caring for herself financially.

June

June, thirty-five, was teaching English and dramatic arts in a high school when she began sorting out professional and personal goals with a psychoanalyst. When the male analyst opposed a risk-taking career change to theatrical production, June fired him. Today she is the artistic director for a major philanthropic institution, for which she produces theatrical benefits, in San Francisco. June creates operating budgets, persuades high-powered corporation executives to fund each production, and nurtures the fragile egos of performers and directors. Clearly, June is not afraid of risk or success. She is, however, afraid of money.

Recently she hired an assistant at a salary higher than her own. Why? "We needed him and he wouldn't work for less." When the new assistant, who took over June's budgeting responsibilities, recommended a $5,000 raise for her, June trimmed it to $2,000. Why? Her salary could be put to better use within the structure of the institution. Finally, the president of the board of directors persuaded her that she deserved the more substantial raise.

Now earning thirty-nine-five—a modest salary for a man, but more than what 75 percent of women earn—June's savings total zero. She has no investments, owns no property, and hasn't the slightest idea where retirement funds will come from.

Where does her money go? She shrugs her shoulders. How would she react to a fifteen thousand dollar raise? She replies, "I'd feel that everyone would hate me and I'd be completely alone." June, a successful professional woman, who has worked her entire adult life, is money squeamish, money eluding, money denying and money confused. To understand why, she needs to examine the messages she received from her family and society about money and earning power, and how they became part of her psyche's script.

Darlene

Darlene, forty-three, was divorced in the eighties. She had been supported by her husband for most of their thirteen-year marriage. Although she had supplied most of the family income in the first few years, and then neglected her career as a graphic designer to work in the home and nurture two children, she felt too guilty about wanting out of the emotionally dead marriage to contest her divorce. As a result, she was awarded less than an equitable share of her family's wealth.

A striking beauty, with warmth, vitality, and articulate intelligence, Darlene has achieved much on her own. She has raised her two teenagers, earned an advanced degree in graphic design, and holds a job as assistant layout editor for a glamorous fashion magazine, despite downsizing and cutbacks. The magazine, however, pays her a not-so-glamorous salary of $24,300 a year, so she is largely dependent on the maintenance and child support payments awarded her by the court.

When we met Darlene, she had not checked her divorce agreement to see when the maintenance payments were scheduled to end, making her completely self-supporting, or calculated the amount of money she would need to earn, or decided exactly how she would earn it, although she fantasized going freelance and becoming well-known in her field. While she avoids thoughts of her future responsibilities, she spends every dollar she has, and some she doesn't have, racking up credit card debts.

She told us, "Right now I have no money, but I'm spending money. As soon as I get involved with a man, I feel that I don't have to worry about money, because he's going to take care of me, even if I know that's not true. And even though I know I don't want him to, since being supported was part of what was wrong with my marriage. I feel I shouldn't have to be concerned with money . . . that I should be able to live my life and get a check in the mail for doing my best. I wish I could market who I am, instead of fitting myself into a job that has nothing to do with me, just to make money." Darlene is money blind, money denying, and has a serious case of money folly too.

The Underlying Anxieties

Why do Sally, June, and Darlene all suffer from Money Phobia? Money Phobia is not "typically female" financial behavior, as some men might suppose, or due solely to a lack of training in money related skills and practices. Troubling conflicts are at work when women are afraid of money. Our research shows that these conflicts are inevitably related to a woman's stress-filled attempts to unify the mixed messages from her family and a continually changing world into a personally satisfying life plan. Money Phobia, then, is not necessarily negative behavior; it is part of the way women are adapting to their changing role in society.

For women—particularly for those thirty and over—the old cultural picture was transmitted by families. In order to separate from traditional definitions of what women are and what they do, then, these women had to separate from their families.

Separation-individuation is a term psychoanalysts use to describe the internal process by which children gradually become independent adults. Those who are loved and given proper nurturing are better able to achieve this distance, so necessary to their emotional well-being, and, ultimately, to their sense of closeness with their parents. Every child separates from parents to some degree, but some children remain much closer and more dependent than others, and more accurately embody parental concepts of their identity, even if such concepts are not personally satisfying. (Unseparated children, in fact, may resent their parents.) A separation process that involves becoming a different kind of woman than one's parents had in mind—the kind of separation we are talking about here—is inevitably a difficult and dramatic process, fraught with anxiety and potential self-conflict.

A "good enough" mother is one who lets her daughter explore the world on her own, yet remains a reliable, comforting base. As the little girl separates, she internalizes this "good enough mother," whose soothing qualities give her confidence and protect her. During the separation process, the little girl is supposed to learn that the world is a place where she is loved and valued, and where she can fulfill her own potential, have satisfying personal relationships, and become the person she wants to be.

Because so many mothers were deprived of meaningful social roles and real power both in relationships and in the world, they could not teach these positive lessons. They passed along to their daughters their feelings of powerlessness, including depression, shame, anger, and fear. Some, who became heads of households, or stayed married to men who did not provide, were powerless because they were poor. Their fears included symptoms of Money Phobia—anxieties about money. These mothers, who felt "stuck" in the home, or in low-paid sex-segregated jobs, or who worked for their husbands without getting paid, communicated the ways a "stuck" woman lives and feels to their daughters, narrowing their psychic horizons.

These mothers, whose lives were largely defined by their domestic roles, emotionally needed their daughters to be like them. If the daughter turned out to be different, the mother risked losing her own sense of worth; she would feel that what she stood for was no longer important, even if her daughter was fulfilling her own secret dreams. She might feel that she no longer existed at all. Daughters, then, got the message that they could validate their mothers' lives by following in their footsteps.

What happens when a daughter—who wants to stay close to her mother, yet break away because she perceives the powerlessness of her mother's situation—decides to lead a life tailored to new aspirations? Flooded with a tidal wave of anxieties, she feels:

- Disloyal
- Guilty
- Out-of-Control
- Worthless, without self-esteem
- Afraid her mother and other women will envy her
- Trapped by boundaries as her mother has defined them, yet
- Terrified of the unknown that lies outside.

Fathers, too, played a crucial role in modern women's psychological development. Unwilling to identify with their powerless mothers, daughters often identified with their more sophisticated fathers. Naturally curious about the intriguing outside world, these daughters imagined themselves learning about it by forming relationships with men like their fathers, or by going out into the world themselves, or both. The world, of course, included the marketplace—the new *agora*.

Ironically, fathers often encouraged their daughters to be quite different from their noncompetitive mothers, and educated them, providing the essential base for future accomplishment, including, in some cases, accomplishments in fields previously dominated by males. But the girl who identified with her father, and tried to emulate his experience and goals, fell prey to other confusions. How could she imitate male behavior, which involved competing with men, and have satisfying relationships? How could she relate to men, who were like her father, without becoming "stuck" like her mother? She grew up fearing loss of love, as well as loss of femininity and sexuality.

As they struggle to lay these troubling anxieties to rest, women maneuver to find a space in the world that feels different from their mother's space, yet feminine and comfortable. They try to relate to men and other women in satisfying ways, and acquire tools that will help them function and equip their new space—both its psychological and its physical dimensions—with what they need. One of these tools is money.

Her relationship to money, then, reflects a woman's anxieties about her relationships to family, men, other women, and her own femininity. Her financial behavior is more than an easily altered pattern of earning, spending, and saving habits; it is a mirror of her psychological state in a world where women are changing.

"The Shower of Gold": An Old-Fashioned Parable for Modern Women

"The Shower of Gold," a fairy tale by The Brothers Grimm, portrays a "junior bag lady," who represents the way many ambitious modern women, conflicted between old and new definitions of their role, relate to money and to the frightening prospect of taking care of themselves.

The story, in brief, tells of an orphaned girl so poor she has no place to live. She has no clothes, except those she wears, and nothing to eat, except for a piece of bread given to her by "someone who had a kind, pitying heart." Pious and good, she prays, knowing that God will take care of her.

The poor homeless orphan sets out on the road. She doesn't get too far before she gives the donated bread to a hungry beggar. Soon she gives her hat to another shivering child whom she meets on the roadside. Still another freezing urchin acquires the generous maiden's jacket; when another begs for her petticoat, she gives that away, too.

When the little girl enters a dark wood to sleep, she bestows the few rags she has left on another abandoned child with no clothing at all, thinking, "It is quite a dark night now, so no one will see me."

. . . she was turning to go into the wood and cover herself with fallen leaves, when all at once a golden shower fell around her from heaven. At first she thought that the stars, which looked like golden money in the heavens, were falling, but when the drops reached the ground they were real golden dollars, and as she stood still under the golden shower she found herself covered from head to foot with warm and beautifully fine clothes. She gathered up the golden dollars, carried them away, and was rich instead of poor all the rest of her life.[10]

The orphaned maiden, lost in the woods, symbolizes the way many women feel when make their way in the world. Unprepared for the journey, they confuse traditional concepts of what women should be, and how they should behave, with the assertive action necessary to provide for their needs.

The good little girl suffers from almost all the symptoms of Money Phobia: She is money blind because she does not calculate her needs or take stock of her limited resources. Money squeamish, she considers it natural to keep her own needs to a minimum. She is money denying, too, because she believes fate will take care of her needs, provided she remains "pious," which can be defined as "having or showing duty and loyalty to friends, family, and others." Her neediness, she seems certain, will, in itself, ensure her well-being. She is uncomfortable outside the home, and prefers volunteer work to creating income-producing opportunities—money eluding! She suffers from money folly because she generously gives away or wastes her resources. Last but not least, she is money confused; when others demand what she has, she feels it is more important to take care of them than herself, and does not negotiate. (She could have done a charitable deed, but kept half the bread for her lunch.) The only symptom she does not express is money paranoia, which usually afflicts successful women.

The end of the fairy tale leaves us with doubts. When the maiden is magically rewarded with a "shower of gold," it is unlikely that she will be "rich instead of poor all the rest of her life," as the fairy tale claims. Given her serious case of Money Phobia, it seems more probable that the maiden will continue to mismanage and give away her resources. She will regard her magical money as "filthy lucre" and go on being comfortably pious and poor.

As we shall see, so much of the mythology about women and money, like this old-fashioned tale, depicts women's financial well-being in the hands of fate, and encourages us to take care of ourselves by believing in magical rescue plans and traditional definitions of women's roles.

Developing Money Awareness

Modern women, who have worked so hard to achieve new professional and personal identities, do not have to relate to money like poor, pious maidens. The healthy, flexible financial identities we want and require can be achieved by looking into our money mirrors and asking how money reflects the dark side of our personal fairy tales.

Like the heroine of "The Shower of Gold," Gloria Steinem left a poverty-line home for a successful career in the larger world, where she continued to drown in "a well of neediness" that she carried inside. Like the poor maiden, she gave her money away and didn't plan for the future. Unlike the fairy tale character, however, Steinem, modern, and psychologically aware, could examine how her financial behavior reflected her inner deficits and relate money to her personal dreams and feminist ideals. Eventually, this strong and flexible woman discovered that money awareness could expand her creative possibilities as well as her sense of self. Listen to the change in Gloria's voice after she gazed into her money mirror:

Suppose I were hit by a Mack truck tomorrow; how would my checkbook stubs reflect what I cared about? I liked to think I put my money where my beliefs were, but when I looked at those stubs, I wasn't pleased . . . I was . . . treating money as if it were a passive thing to be needed or demanded, not an opportunity to initiate, give, and pursue change. . . . From that day forward, I found myself thinking about economics . . . as a form of expression.[11]

Chapter Two

Seeing Money with Clear Eyes: Overcoming Money Blindness

A woman with money vision sees her financial life clearly; she also understands that money has emotional and symbolic value, and reflects her inner self. Her wide angle view takes in a past, present, and future with money that includes earning and saving goals, spending patterns, and a support plan for retirement years. She maintains a sharp picture of her needs, knows how much she earns, and where her money "goes." If she is married or in a serious relationship, she is also aware of how much her partner earns and spends. Having investigated investment opportunities, she doesn't blink when bank and brokerage statements arrive. She reads her tax return—individual or joint—before signing it. As she journeys through life, her lucid money vision enables her to adjust her focus to match her changing financial panorama, and new priorities supplied by time. A money-sighted woman puts herself in an optimum position to make important decisions about money, in an intelligent way, and at the right time.

Despite the creative advantages of acquiring 20-20 financial vision, some women unconsciously close their eyes and grope through murky forests of tangled dollar signs. Why? Thanks to negative, internalized messages from their families and society, "seeing" money makes them anxious. In fact, for some women money blindness is a creative tactic to avoid stress-provoking people, thoughts, and situations to which money is inextricably tied.

Detecting Money Blindness

It is easier to detect money blindness by what a woman does not do with money than by what she does. The money blind tend to avoid serious thought or conversation about money and view it, especially in large sums, as esoteric, vague, or unreal. They do not keep a close watch on the money they spend or have a clear picture of their financial needs. They may not know exactly how much they earn, much less how much their husbands or partners earn. When asked to name an ideal income, they cannot give a specific figure. Like Elizabeth Taylor, who didn't learn to balance her checkbook until after her second marriage to tycoon Mike Todd, they seldom take time or initiative to accomplish financial tasks. One woman confessed throwing financial statements away instead of reading them.

> I like my passbook savings accounts and my checkbooks, but these stupid money markets send you a statement—like a light bill. You don't get a bank book, you get these stupid little papers. They come in and I throw them out. I think they're junk mail. I never open them. . . . I just rip them up and throw them out.

Additional evidence of money blindness is the invention of elaborate systems for juggling and managing sums. Some women have a plethora of bank accounts, credit cards, and checkbooks, devise petty ways of robbing Peter to pay Paul (all with their own money), and attach different meanings to their different caches. As they focus on the myriad pieces of their financial puzzle, they obliterate the whole.

By contrast, the non–money sighted can also be capable of remaining blissfully unaware of the system that they use to allocate day-to-day resources. They unconsciously leave the cute waiter in their favorite espresso bar a 40 percent tip; credit card debts sneak up behind their backs; and end-of-the-month bills are an unpleasant surprise. Those who don't see money are not really able to add and subtract because their emotions have partially erased the figures.

Another characteristic of money blindness is lack of interest in the topic of money. Money in the form of disposable cash is "fun," but finances are "boring." Though most women are aware that good investments could provide a necessary hedge against inflation, the money blind secretly roll their eyes heavenward when talk turns to the 401(k). Even those who have been in therapy or analysis, and are able to ferret out nuances of other emotional conflicts, discuss conflicts with money on a surface-scratching level. We have noticed how tempting it is for them to change the focus of any conversation about money to a related subject. Begin delving into the deep-seated reasons for a binge-shopping syndrome and the shopper starts talking about clothes—Martin Margiela versus Donna Karan and those black heels with the little straps she is dying to own.

The non–money sighted women who filled out the lengthy questionnaire for our study did not find it interesting. One California artist, an Ivy League graduate rescued from a hand-to-mouth lifestyle as a street vendor by her romance with a wealthy man (whom she had not yet married), termed our questionnaire "lackluster." She explained she may have found the subject non-illuminating because money had never been a "priority" for her. Even women who had always worked and seemed competent with money were shocked to see unexpected gaps and discrepancies in their financial picture when asked to account for income status, goals, and spending, saving, and earning patterns in a comprehensive format. What they did not see, and what they saw for the first time, made many of them anxious; some said the phantom figures made them "nauseous."

Keep a day-to-day budget and note where their money goes? Call the bank and ask questions about the investment they don't understand? Withdraw money from a safe CD and purchase a growth fund with a better ten year performance? The non–money sighted agree these suggestions are good ideas, but they have difficulty carrying them out. They think financial action is a nuisance and a bore (and let's face it, for many it is exactly that, but then, doing the dishes is, too), so they postpone these uninspiring but necessary tasks. Their money, they believe, has a life of its own and will go on living it without their intervention. When we asked the women in our study if they had kept the budget they agreed to keep, or called their broker, etc., they let us know that their lives were full of obligations far more intense and pressing.

Why Women Are Money Blind

The family and society unwittingly conspire to make sure that many women become money blind. The problem first develops in the family context: Children of both sexes are seldom made privy to the actual process of resource allocation, the amount of income the family receives, how it is budgeted, or the discussion that goes into making financial decisions. The dollars and cents of family finance are more often than not a cloak-and-dagger affair from which children are excluded (presumably because the worldly knowledge of money would sabotage their innocence).

Women from working-class families often grew up with much more awareness of how money was obtained and spent than middle-and upper-middle-class women, from whom the facts about money were obscured. Secrecy about money and financial maneuvers breeds anxiety at an early age. Women we interviewed said that although they appeared to be living in comfortable circumstances when they were girls, they could not help fearing this comfort was illusory and that their family's financial stability was actually precarious. Whereas resources available to the family, and the logic that determined their use, remained invisible, the parents' own neuroses about money were all too obvious. These parents projected their neurotic concepts of money onto their children, who absorbed them unconsciously. Janice, for example, registered her upper-middle-class parents' guilt and confusion about money; by the time she was a teenager, she had an unrealistic concept of how much money was available and what it was worth.

> I never wanted to take money from my parents. I always felt I was taking it out of their blood. . . . If they bought something for me, I felt very badly. The way I chose my prep school was to go through the catalogue and pick the one that cost $100 less, even though I didn't like it. My mother said, "Oh, don't worry about it. We have enough money. Go to any school you want"; but I didn't feel worth it. I didn't feel I was a good investment.

The emotional conflicts Janice had already absorbed about money distorted and inflated its real value, so that she had no way of ascertaining how much $100 was worth in relation to the family's financial picture, and the sum became a negative symbol of her own worth instead. Most of the women in our study were able to describe their parents' "quirks" about money, yet were often unaware that they exhibited the same quirks themselves.

As boys get older, their fathers may teach them facts about finance, but they rarely teach girls. While the family failed to give its daughters any financial training, or an objective idea of the value of money, the schools, too, failed to include information about money in their curriculum and encouraged women to blind themselves to the area of study most related to finance—mathematics.

Historically, boys and girls tend to do equally well in school overall, but girls make better verbal scores on college entrance exams, while boys score higher in math. Studies have indicated that beginning in infancy boys are better at spatial perception—or the ability to visualize objects out of context—a skill related to the abstract, analytical logic required by the sciences and math. Psychologists believe that although boys are born with an edge in this area, this reasoning ability is not an innate "masculine" talent so much as a result of the way little boys are socialized to relate to the world. Mothers are usually less protective of infant sons than they are of daughters and allow them to explore more freely, giving them a more expansive and varied concept of space and objects at an early stage of their development. Schools do much to promote the boy's "natural" mathematical ability and to discourage the girl's, because teachers see numbers as masculine territory. Now that women are finally becoming visible in business and in the sciences, hopefully this prejudice will soon be obsolete; however, we suspect this baby boomer lawyer's horror story is typical of the experience many women of her era had with math:

> I had scored a 99 in the Geometry Regents and was put in an advanced placement class in intermediate algebra and trig. There were five girls in the class and fifteen boys, several of whom went on to MIT. The teacher, Mr. Leone, had a reputation for being strict but fair. Though I began the class full of confidence from my recent success with geometry, after about two weeks I found myself huddled in a corner with the four other girls for protection. Mr. Leone was out to prove that math was no place for a woman. And he did! He would ridicule any girl who got a right answer, making sure to tell us he would give us good grades just for being able to sit through his class. He made these five girls (all of whom graduated at the top of the class) feel like dummies, stupid and ashamed. I had to take a statistics course in college, but I never again felt confident about my ability to understand mathematical concepts.

The school's pejorative view of a girl's math ability often becomes a self-fulfilling prophecy. Many women fear financial tasks because they believe it is impossible for them to comprehend any number-related concept and are surprised when they can. One woman, whose female algebra teacher made her "promise" not to go on to more advanced math, told us

> I'm forty years old and I just learned that 45³/₄ in the stock market report means $45.75. Nobody ever bothered to tell me that all my life. I thought it was an esoteric algebraic formula.

The socially instilled belief that they are "dummies" at math and, by implication, finance, and that men are the smart ones, leads women to make men their financial "guide dogs," and abdicate control of their money to male advisers, relatives, and friends. A forty-three-year-old interior designer recalled:

> When I started earning a lot of money I didn't deal with it at all. Any financial decision I could leave to my husband, I would. The myth was that he was the one who was competent to do that, and I never noticed he made a complete mess out of it. I can't see why I couldn't take control over the money when I was earning it. Could it have been the simple calculations, the math part? I never was good at math, but I'm not that terrible at it.

Socialized money blindness also often influences a woman's choice of career. Until recently, educated middle-class women seldom took the monetary value of the career they chose into consideration. In our study women expressed job dissatisfaction when limited earning power was built into their profession; some teachers and nurses felt "burned-out" on their jobs because they saw a definite ceiling to their income level which did not reflect their talent or devotion. Most said parents and guidance counselors had pushed these "secure" jobs, appropriate for women of their baby boom generation, and without support or information, they were unable to see other options.

In the eighties, young women went to the opposite extreme and selected careers primarily for the high salaries they offered (which also resulted in "burnout" and job dissatisfaction). Today, faced with downsizing in many professions, rapidly changing technologies, which, over time, may require employees to acquire new, specialized skills, a woman planning to work for most of her life may be uncertain that any career she selects will provide a predictable source of income.

Most women, then, enter the marketplace with a distorted image of money. On the one hand, money seems an abstract, incomprehensible science, terrifying in what it says about their lack of ability to manage or understand it, and on the other, it is an all-too-personal symbol of parental neuroses and their own attempts to reconcile mixed messages about women and earning power. No wonder some women feel the best way to deal with money is to close their eyes to it!

Doris Day: A Tragic Case of Blind Faith

One rich and famous woman who suffered from money blindness is Doris Day. Like many of her less wealthy women counterparts, the hard-working performer made the mistake of joining her heart (and bank account) to a money blind man's. She entrusted the millions she earned to her third husband, Marty Melcher, who, in turn, entrusted them to an unscrupulous Hollywood shark, Jerry Rosenthal. Rosenthal, who was later tried for ripping off other superstars, "invested" the Day money in mythical oil wells and other bogus or ill-fated properties. From the beginning Doris had doubts, not about the character of either of these dudes but about their choice of investments, and wanted to buy art. She felt she had "no business in high-risk ventures." Whenever she protested her husband told her it would take too long to explain complex contracts to her, defended Rosenthal, and asked a crucial question, "Don't you trust me?" Although many of Doris's friends and fellow actors did not trust Melcher, who earned no money of his own, Doris did trust him.

Although I didn't like being in oil wells and hotels, there was no question that I did trust Marty.

When she didn't understand the investments Melcher made, she did not consult outside sources to obtain this vital information.

I did arrange a couple of confrontations with Rosenthal to protest his investments, but his explanation of what he was doing, and how it would benefit me as a tax shelter was too technical for my comprehension . . . (When people mention tax shelter to me I always have a mental image of a little lean-to somewhere where you run to hide when the tax collector comes.)

After Melcher died, Doris discovered she was all but broke and that the investments she had instinctively distrusted were meaningless pieces of paper. To make matters worse, Melcher had signed her up to do a television series she did not want to do to pay off his debts, and had borrowed against her future salary. Doris, grief-stricken over her husband's death, now had penury to contend with.

Who was Marty Melcher? That was the question that constantly thrust itself at me. How could I have lived with a man for seventeen years and not known who he was?

Good question! How had such a bright, talented woman, who had been so farsighted in developing her career, become so nearsighted, not only about men, but about money? Though Doris blames her lack of interest in money and Melcher's foolishness for the destruction of her financial empire, like many of us, she had compelling emotional reasons to put blind faith in a man.

When she was young, her father, a remote musician who never paid much attention to Doris, proved untrustworthy; he abandoned Doris, her mother, and brother because he was having an affair with a family friend. Throughout her childhood Doris dreamed her father would return, and the family harmony she so desired would be restored. Sometimes we use the power of our imagination to manufacture our dreams—in Doris's case, a loving, protective, trustworthy man—and close our eyes to the glaring difference between reality and myth. Unfortunately for Doris, money got mixed up with her unresolved emotions.

Doris Day and Marty Melcher provide an interesting example of the blind leading the blind. Though Melcher had no greater money vision than did his wife, he was money blind for typically *masculine* reasons: He saw money as a source of power and prestige, and getting rich as a way of maintaining his superiority in a marriage to a woman who was far more talented and successful than he was. Doris, however, like most women, was money blind for more feminine, emotional reasons—because, despite her nationwide fame and her millions, she was still a lonely little girl, yearning for a daddy she could trust.[1]

Getting Robbed Blind

Many women who don't see money, unlike Doris Day, are married to trustworthy men who have their best interests at heart. However, if these women consistently close their eyes to family finances, they can confront disaster in their later years. Virginia Wasser, second vice-president of an international brokerage, has many women clients who arrived at her doorstep after their husbands died. Grief-stricken and alone, their inner turbulence is increased when they are faced with a complicated portfolio of investments that they do not understand. Their financial as well as emotional stability is suddenly precarious. These widows, according to Virginia, often fall to the mercy of male bankers, accountants, and advisers who, preying on their sense of loss and desire for a surrogate husband, "rob them blind."

One of these potential sacrificial lambs was Virginia's own aunt, whose husband died unexpectedly without apprising his wife, also ill, of the details of his electrical supply house business. So preoccupied was this good and loving man with his wife's illness that he let his business go to pot and spared her his problems. Virginia said, "My aunt didn't know the difference between receivables and payables, and was in terrible physical and emotional shape." Virginia came to the rescue, and called a meeting of her uncle's attorney and accountant and the company's major stockholders

> It took me four minutes to ascertain that the lawyer and the accountant were suffering from tavern burnout. The lawyer walked in with liquor on his breath and minus a briefcase. He hadn't done any of the paperwork, or brought the will or legal papers. We had to remind him to take notes, and give him a pad and a pencil. He advised liquidation of the company. I advised my aunt that if she liquidated she'd get 10 cents on every dollar of what the company was worth and I suspected the lawyer had his network of good old boys lined up to buy. He gave my aunt no alternatives as to what to do with the business. I fired the attorney and the accountant, and hired others, and am now getting the company in shape to sell, collecting my uncle's debts, and putting the workers on an incentive-based salary plan. Imagine the nightmare that could have occurred had I not been available to take charge.

Needless to say, few widows are fortunate enough to have VPs of brokerage firms in their families, and may become victims of those who, through evil intentions or innocent incompetence, rob them of their assets.

Women who close their eyes to money, however, are thoroughly capable of robbing themselves. A participant in our New York money group agreed to learn to read her monthly statement from a large financial firm as a "personal goal." Carolyn, though a cautious binge spender, had managed to accumulate some savings, the bulk of which she had invested in Ginnie Mae units, or the Government National Mortgage Association, a safe investment that pays interest. Carolyn had been advised by her father and male stockbroker to put her money in Ginnie Maes, but had never understood the basic concept involved. Essentially, she had loaned money to the government, which, in turn, loaned it to people who needed mortgages to buy homes. Every month the borrowers paid the government back, and the government divided up the sum it received and paid back the investors, along with a monthly rate of interest.

Carolyn, however, did not realize the monthly checks she had requested and automatically received from her financial firm included the repayment of her principal plus the interest. She believed both were pure profit, and blithely spent the money, usually on clothes, regarding it as "mad money." About the time Carolyn decided to enlighten herself, her male broker retired. A new female broker set her straight.

> She told me that I'd already spent $4,000 of my principal, and if I kept it up, I'd soon have Ginnie Mae units without any money in them. Since I am a freelancer without a pension or unemployment benefits, it is important for me to keep these savings intact. When I really looked at the statement, I couldn't understand how I'd gotten so confused. Right there in black and white it said principal, and on the line beneath it said interest. Every month the total sum of my assets was decreasing on the statement, and I never noticed that either. Boy, did I feel dumb! I called my father and accused him of not explaining the Ginnie Maes to me, and he accused me of not being interested, just like my mother, who always protests that she's cooking dinner or folding the laundry when he tries to explain their finances to her. He said women were "congenitally uninterested in finance." I had to admit he was right. I was the one who never asked questions. I wonder why not?

Roget's Thesaurus lists *blindness* as a synonym for "ignorance." But, as Carolyn intuited, there are hidden reasons why intelligent, sophisticated, professionally competent women are money blind.

The Case of the Money Blind Photographer

Beth is an unusually self-aware New York photographer, with a talent for analyzing her own inner landscape and the world outside with a perceptive eye. This vibrant, intense, thirty-four-year-old woman seemed to be leading an enviable life, doing exactly what she wanted to do and doing it well. After a difficult divorce, she was living happily with a supportive man she truly loved and with whom she shared all basic expenses. Her years of persistence were paying off and she was beginning to show her black-and-white portraits in prominent galleries, supplementing her basic income photographing weddings with sales to collectors. Though money was not "growing on trees" it did not appear to be an immediate problem; Beth had enough and expected her work would soon produce more. Why, then, was she so anxious about money? When we met Beth and asked her to look into her money mirror, she was intrigued but very scared.

> I feel nervous; really nervous. I just feel very nervous and anxious about this subject. I don't know why. I don't even really want to know why. Money, to me, is like a bottomless lake. I know there are slippery fish down there. I don't know what kind of troglodytes and eels we'll find . . . but, yes, I want to talk about it.

Despite her clear vision about her self and her goals, Beth was not money-sighted. She didn't balance her checkbook, or have the slightest idea how much she spent in a month, or earned in a year, until her accountant did her taxes. She didn't know how much the man she lived with earned either, and didn't want to know; they never discussed money, and both considered their income a "private affair."

Though Beth's money blindness seemed harmless enough, when we probed a bit deeper we saw other problems with money lurking beneath the surface. Her self-imposed blindfold had resulted in some destructive financial attitudes and actions. An occasional over-spender, she described herself as "penny wise and pound foolish." She had supported her former husband for many years, yet when they separated, she had let him take half the worth of their house, which she had paid for. She found it difficult to price her work, which she often felt she had sold for less than its value. Her belief that money she didn't earn was "tainted" had prevented her from applying for grants and awards in her field because she thought other artists were more deserving of the money than she because they "struggled." She refused to tell us or anyone exactly how much money she had at her disposal, pleading inexact knowledge of the amount. These problems, as well as her anxiety and guilt about the money issue, tipped us off that there were indeed "slippery fish" in Beth's lake. She was, however, willing to dredge them up from the bottom.

Beth had a money secret. She confessed that the income she earned by teaching and selling her prints was supplemented by "family money"—interest on a trust fund left to her by her paternal grandfather. Though this stipend was small, she was worried that friends and colleagues might find out about it and view her negatively.

> I feel guilty about the free money I get—money I don't earn. I don't want people to know I have the backing of powerful money. It's really easy for people to feel resentful and jealous, and make you into someone who has an easier life than they do. It would negate the fact I work so hard and take my career so seriously for them. I want to escape blame. I want to be in the spotlight, but not the hot seat.

We wondered about Beth's use of the term "powerful money." She told us that she associated money with masculine strength; she felt earning power might make her feel less feminine, and change the balance of power between herself and her partner.

> I want fame more than money. I think of my ambition, which is so fierce, as being very male, and not naturally female. And to want to make money, too, in addition to being recognized for my talent, is, at the moment, more than I can handle. I don't want to be thought of in that powerful way. Being helpless is fake . . . everyone knows that . . . but it's a game that I play.

Beth had absorbed society's not-yet-obsolete message that money is synonymous with male power, but, as we soon learned, her own unique background had reinforced that message in a significant way. Beth had another money secret. Her father, she told us, had suffered from episodes of severe manic depression in her childhood and had occasionally been hospitalized.

Though he was not always mentally stable, he had been a powerful family figure who had garnered most of the attention. And one of his major sources of power was his talent for finance. He had quadrupled the family inheritance by making astute investments, even when his psychological problems were most apparent. Though he, too, felt guilty about the family money, calling it a "curse," he maintained total control over it, spending it, even giving it away, as he saw fit.

> He got his identity from showing he was available to give money away in the town that we lived in, and he put people through hoops for it.

While he used money as an instrument of power and manipulated others with it, Beth's father instructed only her brother about the complex art of finance, and kept Beth and her mother in the dark.

No wonder money made Beth nervous! Unenlightened about the financial skills that created money, she was able to see money only as a symbol of guilt and a manipulative male omnipotence, threatening and out-of-control. Though she was aware of the ambivalent emotions she had about her father, she was not aware of the way she had confused money with her feelings about him, or the way that confusion had scrambled her financial vision.

> There is a connection in my mind between money and mental illness. Maybe I fear that line of succession. I have this inherited money, my father inherited money ... maybe, therefore, I am like my father. I do identify with him in so many ways.

Beth had become money blind, then, as a way of avoiding the anxieties and fears that money symbolized in her personal world, which, as it happens, was a reflection of the way money has traditionally appeared in the larger world mirror—as a symbol of male power. Though few money blind women have fathers with severe psychological problems, or an inheritance to inspire guilt and confusion, most close their eyes to money for exactly the same reasons: Because money conjures up alarming images of psychic "troglodytes." Sometimes, however, not seeing money proves to be an ingenious way for a woman to adapt to anxiety-producing changes, like separation from her family, a period of transition, death, and birth.

How Ann-Marie Survived Change and Loss

Ann-Marie, a Connecticut social worker, had been a self-supporting single woman for fifteen of her thirty-seven years. She had carefully budgeted her modest salary to include courses toward a master's degree and foreign travel. Then her aging mother fell and broke her hip, and Ann-Marie rediscovered an old high school pal—her mother's orthopedic surgeon. They fell in love and soon were married. Though this may sound like a fairy tale with a happy ending, Ann-Marie's new lifestyle involved some difficult adjustments.

In five years she had moved from her tiny "bachelor" apartment in the community where she had always lived into a luxurious suburban home, given birth to a daughter after a difficult late-life pregnancy, and lost her mother, father, and a favorite uncle, all of whom had died after lengthy illnesses. Between coping with a young child, who suffered from constant earaches; the medical problems of her relatives; a bad back of her own; and the responsibility of managing a large house with little help from her doctor husband, who was at the hospital until late at night and often on weekends, Ann-Marie found it impossible to continue working. After a stressful year of trying to balance so many priorities, she quit her job.

> It wasn't realistic; something had to give. Our society was saying, "Yes, you can have it all," and I was saying, "How can I have it all? I have all this stuff going on here."

Ann-Marie had been raised to believe she should be financially self-sufficient, work, and take care of herself; when she found herself thirty-seven and still single, she had not really expected to marry. Suddenly her identity had changed. She was no longer a hardworking, low-paid social worker, but an affluent wife and mother.

> I am not one of those people who go around saying motherhood is wonderful, because, oh God, it was a shock to my nervous system on top of everything else. It has its rewards, but when my daughter was tiny, it was very boring. I was going nonstop before she was born, and then here I was at home with this baby that didn't do anything except spit food at me and sleep. When she got to be a year old, I realized how much work it all was, and then I really started going crazy.

Ann-Marie's economic identity had also changed. She had crossed the boundaries of the working-class family and community into which she (and her husband) had been born and moved into upper-middle class territory. How much money did her husband make? Ann-Marie didn't know, and didn't want to know.

> He's making it, and in my mind, it's his money. He puts it all in these money market things, and he has this corporation, and it pays him a salary and buys a car. . . . I don't understand, even though I'm secretary of the corporation.

She worried that people she had known all her life as well as new acquaintances would see her as a *nouveau riche* doctor's wife, with all the economic advantages that title implied, and feel "distant" from her. She was determined to raise her little girl in a way that reflected her own childhood values.

> I see her as being able to get along with everyone. There are people who define themselves by how much money they have, how many expensive possessions they have, what kind of house they live in. . . . I don't want her ever to define herself or other people in those terms.

Ann-Marie had found a very creative way to adapt to these difficult transitions and losses: She became money blind. She began to run her financial life in an ingeniously complicated fashion, which first involved shutting her eyes to her husband's enormous income. Instead of regarding what he made as hers, too, she asked him to pay her the same salary for managing the house that she had earned as a social worker and deposited it in a checking account in her own name. Every year she called her former boss to ask him how much she would be making and charged her husband the same "annual salary," which he paid her on the fifteenth and the thirtieth of the month. The income she got for working at home validated the worth of this new job in objective terms and made her feel less supported.

> I had this real thing about being supported. I've never been supported in my life. I just couldn't sit around in the lap of luxury.

Though Ann-Marie's husband would never have denied her anything she wanted, she felt that earning an actual salary for homemaking and child raising activities gave her the right to do exactly what she liked with money she thought of as her own.

> I went to Macy's and had the Elizabeth Arden treatment to the tune of 200 bucks. It's on my charge and it's going to be paid for with my money. I could never present the bill to Dick and say, "Here, I just ran up $200 at Elizabeth Arden." It's not how I see myself.

The barrier Ann-Marie constructed between herself and her total financial picture was elaborate. She also maintained a second checking account, in which she deposited the money she got from renting her deceased father's house.

> I said, "Look, honey, I don't have enough to pay the guy who paved the driveway," but he forgot to leave the check, so I had to go into my other checking account—the one with the money in it I get from renting my father's house. I have all these checkbooks that I'm fritzing around with and it's probably loony. It's really small sums that I'm dealing with. It gets confusing, but I won't take money from my father's estate and deposit it in my personal checkbooks.

Ann-Marie's financial management techniques appeared, as she suggests, a trifle "loony," but there was a definite method to her madness. By getting paid an actual salary for her job at home, she validated its worth and sustained the sense of financial independence she had had as a self-supporting social worker. By blinding herself to her entry into a higher economic class, she preserved the more comfortable boundaries—and values— of the old one. Finally, by separating the money from her father's estate from her husband's money and her salary, she maintained her emotional link with the family she had lost. Her checkbooks represented boundary lines that kept the borders between her old self and her new one from blending into a disorienting confusion; they kept Ann-Marie intact in her changing world.

There were, however, predictable problems with Ann-Marie's money blindness. First of all, since she was using an elaborate financial system to mask the real cause of her stress, money was making her feel very anxious. She told us the very thought of money made her "physically sick." Second, though her financial nearsightedness made her present more emotionally comfortable, it was making her future more risky. By closing her eyes to her husband's money, she was ultimately hoodwinking herself. By not becoming actively involved in his corporation, she was setting herself up to play the tragic role of money blind widow in the event that he should die. By refusing to look at her family's financial picture, and insisting on maintaining the illusion of self-supporting independence, she had unwittingly donated money to the IRS.

> Before I quit my job, people were telling me to put my money in these tax-deferred annuities and things like that, but I was still operating with the idea of cash in hand. If my paycheck had gone down to $500 because I was putting my money in cash deferred annuities, then it wouldn't have been cash in hand. It made sense, but I needed the cash, and I liked fritzing around with these checkbooks. When my husband told me how much we'd paid to the IRS that year, it was more than I'd ever dreamed of making.

Instead of opening her eyes, however, this experience provided Ann-Marie with a villainous scapegoat: She could now blame other money blind actions on the IRS. She sold her father's house to a rather distant cousin for much less than it was worth on the open market, justifying this action by saying, "Why not? After all, the IRS is only going to steal the profit." Clear money vision would have enabled her to do her financial homework, and learn that in reality, the capital gains tax at that time actually worked in her favor, and she would have given only 20 percent of the profit on the house to the IRS in the year that she sold it.

On the other hand, we respected Ann-Marie's desire to preserve her all-important sense of personal and community relations by keeping her father's house in the family; we believed, however, that it would have been more personally satisfying for her to do so with her eyes wide open. The IRS also became the evil specter that kept Ann-Marie from seeing the truth about another important decision: Where would she put her talent and prodigious energy once her daughter started school? She had no intention of remaining a salaried housewife, but she protested that she didn't want to return to her previous job because the IRS would "whack her income to bits." Yet, given the importance she had always placed on getting paid for what she did, she felt uncomfortable volunteering.

> Volunteering would be fun, but you can never take it seriously; at least I never have. But I'm not going to work for the IRS either. To hell with them!

Beneath this conundrum lay an important truth, difficult for Ann-Marie to acknowledge. She was slowly admitting to herself that she did not really like her career.

> My father wanted me to be a social worker. I don't really feel I was suited for that, but I needed something secure so I could support myself. I went ahead and did that, and I wasn't really sure I liked it. It got worse.

We hoped that as time and increased self-awareness allowed Ann-Marie to adjust to the changes in her life, she would be able to view her husband's large income as a resource she could use to develop new skills (which would eventually produce the paycheck she personally needed to validate her sense of self-worth and independence), instead of continuing to blindly maintain the illusion that she was still a single woman from the working class, struggling to support herself.

Becoming Money Sighted

As Beth and Ann-Marie participated in our money study, both began to open their eyes. Beth was relieved to find she was not judged harshly for her small family stipend, either by us or by members of the money-awareness group she had joined. She said talking about money had helped her determine when she wanted to stay money blind and when she did not. With this new perception she was able to invest money she received from her ex-husband—payment for her share of the house they had owned—in a condominium, which she intended to rent. She enlisted her father's advice, and learned what questions to ask the financial adviser and the lawyer who assisted with the purchase. She decided that she did not want to invest the time and energy necessary to master the art of finance herself, but she wanted to know enough so that she could choose competent, trustworthy professionals in the financial field.

While we were working with Ann-Marie she began to help her widowed aunt cope with her large estate. She discovered that financial matters were not impossible to understand, once one was willing to look at them.

> Once I got myself through the technical jargon on the forms I saw I could do it. The technical jargon made me nervous all summer. I had to figure it out. Lawyers who charge three or four thousand dollars to set up an estate are ripping old people off in a way. It's not that simple, and it's a lot of work, but all you have to do is figure out how much tax you have to pay and pay it.

Her experience with her aunt's estate, and her willingness to examine her own money problems, made Ann-Marie decide to learn what was happening in her husband's corporation.

> Hell! I'd better get up there and not let those fellows keep bamboozling me . . . the lawyer and the insurance guy. . . . Next time they have a meeting I'm going to have questions to ask them.

Also important, Ann-Marie got involved in community restoration, a long time passion she had been unable to indulge in the days when she had to be self-supporting, by organizing a volunteer group of concerned citizens herself.

Both Beth and Ann-Marie, then, were able to begin the slow, often painful process of acquiring money vision, because they were conscious of their anxiety about money and were willing to tolerate this unpleasant sensation long enough to investigate its cause. In other words, both had taken an important step toward money-sightedness before we met them, because their money mirrors had begun to reveal that money was a problem in their otherwise successful lives.

Chapter Three

The Sweet Smell of Success: Transforming Money Squeamishness

A woman who sees her financial profile clearly is free of attitudes that distort the meaning of money in her life. She recognizes that money is a medium of exchange and a measure of value—not a charged symbol of good and evil, or of its owner's moral virtues or defects. Once a woman realizes that money is a tool—no more, no less—she can define how much of it she needs and use it as a source of fulfillment, to implement present and future goals.

Unfortunately, Victorian cultural definitions of how women should relate (or not relate) to money can make them see it as "filthy lucre," quintessentially soiled. The money squeamish confuse green backs with wicked evil-doers who, throughout time, have mishandled them, and harbor secret beliefs that money itself represents corruption. This Money Phobic woman is apt to believe that to desire more than a pittance is selfish or greedy, like an out-of-control urge for food or wanton sex. She thinks discussing money in specific detail is "tacky." Although openly or secretly she may lust after money, and the aura of power and comfortable lifestyle it creates, the money squeamish woman maintains to herself and others that a desire to be well-off isn't a "pure" or "proper" value.

A holier-than-thou attitude toward currency might seem like an obsolete viewpoint in an era when most women expect to work and dream of success in their chosen career; but a surprising number of women that we interviewed still believed that money isn't "nice." A 1993 UCLA sociological study of 605 middle-class college students confirmed our findings, revealing many saw money as "tainted." They said that earning more than their parents would make them feel guilty, considered high-earners "immoral," and confessed to be repelled and intimidated by them. (By contrast, the same study found that money made men students, who respected top earners, feel lovable, happy, and in control.)[1] Unfortunately, even traces of the feeling that money is dirty can have a negative impact on the way ambitious women earn, negotiate, and spend.

The Origins of Money Squeamishness

Money squeamish ideas and practices were introduced into our culture by the Puritans, whose fervent ethic placed no bounds on the amount of property an individual could acquire, but tempered the ways money could be made and spent. Although the clergy saw no conflict between wealth and religion (in fact, some of the upstanding members of the congregation were merchants and tradesmen), they opposed frivolity, ostentation, and corruption. A Puritan's fortune was proof that God had elected him for salvation, but he was forbidden to make it dishonestly, squander it, or devote his life solely to the acquisition of wealth. A rich man who was also godly did not indulge in luxurious living, but used his money for the public good.

Books could be written speculating why the Puritan money message survived our social melting pot, and how it has changed. Suffice to say that remnants of puritanical attitudes still color the way both sexes think and talk about money today. Like the Puritans, we believe that people who have made money through hard work and intelligence are privy to a special, almost mysterious wisdom, and are morally superior to those who got it some other way. The wealthy are still expected to be charitable. Though we may envy ostentatious spending, we do not really admire it. We also practice puritanical discretionary policies in our money talk, and believe the total amount we have and how we spend it—particularly large sums—is private information. Sigmund Freud once said, "Money matters will be treated by cultured people in the same manner as sexual matters, with the same inconsistency, prudishness, and hypocrisy."[2] Yet a century after Freud made that statement, most of us would feel more comfortable asking for, or confiding, the intimate details of a sexual relationship than the figures of bank accounts.

Money squeamishness is explained by our psychoanalytical as well as our historical tradition. Freud, the first analyst to look at the meaning of money, theorized that it was linked to sex and filth in the unconscious mind, and interpreted money as a sanitized symbol of an infant's feces. He said that the significance of money for each individual is based on the way he was toilet trained, and the emotional responses this training induced.

The slang we use for money and getting rich seems to bear out the Freudian idea, indicating we think of money as "dirty." We talk about "making a pile" or "rolling or wallowing in money." Those who make money illegally have to "launder it," and the financially powerful are sometimes described as "filthy rich."

Why Women are More Money Squeamish than Men

Women are more likely to be money squeamish than men because the attitude is part of our society's traditional definition of middle-class femininity.

As far back as fifth-century Greece, a paragon of true womanhood was "frugal, chaste, and silent." It was in Victorian times, however, that a "lady," in the American sense, was defined by the distance between herself and the marketplace. Before the Industrial Revolution, Colonial women worked side by side with their husbands to run household economies; the labor of one sex was not valued more than that of the other. When men began working outside the home in the nineteenth century, what women did was no longer perceived as an invaluable financial activity because it did not bring in money. Paradoxically, it was from this worthless "idleness" (often not idleness at all, but an endless round of unpaid household chores), that women derived a new sense of status and class. Middle-class women, dependent on their husbands, were elevated to "ladies" and considered superior to poor women who worked.[3]

The church conspired with economic history by praising women who stayed at home as upholders of society's moral virtue. Since the seventeenth century women had been viewed by the Anglican church as "weaker vessels," or morally delicate creatures, whose pure and fragile souls were likely to fall. In America, Protestant ministers expanded this concept to include the idea that contact with commerce and government made men "base." Women, naturally more modest and benevolent, could preserve their own morality, and mold the characters of their husbands and children, by remaining untainted by worldly pursuits. Money-making was seen by the church as a "contagion" from which women were free. Even important spokeswomen like Sarah Hale, an impoverished widow who had supported her children by founding the popular *Ladies' Magazine*, urged her readers to stay at home and devote themselves to "the chaste disinterested circle of the fireside."

The nineteenth-century lady's attitude toward sex was the same as her attitude toward worldly pursuits—disinterested. Encased in organ-crunching corsets and stays, she was not supposed to exercise or have sexual needs. Restricted by her virtue and class to the fireside, what did the middle-class Victorian lady do with her intelligence and time? She gave birth, instructed her children, managed her household if she had help, and did her own chores if she did not. She joined literary discussion groups and formed intense friendships with other women—the basis for later pro-suffrage organizations. She also got sick! (The nineteenth-century ideal for feminine beauty was a pale and ethereal wraith.) Even early feminist pioneers like Jane Addams, the founder of Hull House, and Charlotte Perkins Gilman, who campaigned for women's rights, languished with undefined nervous ailments before they had the courage to move away from the fireside and out into the world. Gilman continued to have nervous problems. Later, when the Weaker Vessels did leave the hearth, it was not to try to make a place for themselves in an economy that almost totally excluded middle-class women, but to expand their virtuous influence and help the needy victims of the marketplace—the poor. As a result, the tradition of women in volunteer work was born. A century later, married women still volunteer, but they also work for money, at least part-time.

Today, most of us regard the Victorian lady as a ghost from the past, with no relationship to modern women. Few of us would be able to recognize in ourselves a conscious desire to be frugal or chaste (let alone silent) by the hearth. Most of us want to work outside the home for as high a rate of pay as possible and believe sexual pleasure is one of our birthrights. Yet, the power of the Victorian lady—and the persistent forces that keep her alive—cannot be dismissed or underestimated. Her small voice inside our historical unconscious can still sabotage our modern selves by whispering that our desires for worldly power, money, and sex are not ladylike.

Detecting Money Squeamishness

There are four ways women embody money squeamish attitudes.

The Financial Virgins

Financial Virgins view financial acts the way the Victorians viewed sex—as dirty or forbidden—and the desire for money not unlike an uncontrollable sexual urge. They may see spending as "giving in" to seductive forces and saving as "holding out." Said one:

> If you have money in the bank you are always all right. It's virtuous. It's like virginity. You are saving yourself.

Unlike the money blind, who are bored by financial discussions, the money squeamish do not like to talk about money matters because they feel they are "personal," or "private," like sexual behavior. If the Financial Virgin earns more than her mate, she may keep her annual income a secret. One was titillated by the topic when she discussed money with the man she was dating for the first time.

> Actually it was sort of fun. I realized that this was taboo . . . something you didn't talk about. There was this shiver of delight—the same feeling as when you talk about sex. It was so delicate, so loaded in terms of identity and ego. The interesting thing was that we both understood that each of us respected the other's privacy.

Because the Financial Virgin associates spending or making money with dangerously greedy visceral desires, likely to compromise her feminine attractiveness, she may describe financial feelings in terms of food as well as sex. A law student with ambitious goals confided that she felt uneasy after our interview. She thought she had sounded "piggy" or "money hungry" and that talking about money was like "talking about oral sex—not really appropriate." She told us that she thinks of a diet as a budget and vice versa.

> I like the structure of budgeting calories. When I buy a candy bar I ask, "Is this a good way to spend forty-five cents?"

Financial Virgins who think of money as a visceral "temptation" may find even the look and feel of it distasteful. Naomi, a Boston physical therapist, dislikes handling cash, a money squeamish symptom she inherited from her mother, who would follow a monthly trip to the diet doctor with a shopping binge for clothes on sale.

> She'd buy tons of stuff, bags of it—all cheap shit—and she'd use plastic to pay for it. I can't see my mother's hands with cash in them.

As an adult, Naomi, who also has a weight problem, avoids cash, too, and pays for purchases with credit cards and checks. Whereas her mother used "plastic" to rebel against dietary restrictions by bingeing in stores, Naomi uses it to make money less "real," and to move it out of the range of spending impulses she fears are uncontrollable.

> With cash, there's a sense that I could succumb to impulsive spending. Dealing with plastic takes it a step above.

Financial Virgins like Naomi are suffering from social restrictions they have unconsciously internalized. They are no more comfortable with their needs to earn and spend their own money than they are with their bodily needs for food and sex. Ladylike women, some part of them believes, should not have these "wayward desires." The modern, independent side of a Financial Virgin, however, rebels against the prohibiting voices within herself by overindulging, then pays with guilt and self-denial. For Financial Virgins, money becomes a symbol of inner conflict, instead of a source of pleasure and fulfillment.

The Weaker Vessels

Seventeenth-century Anglican clergymen termed women "weaker vessels" because their naturally pure souls were susceptible to corruption. Contemporary Weaker Vessels still profess that the purity of their lives or work could be spoiled by money. Though these money squeamish women may have commendable ideals and come from religious backgrounds, they live in a cultural and economic climate which makes it hard for them to go on believing that money is the root of all evil. In fact, the Weaker Vessel's protestation that money and the people who have it are corrupt is often a rationalization for her own failure to earn, fear of success, or career confusion.

Weaker Vessels are prevalent among women who have chosen low-paying, social service professions, or financially capricious vocations that promise glory, like one of the arts. Artists believe, often with validity, that financial rewards are bestowed on artistic products that are not the best. They say that they have not earned much money for their work because, by contrast, it is "good" or "pure." A California artist who supported herself on a poverty level while she painted, wrote:

> I felt, from age twenty-two to thirty-five, at least, that making money would be too powerful a goal for a fledgling artist—that I was not making commodities, and wanting money might pollute my art-making process.

Age and necessity often urge the Weaker Vessel to revise her counterproductive attitudes. Sue, a single Maryland social worker, began to modify her belief that money is not "pure" when she turned forty and realized that if she did not take care of her old age, no one else would. She told us that she still wanted a "socially useful job," but one that "pays a lot more."

> I always felt, until now, that if I earned a lot of money it would inhibit my spiritual development. I never wanted to be dominated by money, and was always proud that I never needed much. I also realize that it's not a sin to be worth it; it's a sin to take it from someone without earning it.

Originally Sue subscribed to the Victorian definition of a lady by keeping her needs to a minimum, then graduated to the Puritan idea that it was acceptable to earn, provided that you did so honestly. Why did she believe that money would "dominate" her? For Financial Virgins, money threatens loss of self-control; Weaker Vessels, on the other hand, believe that money would control them by subjecting them to changing forces.

Andrea, a participant in our New York money group, also feared the controlling powers of money. She had broken away from a Southern Catholic working-class background, put herself through journalism school, and was working as a reporter for a metropolitan daily. She told the group that she had recently discussed the possibility of ghostwriting a celebrity biography with a male friend, an editor for a major publishing firm. Andrea rejected the idea when she learned she would not have "total control" over the editorial content.

> He said, "There's two hundred thousand dollars there, Andy. Come on! You wouldn't do it for that kind of money?" And I said, "No, I made that mistake once, and it wasn't even for that kind of money."

A member of the group questioned Andrea about her money squeamishness:

> But Andy, that kind of money would let you buy an apartment, and take time off to write a novel, like you told us you wanted to do, and the job would be over within a few months. Your name wouldn't even be on the book!

Andrea replied:

> Famous last words! Maybe that's my Catholic upbringing. I would love to make a lot of money, but I want to make it in a pure way.

Though there might be good reasons for Andy to turn down a lucrative opportunity, we did not think loss of purity was a convincing one, given her ambitious financial goals. Andrea's "purity," even as she defined it in professional terms, preserved her relationship with her religious, working-class family. Two hundred thousand dollars, however, represented a potentially terrifying unknown—a new world with unpredictable boundaries, light-years away from her family's world. Andrea had wanted to get away from her family, but not that far away. It was not editorial "control" she feared but the irreversible changes, and the lonely feeling of total separation, she imagined money would impose.

The Genteel Poor

The money squeamish women in this category believe there is a righteous nobility to impoverishment. Often well educated, they regard scrambling after money as a sign of ill-breeding and pride themselves on keeping their needs to a minimum. They achieve taste and style on a shoestring and think it worthwhile to try to be happy poor. Being happy poor does not exclude having middle-class comforts, however, and the Genteel Poor are rarely found living in slums or shacks. Some will resort to exploitation, if necessary, to survive in the style to which they are accustomed.

Among the Genteel Poor are house guests who do not contribute for groceries and women who dislike picking up their share of a check on a date. They also resent "dirtying their hands," or taking jobs they consider beneath them; they may refuse to carry their financial weight in a marriage. Beneath their facade of virtuous abstention from income-producing tasks, these women may actually doubt their ability to achieve financially.

The Money Martyrs

Money Martyrs think it is "morally superior" to ignore their financial needs and often become victims. They believe those who rip them off, or hustle to get the material advantages they would secretly like to have, are lower on the moral hierarchy. The supposedly guilty conscience of those who exploit them is adequate compensation for the Money Martyrs, who prefer to remain passive and pure in relation to money. Doris Day, who was also money blind, was unable to focus on her financial picture partly because she was a Money Martyr. Throughout her life, as we have seen, she was exploited both personally and professionally. Even the manager of the first band she sang with pocketed half her pay. Doris explains her failure to demand justice in moral terms:

> I suppose from the very beginning I was just too naive and trusting in a business that attracts predators. But it is my nature to be trusting—I wouldn't have it any other way. . . . Those who have abused it—well, I pity them, for I am none the worse, really, for their abuses, but they are.[4]

Money Martyrs have trouble negotiating for raises, or finding high-paying jobs, because they believe their talent and hard work should be rewarded automatically. Like the Genteel Poor, they think that those who fend for their own economic interests are "crass." Edith, a Washington lawyer who works as a fund raiser for political candidates, did not ask for raises (though she often worked grueling sixty-hour weeks) or use her highly placed connections to steer her to lucrative and challenging jobs.

> The people I know who've made it have been single-minded about it. They've done it by shoving other people around, backbiting, demanding money, and making a lot of noise and fuss. It's clear to me that people get money, not

for what they're worth, but because they know people and promote themselves. I don't want to degrade myself. I just want to be paid what I'm worth.

Edith gets vicarious satisfaction from being slighted professionally, because she remains confident that she has conducted herself in a ladylike manner and done high-quality work. She vents her frustration at not getting what she is worth by criticizing those who have for their inappropriate behavior. Meanwhile, her virtue does not pay her rent.

The Problem with Money Squeamishness

Because money squeamishness is a rigid, moral attitude, and those who hold it are convinced it is correct, it is hard for women with this problem to see that their financial ideals may be working against their best interests. We do not mean to imply that a healthy morality in relation to money—and what one does with it—is inappropriate. Nor would we encourage women to model themselves after unscrupulous robber barons, or Mafia godfathers, or to sell out their true interests or the people close to them in order to become "filthy rich." Women, we believe, have to create a financial identity that expresses their feminine values; otherwise they risk imitating the traditional life formulas of men, which have not always been satisfying to them either.

However, if a woman lets herself believe that it is immoral, greedy, or selfish to act in her own behalf, she may never be able to examine the fears that stand between her and financial success. Today's marketplace often asks a woman to compete with men for the same job; an inner conflict that results in a lack of assertiveness puts her at a disadvantage. If she views talking about money as "tacky" she may deprive herself of useful information, which will help her price her contribution and make profitable investments. Money squeamishness in her personal life may lead to uncomfortable feelings of exploitation. Last but not least, to place oneself "above" financial needs and problems is a way to deny they exist; it is not a constructive approach to seeing or solving them.

Who Keeps Money Squeamishness Alive

Women can inherit money squeamishness from unsuccessful fathers, who condemned earning power in others and professed to believe that job satisfaction is more important than high pay. Mothers who stopped working after marriage, and proclaimed that their homemaking jobs were a "sacrifice" they made for their children, communicated the attitude, too.

Money squeamishness learned from parents is reinforced by men who believe that women should earn less than they do. An ambitious woman may get money squeamish messages from her male partner, particularly if he is earning less than she is, or less than he would like. Gabrielle, for example, an assertive New York woman with her own direct-mail advertising company, said her ex-husband accused her of "moneygrubbing" even before her fledgling business operated in the black.

> His career was on the rocks, yet he gave me long-winded speeches about my superficial values. Though he accused me of being a moneygrubber, if there was ever a man who liked to go to fancy restaurants and have beautiful things, it was my husband. I didn't care so much about all that. Every once in a while he would talk about how he really felt he owed me a fur coat. I contribute to the World Wildlife Fund, and never said boo about fur coats.

Grub is a word with Germanic roots which means "to dig in the ground." By calling her a "moneygrubber," Gabrielle's husband reduced her talents and goals to a low form of menial labor, and yearned to restore her femininity (and his male ego) by giving her the gift high-earning men have traditionally given their wives. Yet if Gabrielle had married a richer husband in order to get expensive gifts like fur coats she might have been accused of groveling in the dirt for something else—or "gold-digging."

The Story of "J": The Rise and Fall of a Financial Virgin

Who wouldn't want to make a fast fortune by writing a best-selling book? Many of the women who filled out our questionnaire named this as their financial fantasy. However, as one author who went from rags to riches discovered, hell hath no wrath greater than Victorian reactionary forces, which can seem mythical until a woman makes a pile by saying something in print that is not considered "nice." Terry Garrity's problem was that the book she wrote under the pseudonym "J," *The Sensuous Woman*, told women how to manipulate men by enjoying sex. When the book became a blockbusting success, Terry was so overwhelmed by the furor that ensued, and the repercussions in her personal life, that she found it easier to go back to rags than to go on being "unladylike." Let's look at how money squeamishness destroyed Terry Garrity.

A product of the pre-feminist 1950s, Terry grew up in a Minneapolis Catholic family, where one of the lessons she learned was that men didn't marry girls who were not virgins. In the freewheeling sixties, star-struck Terry came to New York to pursue an acting career and worked as a hatcheck girl, secretary, and publicist for the publisher Lyle Stuart. Later, Stuart, who knew that Terry was struggling to start her own publicity agency, offered her the opportunity to write a publishing first—"a sex book by a woman for women"—for a meager $1,500 advance.

Terry agreed. As she explains in her autobiography, *The Story of "J,"* she was an excellent candidate for this novel assignment. Although she had experimented with a number of sexual partners, she had never succeeded in enjoying sex and had always faked orgasms. Old-fashioned doctors and psychiatrists advised her that, like many women, she suffered from a low sex drive. One day, while shopping, it dawned on Terry that having an orgasm was an art to be learned—like unearthing a pair of expensive shoes from the bargain table at a department store, which she was in the process of doing. She proceeded to teach herself to have transporting climaxes by masturbating, and then in bed with a man by "learning a higher degree of selfishness" and "focusing on her own sensations."

Terry saw the Lyle Stuart contract not as an opportunity to make a quick buck, but as a worthwhile campaign to initiate other frigid women into the joys of sex. She did, however, insist on a pseudonym: "I felt squeamish about being identified as a sex book author," she said. Stuart agreed, and Terry churned out *The Sensuous Woman* in record time. It was published at the peak of the Sexual Revolution—in 1969.

Compared to more radical and graphic sex manuals that followed, *The Sensuous Woman* contained little that was shocking. Basically, it advised women how to get and keep a man by resorting to time-honored feminine ploys, such as wearing slinky lingerie and changing the bedroom decor to keep sex exciting. However, it also described masturbation and fellatio techniques, such as "The Butterfly Flick" and "The Silken Swirl" and anal intercourse. Though it was these details that ostensibly shocked sixties Puritans, we think what really shocked them was the more radical political message that Terry had unwittingly preached between the lines.

In essence, *The Sensuous Woman* declared that a woman could manipulate and control a man by demanding—and achieving—her own sexual pleasure. And that had been, since time immemorial, a male prerogative. Ugly women, according to Terry, could wield power over rich and handsome men by brushing up on their sexual stimulation skills. Women with straying husbands could recapture them by making sex an "adventure." The Sensuous Woman could even obtain material wealth—"great loot like diamond necklaces, ruby bracelets, and mink coats"—merely for the sexual satisfaction she was experiencing herself.

This is scarcely a feminist message: Terry was telling the ladylike women of her generation to engage in what amounts to a domestic form of prostitution. Unlike the prostitute, who is using her body only to make money, however, Terry's Sensuous Woman gets personal pleasure from her manipulative act. Terry had strayed quite far from her Catholic girlhood in

Minneapolis, but since she had done so in disguise, she at first took the outraged reaction to her book in stride.

> People wrote "J" and quoted Biblical injunctions that seemed to prohibit all sexual contact between humans, up to and including handshakes. They connected masturbation with venereal disease and madness.... My more progressive critics conceded that performing these sexual acts might be acceptable, but describing them was not.... Radical women's libbers ... blasted me for perpetuating the image of women as "mere" (their word not mine) sex objects.

When the paperback rights to the book sold for $100,000, however, Terry had something else to worry about—money—which she, like other money squeamish women, feared might control or change her life.

> This money was exciting, but it made me nervous too. I didn't want my life to change radically.

As she embarked on the first of many compulsive spending sprees, Stuart broke his promise and revealed "J"'s true identity to *Time* magazine. Terry's greatest fear was now realized: Her mother, to whom she was very close, would, along with the rest of the world, find out that the author of *The Sensuous Woman* was Terry Garrity, a girl who had prided herself on being as "wholesome as apple pie."

> Mother had never discussed sex with me. She was a very cosmopolitan, sophisticated woman in most matters, but she had a Victorian moral outlook ... everybody respected the fact that she was a "lady," and that certain matters had to be treated delicately.

Terry decided to confess before the *Time* article appeared:

> I was right to have dreaded that moment. She was shaken. Confused. It seemed completely unreal to her. For years I had hidden a side of my nature from Mother, knowing she would disapprove. I had told myself—in fact, I told everyone—that I was not ashamed of *The Sensuous Woman*. But with Mother? I felt shame. I had associated myself with something that was dirty in her eyes.

Though Terry's parents were divorced and she apparently had little contact with her father, she also feared his reaction:

And Daddy? How would he feel when he heard that his little girl had written a steamy sex manual?

Terry, then, had taken giant steps away from her mother's Victorian world. In the end, however, her orgasms had not transported her very far; she had not really separated from her family and society's message about women's roles. Now personally connected to the "steamy sex manual" that she had written, Terry was caught in the most dramatic possible confrontation between her need to forge a workable modern identity for herself (which included making money and satisfying her sexual needs), and old-fashioned, restrictive definitions of "ladylike" behavior. To make matters worse, Terry's mother (who, it ought to be said, took the news of her daughter's fall from grace with a stiff upper lip) developed terminal cancer and died shortly thereafter. Though her mother had been ill before, perhaps Terry thought *The Sensuous Woman* had dealt the mortal blow.

A miserable nervous wreck, and suffering from gynecological problems (which resulted in her being unable to have children), Terry nevertheless began stumping bravely for her book, appearing on television and radio talk shows throughout the country. But she no longer felt in touch with herself. The fifties Victorian virgin and The Sensuous Woman were now split in two:

> "J" signed aerosol cans of whipped cream that male fans thrust at her at bookstore appearances; Terry would have blushed and fled . . . [Terry] bought beautiful clothes and objets d'art with the money "J" was making hand over fist.

It was probably the more modern "J" who discovered that Lyle Stuart was not paying the royalties he owed on the book and instituted a lawsuit, but Victorian Terry justified the suit in moral terms—it would vindicate other authors who had been ripped off by their publishers but could not afford to sue.

Terry's squeamish feelings about having written a sex book extended to its profits, and she began to use her money to restore herself to a more ladylike status. She became Lady Bountiful, buying extravagant gifts for her family and friends. She shopped compulsively. She became the "caretaker" of the important men in her life, legally dividing her earnings on *The Sensuous Man*, the next book Stuart commissioned her to write, with her brother and boyfriend. Keeping her needs minimal, as a good Financial Virgin should, she accepted a piddling advance for this project. She signed 10 percent of her earnings on *The Sensuous Woman* over to her boyfriend, whom she named as "agent"; he, in turn, promised to use the cash to take the two of them on luxurious vacations. By getting rid of the most concrete evidence of her unladylike success—the "filthy lucre"—Terry tried to atone.

But she still had additional "wages of sin" to pay. Her boyfriend never used the money he made on *The Sensuous Woman* to take her on trips; instead they split up. Terry began to suffer from mental confusion, health problems, and professional paralysis; she found it almost impossible to produce a new book on love that Simon & Schuster had paid her a whopping $200,000 to write. Living in isolation in a Palm Beach apartment, Terry spent most of her time binge-shopping and binge-eating. Soon she was surrounded by a virtual fortress of shopping bags containing "fire engine red moire gowns, Baccarat millefiori paperweights, and four pairs of shoes, all exactly alike." Sometimes she could not remember paying for these purchases and thought she might have succumbed to kleptomania during her "blackouts." To pay her department store bills, her financial adviser began to sell the stocks and bonds be had bought to provide for her future security. Terry was using her riches to buy rags. Sex had fled from her life, and the woman who had earned a million by becoming The Sensuous Woman now slept alone. The lawsuit against Stuart, which was resolved in her favor, was a dubious moral victory. By the time legal fees were paid, it netted her only $30,000 and additional humiliation. During the trial a vicious article Lyle Stuart had written for *Screw* magazine was introduced as evidence. Stuart said:

> Terry Garrity is suing me as a woman scorned . . . I asked her to write a book that would make cocksucking respectable in America, and we published *The Sensuous Woman*. I've paid her more than $700,000 . . . but the sudden riches seem to have frightened away all the fellows she used to blow, and now she's hysterical because with nothing but bananas and overcooked frankfurters to suck on, her buck teeth are threatening to fall out.

If Terry had not already been convinced that she had defied all notions of common decency by writing a sex book, she might have survived this vindictive attack and judged it for what it was—an enraged sexist's predictable response to being asked to pay her more money than he thought any woman had a right to earn. Instead, she saw it as another Scarlet A branded on her forehead.

> I felt nauseous and tears were welling up in my eyes. I felt that I was a party to some uncontrollable ugliness, and that I was mired in muck and would never be clean again.

Terry eventually succumbed and was treated by a psychiatrist for mental illness—a mood disorder called bipolar cyclical depression, caused by a chemical imbalance and aggravated by stress. She now attributes all of her problems to this disease. Though Terry was indeed depressed, and may have always suffered from her illness, as she claims, it never got the best of her until she defied social mores by making a lot of money writing about sex.

We think Terry was a casualty in a brave new world where women were just beginning to demand the right to fulfill both their sexual and financial needs, and tended to see both as "forbidden." Because in Terry's case, an unlikely chain of events united her desire for money and sex in the public eye, she paid a heavier price than most of us, who asked for, and got, similar freedoms. In order to "repent" for her transgressions, Terry became a modern counterpart of the Victorian woman—nonproductive, confined to the hearth, dependent, with no money of her own, and sick. Like Jane Addams, whose doctors attempted to cure her nervous disorder by isolating her in a dark, quiet room, Terry Garrity "cured" herself by closing herself up in her soundproof Palm Beach apartment and letting her brother and male psychiatrist take care of her.

> I now settled into being sick. The weight of responsibility seemed lifted off me.[5]

And so, in this way, one terrorized Sensuous Woman fled back to the safe but restrictive nineteenth century. Terry's story, although it may seem ancient history in the post-Sexual Revolutionary era, has a lesson to teach about the perils of unacknowledged money squeamishness. Those who would dismiss her as "weak" or "crazy" should ask themselves how they would feel if their mothers found out they had written a best-selling sex manual.

Overcoming Money Squeamishness: Candace's Battle with the Curse of Genteel Poverty

When we first met Candace we thought she was struggling with a world-class mid-life crisis. The school of English as a Second Language, where she taught, had folded, and at thirty-six she was collecting unemployment insurance and was unable to decide what she wanted to do next or, as she put it, "What I am capable of doing."

When we interviewed her, however, it became apparent that Candace's career confusion had not begun in midlife. Though she had worked since college graduation, she had yet to dedicate herself to a career or earn a high salary. A few of her many jobs had been equal to her intelligence and education—working as an assistant producer for a television news show—and others had not—selling encyclopedias door to door. Now, her husband, a hardworking, intellectual electrician, who wanted more time to make pottery and "read Plato in bed," was demanding that Candace bring in her share of income.

> I think he understands my inclination to be supported, and this he does not want. The minute the news came in that the school had folded, Richard said, "Well, get to work on your resume." And I put on the façade of looking for a job to make him happy, but I'm not really looking for a job just yet. We don't have a totally honest relationship.

While Candace "pretended to look for a job" and debated what to do with her life, she helped Richard do the bookkeeping and cost price jobs for his small business. When we asked why this vital contribution was not considered income-producing, and why she didn't ask her husband to pay her a salary, we stumbled on the reason behind Candace's career confusion: She was money squeamish. For her, pay would devalue her contribution.

> I don't want to be someone you can pay off and forget about. When people say to him, "What does Candace do for you?" that's what I do. If I got paid it wouldn't be the same at all. I wouldn't be valued for doing it personally. It reminds me of when I was a kid and did the dishes at a dinner party. The guests said to my mother, "Oh, Candace is doing the dishes! Isn't that nice!" My mother, a bit embarrassed by this, said, "Well, I'm going to give Candace a dollar!" And I started to cry.

Like other money squeamish women, Candace did not want to "dirty her hands" unless she got the vicarious moral satisfaction of working for free. She felt guilty that she did not earn and tried to compensate for her lack of income by keeping her needs to a minimum.

> Richard struggles so hard working in filthy basements and driving his wretched old truck around. But his expenses haven't gone up radically since we got married. I don't eat much. It's a question of whether I contribute. I do feel guilty . . . I should be doing more for Richard.

In fact, doing something for her husband was the only good reason Candace could think of to earn a salary. She admitted to a personal "disdain for money" and thought sacrifice was required to "launder" it.

> I think I could go out and earn money if I had a couple of dependent children. If you go out and work and make a lot of money for yourself, I think people are really saying, "Greedy! Tacky! Insensitive! Low values!" But if you go out and support your children, they say, "Isn't she terrific? We

know Candace isn't the type to make $150,000 a year, but she's doing it for her children! . . ."

We laughed at Candace's ironic humor, but we knew that beneath her wit she was also sincere. We learned that her money squeamishness was a trait that went back two generations. Her current lifestyle in a modest Boulder, Colorado, house, and her marriage to a philosophical electrician—even her struggle with money issues—were very different than the atmosphere of genteel poverty in which she had been raised. Candace's story provides a dramatic illustration of the way money squeamish messages are passed from parents to daughters, and how difficult this inheritance is to shake.

Candace was a Montgomery. Her old Virginia family traced its origins back to the early colonists, and lived in a crumbling estate that had once belonged to Thomas Jefferson. Neither of her parents worked for money. Her mother, a biochemist, had earned a doctorate in her field from an Ivy League university, but she claimed that staying at home was a sacrifice that she made for her children.

> She said she couldn't bear missing us take our first steps, and so on, but she was always out doing errands and volunteering-the ladies' this and the women's that. And she was always bad-tempered and angry. She talked endlessly about how she'd sacrificed her own career to be a good mother. "My children are the most important thing in the world to me, and I don't care if they hate me, I'm going to bring them up right," she'd say. "Love is a four-letter word: W-O-R-K! Working hard!" She was always working away, but I think her feelings of inferiority were overwhelming.

Candace's father was an art historian who had never fulfilled the promise of a luminous career. For years he had been finishing an authoritative book on Giotto while curating the collection of the state museum, for which he received more of an honorary stipend than a living wage.

> Every now and then Daddy would say, "I think I'll take a half year off and work on my book," and we all knew not to follow up on that. Nobody ever mentioned the book, and he never got anywhere as far as we knew. Nevertheless, we all thought my father was more gloriously smart than the critics who actually wrote all those books. Perhaps he wasn't as famous, but then, be didn't do the crass thing. Achievement was thought of as a little tacky. You had to be on the inside circle. He was a wonderful curator, and everyone respected him all the same.

How did Candace's family survive? On inherited money that her great-grandfather on her father's side had made in business. The succeeding generations, however, despised the family's source of income. Her grandfather had continued to operate the factory, but for "charitable" reasons—to keep local people employed during the Depression.

> By the time he died there was so much money that it liberated his sons. My father didn't have to do anything for money, and he felt guilty about it.

With a guilty, underachieving father and an angry, economically powerless mother, Candace and her siblings got a confusing negative message about the value of money and how it should be earned and spent. Her parents professed that money signified "low values" and lived in a deceptive state of genteel poverty, which Candace wittily described like this:

> My parents are quite upper class in terms of squalor. They never fix anything. The place crumbles away and is filled with old trash. They let their couch go for twenty years, and the cats scratch it to bits, but they still think it's a grand old couch. It was very oppressive to me.

Because money and material things were disdained as "worldly" or "tacky," Candace was not encouraged to value them.

> They didn't want us to think money was important to have. They were small allowance givers, and I was always very badly dressed in hand-me-downs. I was dying for a horse my whole life, and when I finally got one, it was twenty-one years old and horribly swaybacked. A year later, some colonel who had originally owned it came and took it back. Why didn't they buy me a horse? They could have afforded it! I didn't understand that they were trying to keep my values intact, and instead took all this to mean that I wasn't worth much. My father, however, never hesitated to spend money on himself.

In order to keep her from acquiring another "worldly" value—a sense of competence, known in the Montgomery mythology as "a swelled head"—Candace was seldom praised for her achievements. Because money, "like toilet training and sex was not an item you discussed," her financial life plan was never mentioned.

> We just assumed that life would take its happy course, whatever that would be. They never pushed me into anything, or made any suggestions. I took this to mean that they didn't really think I could do anything. How they

thought I was going to get by in the world I'll never know, because by the time the family money comes to me, they will already have spent it.

Growing up with a sense of worthlessness and impotence, Candace was terrified throughout her childhood that her parents might discover that she secretly held values of which they would not approve.

For one thing, I liked boys. I felt I should have been reading Dante, but instead I was reading *Double Date*. My parents insisted on this upper level, and I grew up thinking my feelings were wrong, and hiding them. I worked very hard at presenting myself as a "correct Montgomery," but I was a pretend person.

No wonder Candace was bogged down in career confusion! She had grown up feeling like a "pretend person," but actually she had been part of a "pretend world," where an inability to work or make money had been reinterpreted to be a superior moral value. In the Montgomery family myth, fathers could be brilliant and respected without succeeding financially, and a mother, however impressive her education, could stay home from the marketplace and be worth more than if she had earnings.

Candace could criticize her parents' values and joke about her painful upbringing. Nonetheless, the Montgomery myth was deeply instilled in her at an early age. Though she could dismiss it intellectually, she had trouble separating from its powerful emotional influence. Because she inherited the family money squeamishness without inheriting its money, she was struggling to realize that she needed to earn and felt her precarious financial state concealed invisible wealth.

I feel there is always something between me and the streets . . . that I am most fortunate in my wealth, and all I lack is the money. Work, for me, is just a little exercise to find out how real people live.

When we met Candace, she appeared to be floundering, but, as she looked deeply into her money mirror, she saw that she had achieved a great deal. She had managed to sever the tight strings of her childhood, and battling great psychological odds, had moved away from her inherited money squeamishness. As she put it:

I've become a real person. I've been able to live in a reasonable, normal way, and by being fairly sound and sensible, I've gotten by.

To ensure her future as a "real person," Candace had married a "regular guy" who insisted that she earn, however reluctantly. Through him, she was learning to value her financial contribution and was proudly discovering that she was "good at business"—a low-class calling by Montgomery standards.

> I told the two guys who work for Richard that the place was under new management. From now on they report to me. I'm going to cost out the jobs and find out why Richard isn't making more money.

Later, Candace wrote to say that she was now charging her husband for her work in his office, which she found "enormously satisfying." She had applied for actual jobs, instead of pretending to apply, and had been delighted to be selected from hundreds of applicants for a personal interview for a good position editing educational textbooks. Candace was traveling further away from her family's imaginary world, where, unlike the world of our Puritan forefathers, hard-earned money was despised.

Chapter Four

Someone to Watch Over Me: Understanding Money Denial

The money aware woman knows she is responsible for caring for herself financially for her whole life. All women want to be cared for, but some want someone or something outside of themselves to do what they regard as a frightening or onerous chore: These are money deniers, and although they deny it, many women are.

The woman who has gazed profoundly into her money mirror sees her financial well-being as a process, personally affirming: She understands that money and her inner needs must harmonize. A desirable lifestyle, she knows, is part of a complex story that she creates herself, not a ready made fairy tale—like "The Shower of Gold"—that she can slip into like an actress takes on a dramatic role. Money, she understands, can nurture her, and give her power if she nurtures herself and controls her life. If she is in a marriage or relationship, she continues to enjoy financial responsibility, not because she expects to divorce, or "end up alone," but because providing for her material well-being is an integral part of her positive self-concept in a multi-faceted world.

Money deniers, on the other hand, fantasize about their financial future. In an age when most women work, they may be assertive wage earners, who have forged career identities, but their financial identities are still undefined. Nothing about the way they see or manage money indicates that they are taking care of their tomorrows as well as their todays. For them, money exists outside of themselves, and getting it represents closure, instead of an ongoing adventure, with inner, as well as external goals. They remain unaware that their earning, saving, and management styles reflect their personal and cultural histories, as well as deeply rooted dreams and fears.

A money denier is likely to entertain fantasies that a generous man will come along and rescue her. The man may be a rich father or aunt preparing to will her a fortune, or an employer, who will reward her talents with a glamorous, highly paid job. More likely, however, the fantasy rescuer is a "handsome prince," a renegade from a fairy tale, who will marry her and happily absorb her financial burdens—or at least half of them. She plans to live happily ever after with him, and leave her checkbook at the altar. For other deniers, the fantasy rescuer is not a person but a "lucky break"—a low interest loan, a big lottery win, a prestigious grant.

Whatever form her rescue fantasy takes, it can be so rooted in the denier's psychosocial history that she lives her financial life as if it was going to come true, while remaining unaware of it. The "handsome prince," inheritance, jackpot, or magical career opportunity sneaks into a day dream, but she would be embarrassed to admit they were there. Working hard today, making decisions about what path to take next, she remains blissfully unconscious that she lacks a realistic financial blueprint, until her fantasies are challenged by dramatic changes, an uncomfortable choice, or expectations that do not get fulfilled. At this point, she may become resentful and angry, not only at the circumstances that have pricked the bubble and brought about the painful new awareness, but at the society and family members that have duped her by not preparing her adequately for life. As we shall see, women who were not taught to develop their financial identities (the vast majority) often confuse emotional needs with their need for money.

Is the money denier an extinct species in an era when most women expect to spend the better part of their lives in the labor market? As late as the mid-1980s, women in their twenties, thirties and forties repeatedly told Ruth Sidel, author of *On Her Own: Growing Up in the Shadow of the American Dream*, that they grew up believing that someone else would take care of them.

The Three Faces of the Money Denier

Women from different backgrounds deny money in different ways, depending on their age, and the messages about women and money that they received from their parents and culture.

The Classic Money Denier

The Classic Money Denier is almost obsolete. Like her mother before her, she expects a man to take care of her financially, and sets out to find one willing to do so. These are the Southern Belles, Jewish Princesses, and Cinderellas, who have remained unaltered by changing times. Few strayed into our study, which was directed toward ambitious working women. One who did, a Massachusetts housewife in her fifties, told us:

> I love being a "kept woman!" I was raised to believe that was the way it was. Man supported woman!

"Kept women" like this one may fall on hard times if their husbands divorce them, or die and leave them impoverished. Like Scarlett O'Hara, they may find themselves digging for turnips in a frozen field. They have an important psychological advantage, however: They are clear about their needs and the way to meet them. We will not say more about the Classic Money Denier because we doubt very many of them are reading this book!

The Modern Money Denier

The Modern Money Denier is less easy to detect. She is usually working, supporting herself, or carrying at least part of her weight in a marriage; but her financial behavior indicates that she does not expect to be doing so for the rest of her life. A victim of mixed messages about women and money from her society and culture in her formative years, she doesn't want to be like her mother—who may have been angry and powerless, trapped in a low-paying job, or a housewife, dependent on her husband. However, she has received no clear guidelines on how to change her mother's script. Caught in a cross-cultural tide, she is pulled toward the future of women (an uncertain territory) and back to the past.

Modern Money Deniers are ambivalent about career goals. Some place boundaries on the amount they feel they can safely earn without jeopardizing the possibility of rescue. One psychologically sophisticated instructional designer voiced her fears of earning "too much."

> I am moderately successful financially, but if I let myself become very successful, then the mythical, wonderful man—the absent father—would never save me. I'd have to give up my fantasy.

Unlike non–Money Phobic women, who see earning as an enjoyable, as well as necessary part of their lives, the Modern Money Denier takes a stoic's view of supporting herself or her family. She regards income-producing as an unjust obligation she must endure. For her, the strain of making money gets in the way of life.

This money denier tends to feel that making money should be glamorous and exciting. A number of those we interviewed had two careers—one that supported them, and another "dream" career, which they thought of as "real"—usually in the arts or an entertainment field. They saw their money-making career as tediously demeaning, and the dream career as fascinating and prestigious. In some cases, they had done little to actualize the "dream career," and in others, they had done quite a lot.

Alice, for example, a Modern Money Denier, age thirty-four, showed no savings or assets on her questionnaire. She had invested all of her hopes, extra time, and cash in a singing career that, after a number of years, had produced some moments of glory, but no living wage. Meanwhile, Alice worked at a "boring" job for a record company. Although she was respected by her employer, and saw opportunities to advance, she preferred to ignore them, fantasizing that eventually she would earn six figures as a recording star, which she planned to give away and spend on clothes. She took great liberties with sick days and lunch hours to pursue her "real" career, secretly hoping the record company would fire her so she could collect unemployment insurance. If Alice did not imagine she would one day be rescued from the onus of self support, she might have taken both her singing career and the job that produced income equally seriously. She would have seen that both were important, and both were real.

Modern Money Deniers are often single or divorced, but they can be married, too. If she has chosen a mate who does not fulfill her rescue fantasies (a prince who is charming, but not ambitious or successful), a denier may feel betrayed by the myth. She becomes jealous of other women for whom the fairy tale came true and angry at her husband. One of the married money deniers in our study worked until she started a family, as she was raised to believe a woman should do. Now that her children are in school, she resents her husband, a psychiatric nurse, for not making as much money as her friends' husbands, and feels victimized because she has to take up the slack in the family budget with a bookkeeping job.

> My husband would rather live on less than take a chance in order to have more. Most of our friends have a great deal more money than we do. Their husbands are more ambitious (a trait I never learned to recognize until I was in my thirties). Our major money problem is lack of it. We simply don't have enough, and I feel he is waiting for me to bring in the extra money we need. I resent feeling that vacations and financial security are luxuries. I never thought my life would be this way.

This Modern Money Denier blames her husband for waiting for her to take financial initiative. Actually, it is she who is waiting—for her husband to change from a frog to a prince—and her anger will not alter her financial situation until she can recognize it as feedback for her hurtful fantasy.

The New Money Denier

At first glance, the New Money Denier, younger than her counterparts, appears to be the Woman of Tomorrow, who sees an ambitious, lucrative career as her destiny—anyone but a woman with no lifetime financial plan. From her mother, who may have been negatively affected by divorce, feelings of powerlessness in a marriage, or limited earning power, she has learned that she must expect to pay her way and take care of herself. A prodigious grandchild of the feminist movement, she believes that a high salary job, one that had a "Men Only" sign on it in ancient times, is an inalienable right, and right for her. Of course, she intends to pursue an advanced degree and become a CEO, surgeon, or partner in a law firm. An old-fashioned "female" career as a social worker, nurse, or teacher? Give her a break! She imagines herself, stunning and slim, in the Gianni Versace suit she saw in *Vogue*, carrying a cool calfskin briefcase, and creating a solid career identity before she connects with a partner—a sensitive, new age guy, willing to do his share of the housework and child care. Then, she fantasizes, they and their kids will partake of the American dream—a beautiful home, luxurious vacations, a spanking new Bronco, the whole apple pie! If she starts now, works hard, and makes the right decisions at the right time, she sees no reason why her dream shouldn't materialize.[1]

Unfortunately, there may be problems with the New Money Denier's assertive dream: Her vision may have nothing to do with her inner needs, her abilities, or, for that matter, with the declining American economy, the government's lack of commitment to equal opportunity or equal pay for women, and the relatively low number of women in high-paying jobs.

Although it may be possible for her to achieve her goal— fair numbers of women have—she may not have investigated the emotional sacrifices a high-powered career will exact, or her desire to make them. How will her dream career conflict with her unique personal needs (like time alone, with friends, family, or children)? How much will the degree she intends to pursue cost? What are her ultimate chances of success in her chosen field? The New Money Denier can't answer these questions, or hasn't thought them through. In short, as she prepares to shimmy up the highest peak, and grab the pot of gold at the top, she is not considering her inner landscape, nor the political and economic landscape of her country today. This money denier has bought the latest media image of a successful superwoman, which for many, is no more real—or, in fact, desirable—than life in a fairy tale princess's tower. For the New Money Denier, however, the handsome prince looks like a law degree. In the meantime, she may depend on middle-class parents to rescue her from tedious financial obligations, like paying rent, and has no doubt that relatives will cough up the down payment on her "starter" house.

Identifying Money Deniers

How can a money denier be identified? Her main characteristic is that her financial biography is written entirely in the present tense. She may work very hard, dream of success, and even make money, but she lives hand-to-mouth. Generally, she is money blind and does not calculate the amount she needs or spends, perhaps because she considers her current financial responsibilities temporary or unreal. She is also likely to be money squeamish—i.e., she believes discussing the details of her financial state is tacky. But money itself? She loves it and would like to have a lot. While she waits for The Shower of Gold, she earns enough to meet her present needs and seldom feels anxious about money.

A money denier can also be detected by her spending habits. Since she secretly believes her future finances will be taken care of by someone—or something—else, she binges, blows, and throws money away. She has a wallet full of credit cards and doesn't hesitate to use them, or ask her parents for money. No one is less likely to save or invest than a money denier. She does not plan for retirement, because to do so would constitute an admission that she might end up alone, or minus a huge windfall, in her (not so) golden years. When asked how she intends to take care of herself in the future, she answers that she will work until she dies—a noble, but possibly unrealistic aspiration. Meanwhile, she gathers her rosebuds while she may. Although she may suffer a financial crunch when she loses a job or overspends, deprivation does not inspire her to review her money *modus operandi*.

If the money denier hopes to be rescued by a prince, or by a glamorous, high-paying job, she is likely to become overly concerned with her weight and appearance. No woman can subscribe as unquestioningly to media images and prescriptions for beauty and fashion as she. An ideal consumer, the money denier may spend most of her discretionary income on clothes, makeup, and hairstyles, regarding these expenditures as necessary "investments."

Though afflicted with a self-image inherited from her male-dominated culture, the money denier often appears rebellious and may lead her life in unorthodox ways. People view her as a "free spirit" because they do not see the traditional side that she scrupulously hides, even from herself. Those who both want to be saved and fear the pound of flesh a rescuer may extract in return, may defend themselves against their fantasies by doing everything in their power to make sure they don't come true. Ironically, no one fears rescue as much as these victims of conflict.

Because of her fear, the money denier may either avoid relationships altogether, or specialize in "inappropriate" non-rescuing men—dashing, handsome, neurotic "princes," who provide charm, intellectual stimulation, even thrilling sex, but who are either essentially unavailable for long-term relationships, or who suffer from male versions of Money Phobia and are poor themselves. Instead of seeing these love objects for what they are, and enjoying what they have to offer, however, the money denier tries to extract from them what they cannot give, and feels furious or humiliated when she fails to get it. The more involved she becomes in these immediate emotions, the less she is able to examine the economic fantasy that underlies them, and her conflict about the fantasy. And as she fails to get from men what she both wants and fears, her dream of a utopian form of rescue, which will not compromise her freedom, remains unchallenged.

Married money deniers who have always worked can still dream of rescue if the family income is inadequate for future plans. They imagine that someone else—grandparents or the government—will pay for their children's college educations, or that an inheritance will bestow retirement funds.

In the course of our money study, we learned that a woman who is not comfortable with the need to take care of herself financially, makes herself known by her psychological resistance to the idea that she may be waiting for someone—or something—else to provide. Though women can easily recognize money denial in others, acknowledging the same symptoms in themselves is difficult and painful, because to do so is to admit that they are not as independent and "modern" as they seem.

One of our New York money groups, insightful and intelligent women, became angry and confused when we presented them with the symptoms of money denial, and asked if they could relate them to their own life experience. At one point in our long description of money deniers, we had used the term "old-fashioned." The women immediately picked this up and took violent exception: How could we use such a derogatory word? They hoped we wouldn't put it in our book! Without revealing why they found "old fashioned" so personally threatening, they then proceeded to analyze the financial habits of their money-denying friends and the difficult plight of modern women. Our discussion had obviously strayed on to dangerous ground, and our group members found it safer to generalize.

After forty-five minutes of beating around the bush, these usually highly focused, self-aware women were finally able to approach the topic of rescue, although not from a financial viewpoint. Ann, divorced for five years, described the time the pipes had broken in her country home, and her feeling that she had been victimized by her husband when it fell to her to cope with the disaster because he was away.

> Though it was in no way his fault the pipes broke, I could never forgive my husband for that . . . for making me deal with the plumber! I felt it important that he take care of certain things and that they never fall on me . . . for what reason, I can't tell you.

Rebecca, who had left her husband, saw a dead cat she found under the porch the first weekend she was alone in her house as a symbol of all the new trials that faced her.

> I thought, What do I do with this dead cat? It seemed like an omen of my life alone. I went out and got a shovel, but when I so much as looked under the deck, I felt sick, as if I was going to faint. I pulled myself together and said, "This is a test of my life! I have to do this! How am I going to live alone if I can't?" Then I thought, How would Bob have taken care of this? and the answer was, He'd pay someone to do it. That's one of the things I've had to learn since I've been on my own . . . that you can pay someone to do something. I've always thought either I have to do it, or someone else has to do it for me. I'd still rather have a guy who does it because he likes me.

Financial responsibilities (like the responsibility of fixing broken pipes and disposing of dead cats) are problems women look at from a different perspective once they begin to disabuse themselves of the rescue myth.

Caring for one's own financial future is the basis of any modern, independent life. Since most women have not been emotionally or practically trained for this complex job, they find it terrifying and intimidating. If they deny that their rescue fantasies exist, or let them lie unexplored, they can conduct their financial lives as they have in the past, without the stress of difficult changes. *The financial behavior the rescue fantasy inspires can also become a comfortable habit which perpetuates itself even after the fantasy itself has been exposed to the light of reality and faded.*

"Mirror, Mirror on the Wall": How Women Become Money Deniers

The rescue myth, in its purest form, is found in fairy tales, which continue to make their profound impressions on little girls today in modern and televised versions. The heroines of the most popular stories are all rescued by handsome princes and have special qualities that enable them to get saved.

First and foremost, the fairy tale heroine must be beautiful. Her mirror tells her nothing about her unique inner qualities, only that she is "the fairest of them all." Her beauty is often symbolized by one exceptional feature, separate from the rest of herself, which identifies her as having "royal blood," or entitlement. Snow White has remarkable coloring: She is as "white as snow, as red as blood, and as black as ebony." Rapunzel's wealth lies in her tower-length hair, as "fine as spun gold," and Cinderella has tiny feet.

Though these selfless heroines are usually unaware of their beauty, it makes them the target of mixed emotions—love, hatred, envy, and possessiveness—and vulnerable to attack. Their beauty, it seems, is the outward manifestation of their only other salient quality—virtue, which is represented by their total passivity. These heroines submit to whatever injustices their beauty foists upon them without complaint. In the original Grimm version of the story, Cinderella obligingly picks bowls of lentils out of the ashes at her sadistic stepmother's bidding. Snow White, rescued from the forest by seven dwarfs, does their housework happily, despite her royal birth. These beauties have no complex thoughts and few emotions, even for the handsome prince who rescues them. When Rapunzel lets down her golden hair and draws up a prince instead of the wicked old witch, she thinks only, "He will love me better than old Mother Gothel." Sleeping Beauty, awakened by her rescuer, is hardly inflamed by passion: She "looks lovingly at him." It is the princes who brave hardship to win their loves and feel all the emotions as part of the prize.

Before she is rescued, the fairy tale heroine's beauty and passive virtue condemn her to persecution and isolation. Sleeping Beauty pricks her finger on a needle, and because of an angry fairy's curse, falls into a deep sleep as a briar hedge covers her castle, closing her off from the world. Rapunzel is lonely in her tower, but when her wicked guardian discovers her lover, she is transported to an even more isolated spot—the wilderness. Snow White ends up in a glass coffin, where, even dead, she is good enough for her admiring prince, who sees no problem with her lifeless state.

Their obedient passivity and enchanted sleep disconnect the virtuous beauties from the furious emotions and violence in the fairy tale's "real world." Sleeping Beauty's would-be rescuers are pierced to death by the briars that surround her castle; Rapunzel's lover is blinded by the jealous witch, and in the original "Cinderella," the wicked stepsisters slice off their toes and heels in order to cram their oversized feet into the tiny golden slipper, leaving "blood on the track."

Rescue, then, saves the heroines from a deathlike state, which, like their innocence, protects them from passions so dangerous to other people. What happens to these beauties after they have been rescued? We know only that they live "happily ever after," and that happiness seems to mean adoration and wealth.

How the Fairy Tale Invaded Our Lives

Several of the women we interviewed for this book referred to themselves as fairy tale heroines, or saw similarities between their lives and the lives of the mythical beauties. These stories were etched so deeply in so many girls' minds because their prescription for the future—rescue by a prince—

was advocated by the family and culture. Many daughters were raised to be rescued and taught that real life would begin once they were "saved." Although the fairy tale vision of women's lives may be fading as women flood into the labor market, it reverberates today.

For women raised in the forties, fifties, and even for some who came of age in the sixties, a career was often thought of as something to "fall back on." Although these daughters were sent to college–a potential stomping ground for "handsome princes"– most were advised that a man would love them because they were pretty and sweet, not because they were brilliant, assertive, or successful. The best careers for a nice, pretty girl were those that required a minimum of long-range planning, apprenticeship, or competition; they waited for her to "fall" with open arms in the event the rescue mechanism failed. (One popular "fallback" career was teaching, which would not interfere with the prince's timetable, or the family's domestic needs in the event that the princess had to work after marriage.) With this future in mind, her family tried to shape her personality into the fairy tale mold, making her a "good girl," or passive, obedient, sweet, and attentive to others' needs, and spending money to buy her pretty clothes, dancing and music lessons, and, sometimes, plastic surgery.

Unlike the fairy tale princesses, however, these daughters often rebelled, some more, some less. They either withdrew, secluding themselves in their rooms with a book, or practiced secret anarchy–drinking, taking drugs, and having sex with men who were scarcely princely by their parents' standards. One of the non-money denying women in our study, a baby boom-generation daughter, raised in the fifties to be a classic Jewish Princess, found a unique way to rebel: She made money during summer vacations, even though her father offered to pay her not to work. Some girls got a heavier dose of the fairy tale treatment than others, but few completely escaped it.

The popular culture–movies, soap operas, women's magazines, romance novels, popular songs ("Someone to Watch Over Me")–echoed the fairy tale theme, as it encouraged young women to fantasize about the future, and compare themselves to a hypothetical "ideal," which had nothing to do with their real personalities, backgrounds, beliefs, and dreams. And society, which then, even more than now, excluded women from highly paid jobs, or erected unapproachable barriers between women and male-dominated careers, indicated that rescue was an economic necessity.

The Dark Side of the Fairy Tale

Many women in our culture, then, were spoonfed the rescue myth, and some, who became classic money deniers, believed it, even lived it, until life opened their eyes to other possibilities. The conflicted Modern Money Denier, however, was able to perceive the fairy tale's dark side, simply by observing her rescued mother. Middle-class mothers of previous generations were rescued by their husbands, and given the lack of opportunity available to women in those times, most had little choice. (Those who did work did not have jobs with salaries sufficient to support a family, which is also true of many working women today.)

In the fairy tale, the princess heroine is often sabotaged by a wicked stepmother, or witch—an angry, envious, frustrated female—distinguished from her real mother, who loves her and is concerned with her welfare, but who is dead, absent, or dozing in an enchanted sleep. What the Modern Money Denier often saw when she looked at her mother was a woman who embodied the characteristics of both the wicked stepmother and the passive real mother. These rescued mothers were not the emotionally satisfied queens, adored by their husbands and living happily ever after, that the fairy tale described; they were frustrated, bored, and irritable, even envious of their daughters' opportunities. The least satisfied were depressed, medicating their depression with pills or alcohol, and isolated with tedious chores, like the fairy-tale heroines before they were rescued. Yet, it was depressed and powerless mothers like these, with their limited view of other options and their legitimate concern for their daughters' economic security, who proselytized the myth: Women who were supported by men, especially rich men, lived happily ever after. Some of these mothers gave their daughters mixed messages, urging them to fulfill their own frustrated fantasies of adventure and freedom before they got "saved."

Though the Modern Money Denier rejected the lifestyle of her rescued mother, she was unable to discard the myth's less obvious, economic theme. *As a result, working women who have managed to design modern, independent lives, can still harbor the deep-seated belief that real happiness includes financial support, and if they have not been rescued, something has gone wrong.*

When these money deniers become parents, they may reverse the message they received, and advise their daughters that security and well-being come from high earning power and self-sufficiency. Unfortunately, because these non-rescued mothers are often in the emotional grip of the myth they disparage, and may be bitter and angry because it failed to come true, they can't teach their daughters the emotional or practical processes involved in using money to implement a lifetime financial plan. As a result, their daughters are apt to become New Money Deniers, who see high earnings as the vague "happily ever after" in a contemporary fairy tale. These deniers, like those before them, continue to fantasize about a non-specific future, based on a story they didn't create about an ideal woman who is not them. Ironically, having discarded the myth that a man should rescue them, some may depend on their mothers to do so when their contemporary version of "happily ever after" fails.

The Withholding Father Prince

Some money deniers were deprived by parents whose inconsistent material support symbolized inconsistent affection. The fathers of these women were unable to give to their daughters because they suffered from unresolved emotional conflicts. Women, who have been deprived in this way in the course of their personal development, may come to see money as a symbol of the love they were denied. They may become enmeshed in a psychological Catch-22 that makes it impossible for them to take care of their needs, because they continue to want them to be taken care of by their fathers. Ironically, the more withholding the father prince, the more terrifying and difficult it is for the daughter to separate from him. Said one very low-earner whose wealthy, sadistic father refused to give her even a birthday present:

> Whenever I think of not seeing my father anymore, or even of not thinking about him much, I get a physical reaction . . . I shake!

Millions of women in our culture had fathers who were emotionally withholding, or mothers who proselytized the rescue myth, or both. For them, financial and emotional needs have gotten confused. Financial rescue has come to represent love and emotional support, and vice versa. They believe that if they take care of their own financial needs, they will no longer appear to need love any more than they need money. A woman who harbors this fear imagines that economic success will frighten potential rescuers away. As a result, a lifetime of taking care of herself financially can signify Rapunzel's isolated wilderness, the glass coffin of a lifeless Snow White, or the thankless toil of a Cinderella, forced to pick lentils out of the hearth.

The Perils of Rescue

In our society, where men have always possessed the lion's share of earning power, women have traditionally improved their economic status and sought security by marrying—up, or, at least, wisely. If a wife performed her role as the family caretaker, her husband and children would usually take care of her. Historically, however, rescue has hardly been synonymous with "living happily ever after," as the fairy tale claims.

Under English common law, introduced to this country in Colonial times, women lost both legal and property rights as soon as they married. Once she was wed, a woman became a piece of property herself, a legal ward of her husband, called a *femme couverte*. Under law, a married couple was regarded as one person—the husband. Though a single woman could own property and money, bring suit, make contracts, and secure deeds, a married woman could not. If she worked, her wages could be garnisheed by her husband, even if they were no longer living together, and she could not buy or sell anything without his permission. Her clothes, household goods, even her children, were legally his, as were her dowry and inheritance, which he was within his rights to gamble or squander. When a husband died, his property passed to his heirs, and although his widow could make use of a third of his estate as long as she lived, she could not will it to anyone else. The Colonial wife did command the right to be supported, but as she was a legal non-person, she had no redress if her husband failed her. The law also declined to specify a reasonable amount of support and never questioned the husband's judgment.

Equity laws provided exceptions to these generally harsh rules, allowing married women to own and control property in extenuating circumstances, such as when the husband abandoned his family and ran up debts. Wealthy fathers could insist on premarital contracts that protected their daughters' inheritance from debt-ridden husbands, and equitable trusts provided married women with untouchable family gifts. These agreements, however, were mainly available to wealthy women, and they had to be made before, not after the husband had wasted his wife's fortune. No wonder early feminists like Susan B. Anthony made property rights the first issue of their spirited campaigns!

A woman lost more than property rights with marriage. Legally she could not choose her own home, was obligated to perform domestic services, and to accept her husband's sexual advances. (He, in return, was forbidden to beat her, though if he did, she had no legal means of stopping him.) Marriage, under law, was a patriarchy: The husband had the authority and power, and his wife was commanded to obey. Both were bound to each other until death did them part; in the event that they separated, divorce was not allowed and neither could remarry. Though then, as now, married couples may have had personal agreements that were more equitable than the law, they never would have held up in court.

By the beginning of the nineteenth century, women's property acts had been enacted, but the patriarchal legal view of marital property had not changed substantially. Today's no-fault divorce agreements result in a reduced economic status for wives as the courts often interpret "equitable distribution" of property from the male vantage point. In addition, estranged fathers continually refuse to pay child support. In 1988 the Federal Office of Child Support Enforcement was able to collect only $5 billion of the $25 billion a year fathers owed.[2]

For modern women, however, the emotional complications of rescue can prove to be the fairy tale's unhappy ending. As many discover, economic and emotional power are inextricably combined. In a ground-breaking study, Philip Blumstein and Pepper Schwartz, authors of *American Couples: Money, Work, Sex*, found that in three out of four of the twelve thousand relationships they studied, the partner who earned more had the most influence in any decision-making process. This was true of married couples, cohabiting couples, and male homosexual couples. (Only lesbian couples shared power equitably, regardless of who earned the most.)

The women in our money study learned that economic dependency deprived them not only of decision-making power but also of valued autonomy and a sense of self. Some reported that a husband's support had made them feel worthless or incompetent, and diminished their ability to make economic decisions that created a feeling of mastery and well-being. As they lost economic bargaining power, they lost control over their lives.

A husband's support rang the death knell for one troubled marriage. Ann, who had supported her husband in their early years together, found herself unable to pursue her career when he got a big-salary job in a suburban area. Although she had resented supporting him, when he was finally in a position to support her, as a fairy tale husband should, difficulties that had plagued their marriage became insupportable to her, and she left him.

> I didn't realize all those years that he was a very controlling person. I could never enjoy being supported. There was too big a price on it for me. Whenever I asked him for something specific that would make life in the suburbs work for me, like a full-time housekeeper, so that I wouldn't have to make complicated arrangements every time I wanted to go to the city to do something, he'd say, "Absolutely not. Out of the question!"

Overcoming the Paralysis of Conflict

A money denier may be earning a living, but her psychological and cultural history has not allowed her to create a lifetime financial plan. Although her relationship with money has not worked out, she is unable to take decisive steps to change it. Often she becomes money blind in order to sidestep the fears that thoughts of her financial future inspire, and concentrates her energies on finding love. She may make bold life decisions, without taking their financial consequences into account, and end up feeling cheated.

Sylvia, a clinical psychologist, decided to have a child alone in her late thirties. She described the feeling of power this radical decision gave her.

I thought, I can really do this on my own. No one can stop me from having a baby, even if the man doesn't want to be involved. I saw it as an act coming out of my increasing strength, and I felt very powerful, and different about myself in a lot of ways.

Sylvia gave birth to a baby boy and used the money she had saved to do postgraduate work in her field to pay a baby-sitter when she returned to her job. When her son was a toddler, however, she suddenly realized that she had never counted on bearing the financial responsibility of child-raising alone.

I started feeling that, in some way, I had been had. I had experienced my freedom, and I was glad that I did, because I have my son. But the other side of the coin is that it was a very masochistic thing to do. Nobody told me that I was going to be totally exhausted, and feel like I'd aged fifteen years in three. What's this empty pocketbook here? I realized my fantasy was that I would do this on my own for a couple of years, and, at some point, I would be meeting somebody . . . that this was not going to be a forever kind of thing, and it would be easier once there were two salaries. I thought it would be temporary. Part of the disappointment has been that it has not been that easy to connect to somebody in that kind of way, and though I feel optimistic that it will happen, I realize that it might be that I'll go through the rest of my life unmarried, or living alone.

When Sylvia admitted she had a rescue fantasy, and it hadn't come true, her financial future seemed terrifying:

The idea that I'll always be as strapped as I am now is scary. I don't have any savings, stocks, or bonds—only a pension. Virtually nothing! This is part of my anxiety. I never thought I'd be forty-one and still living for the time when it's going to get better. Because this is when it should be better. How is it going to get better? I need more and more money for the kid at this point because he needs different kinds of things than he did when he was a baby. I can't afford to send him to private school. What am I going to do about college? It's unbearable for me to deprive him in any way.

Sylvia's anxiety is painful, but not as negative as it feels. Acknowledging, then questioning her hurtful rescue fantasy, is the first step toward affirming the importance of money in her shrinking world. She can now become money sighted, calculate her needs, and attach a price tag to them. She is in the psychological position to create a realistic, future-oriented financial plan that she can begin implementing in the present by looking at specific possibilities for expanding her own income. As a money denier she watched and waited, at the mercy of a psychic red light; as she becomes money affirming, she can give herself permission to move ahead.

The Helpful Way to Read the Fairy Tale:
Becoming Money Affirming

A superficial reading of fairy tales focuses on their conclusions: Beautiful, passive women get rescued by handsome princes and live "happily ever after." These important and influential myths, however, have more to teach us if we ignore their vague endings—and the unrealistic fantasies they inspire—and look at the stories in their entirety as meaningful personal allegories. The helpful way to read fairy tales is to scrutinize all of their images—the good, the bad, and the ugly, too—for their relationship to our lives.

The "blood on the track," the briars, the evil stepmother, the dwarf and wicked witch, as well as the passive beauty, can be viewed as symbols of the diverse parts of our selves that we need to care for. The wicked stepmother might well stand for Snow White's fears of growing older; the dwarf could represent the stunted part of ourselves that we need to develop; the straw spun into gold might be the hard work we do to get what we hope for; the passive golden-haired princess might well be the media image of women who are nothing like we are; the tower can be the isolation and loneliness we sometimes feel, and the briars and blood may symbolize the inner conflicts and external difficulties that modern woman in a changing world must survive.

When women stop dreaming of a fairy tale conclusion to their financial problems, they may at first feel angry, frightened, and hopeless, as Sylvia did. Once they see their financial reality as part of their wholeness and act accordingly, their lives can change in positive ways. Deniers who become money affirming find that their feelings about both love and work are different than before. When income producing is no longer viewed as a Cinderella-like temporary enslavement, women look for ways to introduce new challenges into their careers. Even if their jobs cannot become "glamorous" or "exciting," they may compensate by developing intriguing outside interests. If a woman has two careers—one that produces income, and another that reflects her true vocation—she may find that she resents the salaried job less and regards both careers as "real."

When the money denier develops a financial identity, she begins to see her financial and emotional needs as separate problems, requiring separate solutions. Once she accepts the responsibility of rescuing herself, she is also in a position to search for an appropriate emotional partner. She is free to eliminate (1) the inappropriate rescuer, who derives a sense of power from controlling his partner and (2) the unavailable handsome prince.

A Mini Money-Affirming Romance: How Claire Conquered the Myth of the Handsome Prince

We chose Claire as a case history for this chapter because she had the modern equivalent of a handsome prince in her life, who made it easier for her to recognize and question her rescue fantasy. "Jorge," a world-famous Brazilian soccer player, was not only tall, dark, handsome, and famous, but also exceedingly rich. His father, known in Brazil as the "Sheik of Alcohol," had made a fortune processing sugarcane into ethanol, a petroleum substitute widely used in Brazilian cars.

Though the handsome prince was real, his role in Claire's life was strictly fairy tale. She had been dating Jorge for five years, but only when he visited New York, once or twice a year. The rest of the time the prince was kicking soccer balls around the world or relaxing in one of his father's fabulous mansions in Cannes, London, Bahia, or Martinique. When Jorge jet-setted into town, however, their affair was the stuff romance novels are made of. He squired Claire to three-star restaurants, to the opera, theater, and glamorous parties, where she met other celebrities. Not only was their romance full of excitement, but tenderness, intimacy, and deep communication heightened their passionate hours in bed. No wonder Claire was head over heels! But the intimate passion, as well as the fun, was as fleeting as one of Sleeping Beauty's dreams. The peripatetic prince flew off again, and Claire seldom heard from him until he returned, months later. He never invited her to join him in Rio or Cannes (though money for a ticket would have been no object), bought her gifts, or suggested that they spend more time together. Yet Claire fantasized that the prince was merely afraid of "commitment," and once he trusted her, would be "capable of giving." She hoped to marry Jorge eventually.

> It's not so much a fantasy of him taking care of me, but to live with him and have his baby. It's a romantic fantasy more than a financial one.

As we pointed out to Claire, a romantic fantasy about the son of one of the richest men in Western civilization is, by definition, a financial fantasy. In between Jorge's visits, Claire lived the present-oriented lifestyle of a money denier. Though she was extremely bright, and a talented set designer, this tall, shapely brunette boasted only modest professional achievements and did not have a penny in the bank. She lived hand-to-mouth, charging luxuries on credit cards. On her questionnaire she told us that she thought of herself as a "survivor, who lived on the edge," and did not plan for retirement because she was certain that "the world will be destroyed by a nuclear bomb" before she was sixty-five.

> I'm not somebody who thinks about the future much. I live in the here and now.

Since most of her original set designs had been done for off-off Broadway productions, her vocation had not yet spun straw into gold. Claire felt she had the ability, but lacked the motivation to develop her concepts and the necessary confidence to approach uptown producers. For money, she had a Cinderella-like job: office work for a philanthropic organization, which paid her enough to "survive." The simple-minded tasks she did there, she told us, did not interfere with either her real or fantasy life, and she could daydream while she worked, take time off to "run around the streets," and write in her journal.

Her present-oriented life was enjoyably carefree, but like many money deniers, Claire, now thirty-three, was beginning to feel paralyzed and deprived, like Rapunzel in her tower. She questioned her lack of career motivation as well as her lack of love. Although men pursued her, she rarely dated anyone but her fly-by-night prince.

> In April I said, man, my life is zero, it is totally unsatisfying, and I have to find fulfillment, because I am not happy. I think a big part of my problem has been not allowing myself to want anything but meager stuff. I'm starting to feel more worthy of material things, and other things, too.

She had also begun to see assertive women friends who were more successful than she was as ugly "stepsisters" and envy them:

> I think, Now where did I miss the fucking boat? What is wrong with me? Here's this woman, no brighter than I am, and not better looking. . . . What's my problem? How come I can't push? How come I can't hustle? How come I can't get out there and sell myself? What's wrong with me?

To learn where Claire had missed the boat, we went back to her early years and looked at the way her family had transmitted the money denying message. Claire is the daughter of first-generation, middle-class Jewish parents. Her father, not particularly ambitious, had dropped out of college and taken over his father's plumbing supply business in Brooklyn. Claire's mother worked as a secretary before marriage, and occasionally after her children were grown; she helped her husband in his office without getting paid. As a child, Claire was spoiled, though her parents were far from wealthy. She was rewarded for being rather than for doing.

> I got an allowance just for being cute. Just for living. Just for being their daughter. If I did something extra, I'd get paid for it. I could always get money from them.

Cash came easily to Claire, but she got no information about family finances.

> Everything about money was a big secret in my family. I used to embarrass the shit out of my mother by making announcements at family gatherings like, "I haven't filed a tax return in four years." Afterwards, she would say, "Why do you have to tell everyone your business?"

Claire's mother, a rescued woman, taught her that she could expect to be rescued as well.

> I have this vivid recollection of being on the bus, coming back from shopping. When we'd pass Brooklyn College, my mother would always say, "There's Brooklyn College! You're going to go there and become a teacher so you'll have something to fall back on." I knew the message was that I was going to get married, preferably to someone who could support me. The career was just in case. God forbid! You should live and be vell, dahlink! I did go to Brooklyn College, but I majored in drama and art and never took a single education course.

Like many modern women, Claire began to perceive her powerless, overly protective mother as a "wicked stepmother," and began waging a full-scale rebellion in her teenaged years.

> I see my mother as someone who has to keep total control over her environment. The byword was caution. Don't take risks! Keep everything pure and safe! And be careful! She praised and rewarded me when I conformed to her notion of how I should behave. But when I did something I wanted to do, even something small—like wearing an outfit that expressed my personality—she came down on me with incredibly harsh criticism. I realize now she never showed any confidence in my ability to achieve anything— however modest the goal.

Claire thought her "survival" depended on her escape from this restrictive environment:

The overpowering thing I felt was, I have to get away from this! Because this is a bore! If I have only one life to live, I don't want it to resemble this. I rejected the unsatisfying and oppressive world I came from and survived in a place I defined as my freedom.

The unsatisfying world that Claire rejected, we believe, was not only her childhood world, but her mother's life. Mothers tend to see their daughters as extensions of themselves, and pressure them to reflect their lifestyles and embody their dreams as well as their fears. The daughter, attached to her mother, finds it hard to resist these pressures or to see them for what they are. Unbeknownst to Claire, her security-conscious mother had fantasies of a freer, more exciting life than her own conservative upbringing had allowed her to enjoy. As a result, she gave her daughter a double message: While she emphasized safety and caution, restricting her in the family context, she also gave her the freedom to move away. When Claire believed she was rebelling, she was actually living out her mother's secret fantasies. When she was seventeen, Claire worked as a waitress at a resort.

I was one of the only waitresses at the resort who was Jewish. My mother didn't love it, she hated it, in fact, and if she'd known the details she really would have hated it. It was a wild scene, and it was the first time I'd been unsupervised away from home. I was nuts . . . crazy . . . cavorting!

We thought it odd that a repressive mother like Claire's would allow her rebellious teenaged daughter, still living at home, to do things other Jewish mothers would not let their daughters do.

Funny, as crazy and cautious as she is, she was cool about it. I guess I had to ask her permission, and she gave it to me. There was some story about her bumping into a friend of mine's mother, who asked, "How could you let Claire go off to the mountains? It's wild up there!" And my mother said, "I trust my daughter!" Which gave me no end of amusement, lunatic that I was.

The next summer, Claire used the money she had made as a waitress to travel to Europe, which her mother also "allowed." In her twenties, living a bohemian life in New York's East Village, she continued to receive mixed messages from home.

When I got a job working for the City they were thrilled to death. Security! They bought me a TV, they were so happy I had a normal job. . . . They thought at last I was going to buckle down and fly right. My mother, a big Hadassah lady, had wanted me to go to Israel earlier on. Later, I got tired of doing nothing on the Lower East Side, and I'd heard there were cute guys on the kibbutz, so I decided to go. She said, "No, you shouldn't go. You have a good job now, and security." I said, "Well, if you don't give me the money to go to Israel, I'm going to live on a commune in Colorado." So of course she gave me the money, and I went.

Today, the messages from home still contradict themselves. Claire's mother enjoys hearing about her romance with the prince, but would really like her to marry a doctor. She expresses little interest in her daughter's set-designing career, yet advises her to become a female executive.

After a whole childhood of saying, "Be a teacher," this year she said, "You're so smart. You look so good. You're so capable. Why don't you become an executive and earn fifty thousand dollars a year?" and I said, "Right!" At this point she would love to see me having visibility in the world and earning lots of money, but I'm more interested in being a character in the underground limelight. In being who I am.

This mother's unrealistic career advice to her daughter seems to express the content of her own fantasy life—her unrealized desires for recognition and visibility.

As Claire struggled to integrate the messages she got from her mother with her own definition of a satisfying life, she became confused, partly because the messages were confusing. She became a "character": She was "wild"; she refused to become a teacher or marry a man who would support her. Claire believes she is still rebelling by "living on the edge" financially, instead of developing a secure, future-oriented career and opening a bank account. In fact, she is not. Financially, her underground "limelight" is merely an extension of her mother's world, not because it is "secure," but because it is as restrictive and stultifying as Snow White's coffin. For Claire, "living on the edge" is another way of "playing it safe." Let us listen carefully as she describes the limitations of her financial life:

I realize that I have no bank account and no security, but *within that framework* I can stay in the position of *not really having to change my life too much*. I can maintain my *little status quo* and enjoy myself. I do realize that I can't piss away a paycheck, and that I have to keep up with my bills. *Basically I'm not going to live beyond my means.* But when I'm with friends who have more, I always have this feeling, *Oh, God, I'm a little person without any money.*

Claire's profile of her financial identity emphasizes her smallness and her inability to move freely. She stays within a "limited framework," which does not allow her to change. She does not "live beyond her means," or expand. In effect, she has put herself in a kind of prison. Financially she accepts the very restrictions and limitations she has spent her life rejecting in other ways. How does her fantasy of marriage to the handsome prince fit in? Claire still hopes for the rescue she was raised to expect:

> I've never been taken care of by a man after my daddy, never, so I can't imagine it happening, and yet I know it is my fantasy.

She feels conflicted about her rescue fantasy, however, because for her, being taken care of symbolizes her mother's powerless existence. She expresses this conflict by being in love with an unavailable rescuer, a prince who both promises and withholds a concept of rescue, more glorious than her mother's wildest dreams, with no financial or social limitations. Meanwhile, the real rescuer is still her family, from whom she has not yet separated. We asked Claire what would happen if she got sick, had no money in the bank, and could not work.

> I'd probably have to ask my parents for a loan. I mean, they're not rich, and I'd hate to have to ask them . . . but they wouldn't let me get thrown out of my apartment.

Claire could begin to sever the tie that still bound her to her mother's world, then, by examining her rescue fantasy.

When we interviewed her, the emotional confinement she was beginning to feel was making her question her financial behavior. New events were also helping to stir up the winds of change. The philanthropic organization was cutting back, due to lack of funding, and Claire was about to look for another job. This prospect made her extremely anxious. Anxiety was positive, however, because it stimulated her to act, create solutions, and develop new skills. She decided to train for a position as a makeup artist for a large cosmetics company. Since the new job would pay commissions on sales, it would enable her to make more money than before, while giving her time to pursue her set-designing career. There was a possibility that the company would eventually employ her to train new artists in European countries. Freeing herself from her paralysis, however, involved questioning the fantasy that had inspired it.

> I thought, Makeup artist! Me! Claire Marion Eckstein! I'm destined for bigger things! It's okay that I was sitting there in that pigsty of an office, doing nothing half the time—that was okay, because it wasn't real. I mean, it wasn't

any kind of commitment. But to actually go and learn this new skill . . . it seemed like I was going to become just another automaton, and it was like acknowledging all my fantasies—and they were fantasies—of something fabulous happening in my life would be negated by my learning to be a makeup artist.

The "something fabulous" that would be negated by making a serious commitment to earn more money was a glamorous rescue by the handsome prince.

Unlike many deniers who cherish vague or unacknowledged rescue dreams, Claire had a real prince to put to the test. About this time, Jorge conveniently blew into town. Instead of accepting the "little status quo" and imagining that Jorge would one day offer more, Claire was assertive. She decided she had to "make something happen, or get out of it, and not be in love anymore." She expressed her dissatisfaction with their present relationship and asked Jorge directly if he had ever considered living with her and having a child together. The prince said he was not ready, and answered, "Maybe in five or ten years." Though Jorge's answer was not encouraging, once she had actually asked him if he planned to rescue her, rescue seemed more of a real possibility, and Claire became aware of her conflict. Was marriage to a jet-setting soccer star and motherhood really what she wanted? She wondered what her day-to-day life would be like when she was living "happily ever after."

> He would be doing what he does, but I haven't figured out what I would be doing. I would be someone's wife; what would be expected of me? It became a concern. I mean, it didn't really make sense, or jive with anything I feel right about to be taken care of by a man, although I do think I could easily adjust to having lots of money. I caught myself thinking that maybe I could be a makeup artist in Rio or Cannes! If I became a mother, I suppose there would be a governess; but what if he didn't want a governess?

Months after our interview, we checked in with Claire. She was working hard as a makeup artist, earning a decent wage, and planning her first vacation in years. Jorge, who had apparently become uncomfortable with the more assertive Claire (or with her fantasy), had changed from a prince into Peter Pan and vanished.

Claire still had a long way to go to develop a future-oriented financial identity: She had yet to balance her new income-producing job with the set-designing career that gave her a sense of self-worth and satisfaction. She had not saved any money. We felt she still did not see the necessity to support herself as an ongoing journey without "happily ever after" as a final destination. Nor had she become interested in the kind of man with whom she might share her financial future. She had, however, taken the first important step away from the passive fantasy land of a Modern Money Denier. She told us:

> I've always thought something wonderful would happen to me automatically, without my doing anything, and I would be rich and lead a wonderful life. Jorge was not really the cause of that fantasy, but only part of it. Now I know that if good things happen, it will be because I worked to get them.

Chapter Five

Red Lights on the Yellow Brick Road: The Reasons for Money Eluding

The money blind, the money squeamish, and the money denying have defense systems that protect them from worrying much about money. When a woman emerges from these self-deceiving states, she totes up her present and future expenses and subtracts them from her savings and annual paycheck. If the total isn't enough for her needs, she may become anxious and conclude that she lacks earning power. Other women, no more intelligent or competent, are earning more. Why can't she extract herself from her dead-end job and do what it takes to find a better paid gig? As she becomes anxious, she is likely to become paralyzed—a money eluder.

When the money eluder takes a step in the dollar-producing direction, she feels overwhelmed by confusion and self-doubt. She may castigate herself for being "lazy" or "undisciplined," even as she fritters away potential earning time with long social lunches and shopping bouts. Even if she appears successful to others, the money eluder may not be successful enough to please herself. What is holding her back? She is conscious that she has placed boundaries on the amount of money she believes she can—or should—earn, but she does not know when and how they got erected, or how to tear them down. She may get bogged down for months, even years, by agonizing choices: Should she get an MBA or have another baby?

If she is one of the 7 percent of women who have left the marketplace to care for children, she may waste eons wondering what kind of job would be right for her now that she knows she needs to go back. Every job has disadvantages, or might be perfect under different circumstances, at another time, or in a better place. She rationalizes her "laziness" or confusion in sophisticated ways that make sense to her, but not to a more objective listener. If the nervous money eluder's anxieties become overwhelming, she may be tempted to crawl back into the cozy cocoon of Money Phobia, and become money blind, money squeamish, and money denying again.

Unlike some Money Phobic women, the money eluder does not hesitate to look inward. Often her anxieties do not focus on money but on her personal deficiencies. She may attribute her inability to earn to a common female complaint—low self-esteem—and invoke pop psychology formulas to explain her failures: Like many of her gender, she is afraid of "risk," "success," or "failure." She is struggling to balance her definition of "career" with personal and family priorities, she says. Once she has found a convenient explanation, however, she tends to fog up her money mirror and, instead of peering deeper into it, dismisses the problem. As she contemplates goblins like "risk " or "success," she ignores alarming specters that loom unbidden into her psyche—like her fear of aggression, competition, envy, and power.

Money eluders view all financial problems as earning problems and avoid investigating other reasons for personal economic distress, such as undeveloped money management or investment skills. We have found that women with this symptom of Money Phobia seldom attach a specific price tag to their financial fantasies; they may simply want to earn "more" without having defined exactly how much "more" is, or even why they want to earn it. Some told us that $50,000 represented a "respectable" salary.

As the money eluder blames herself for all her earning problems, she doesn't take women's economic history or current marketplace conditions into account. She may bemoan the low-paying nature of her profession and call it "unfair," without considering that most professions pay women less than they do men, and that many high-paying jobs are still off-limits to the majority of women.

In a discussion about women's earning problems, sexism is an unavoidable word. Women are still victims of institutionalized discrimination, generally earning less than men for doing the same job, despite their invasion of male-dominated professions. Surprisingly, in 1991 The National Committee on Pay Equity determined that the wage gap between women and men was actually wider in "better," higher paying jobs. Job experience doesn't always pay off either: Statistics show that the longer a woman has been at her job, the less she is likely to make in comparison to men.[1] Although from 1970 to 1990 women upped their representation in a large number of fields—including law, economy, pharmacy, medicine, and financial professions—they were not paid the same as men already in them. And "female" professions are by no means history: Since 1940, one in twenty women workers has been a schoolteacher, and 98 percent of secretarial jobs are held by women, a percentage that has remained unchanged since 1950. Seventy-five percent of working women earn less than $25,000 a year.[2] According to the Bureau of the Census, college educated women still take home less pay than a white man with a high school diploma.[3]

Despite these often discouraging trends, middle-class women in our study did not see their earning problems as part of a social pattern with an underlying political cause. They took them personally. When we asked the members of our New York money group why they thought they were solely responsible for their inability to earn larger incomes, one perceptively replied:

> When I think about the aspects of life that are out of my control—the nature of the market and social pressure—it makes me too angry. It's so enraging! And the reason women turn it inward, I think, is that it's too big to handle. It's just a little bit more comfortable to walk around thinking that it's all your fault. If it is your fault, you maintain the idea that you can control it.

No woman is completely responsible for her lack of earning power. The fears that block our money-making potential—fear of envy, fear of competition, fear of aggression, and fear of loss of feminine identity—are not just individual neuroses, but problems that many women bring to the marketplace, because they are the inevitable result of a sexist social process. Though a woman must examine her own unique history and financial behavior in order to overcome her fears, the history of women will help her understand why she suffers from them in the first place and remove a misplaced burden of guilt from her shoulders.

With this in mind, let us look at the contradictory messages history has given us about when and how we are supposed to make money, and how much money we can safely earn without risking our inherent virtues and values.

History's Mixed Messages

The message to women about work has been packed with contradictions. Until recently, society has told us that the middle-class woman's natural habitat is the home. Home was traditionally the place where her God-given talents would best be employed and her moral influence would be most effective. In response to its own needs and our own, society has gradually modified this message, but never without specifying how far we can stray from the hearth, and under what circumstances, before we lose the qualities for which we are loved and admired. Middle-class women who put career interests first, ignoring their option to stay at home, have been stigmatized in different ways and in different languages since the beginning of the twentieth century.

Colleges and universities opened their doors to women before 1925. Education and work experience, however, were viewed as character-building endeavors that better equipped graduates for their ultimate roles as wives and mothers. Though many educated women worked before marriage, few worked afterward, unless the family economy was jeopardized. Married women, who worked because they enjoyed working, were judged selfish and neglectful of their husbands and children. Those determined to pursue careers simply did not marry. Single working women lived at home or with other women in relationships called "Boston marriages," and were regarded as "exceptional," which translated as "unnatural."

Legal restrictions on birth-control devices until the 1930s, however, made it difficult or impossible for a woman to remain childless if she also had sex, or to limit the size of her family. A houseful of children and constant pregnancies, needless to say, were not conducive to a dual role of career woman and wife.

Despite these difficulties, women advanced. Between 1890 and 1920 their presence increased in paid professions by 226 percent. The professions open to women, however, were then (and continued to be) extensions of their housekeeping role—teaching, nursing, library science, and social services. Those trained to be lawyers and doctors were often barred from practicing in these fields. A few frustrated women disguised themselves as men in order to get jobs in their chosen profession.

The Depression years are often thought of as the "Dark Ages" for women. In the thirties, a woman who worked was not merely selfish and "unnatural"; she was considered a thief who was "stealing" a job from its rightful male owner. This stigma was particularly applied to wives. During the Depression twenty-six states had laws prohibiting their employment. Public utilities, schools, and many department stores refused to hire married women, and the federal government forbade more than one member of a family from working in civil service—a law that effectively discriminated against women. Men applied in droves for female-stereotyped jobs, like teaching, and female college graduates were discouraged by their deans from pursuing careers.[4]

The 1936 Gallup poll asked if wives should work if their husbands had jobs. When 82 percent of Americans said no, Gallup declared he had discovered an issue on which voters were as solidly united as on any imaginable subject, including sin and hay fever.[5] Even Eleanor Roosevelt, who saw no reason why a woman's "first duty to her home" should preclude her from pursuing another occupation, conceded that the pressure on women to stay out of the marketplace in the thirties was "perhaps necessary during an emergency."[6]

Though women were told not to work, statistics show that many of them did; the number of women in the work force increased slightly between 1930 and 1939. In male-dominated professions, however, the increase of women was negligible; the number of women doctors actually decreased.

World War II abruptly revoked the stigma against women working. In the thirties, women were warned not to "steal" jobs; in the forties, they entered the work force in record numbers because they were told they could serve society's interests by getting jobs as quickly as possible. With the men at war, 6 million women filled the vacant slots they left in heavy industry as well as in offices. Women did jobs they had never done before: They riveted, ran cranes and bulldozers, and manufactured ammunition and aircraft. Though society encouraged women to work during the war, then, as now, it did not provide the government-sponsored childcare that would have made it easier for them to do so.

Most women had intended to quit their jobs when the men came home, but when the war was over, 80 percent wanted to continue working because their families needed the extra income. Nevertheless, by the end of 1946, millions had been fired. Jobs that were not too heavy for women when there were no men to do them became too heavy when there were, and we were sent back to the fireside to resume our more "natural" ladylike occupations.

In the conservative fifties, then, society did another about-face and rescinded the message of the forties. Women who were black and poor continued to work as they had previously in a marketplace that discriminated against them, paid them badly, and cast them in sex-stereotyped jobs. Those who could afford to stay at home, however, increased in number as male fortunes prospered. Society and the media touted homemaking and motherhood as complex, satisfying, full-time occupations, and even educated women subscribed to the new propaganda.

It soon became apparent that the Betty Crockers of the fifties were not the smiling madonnas they were supposed to be. In 1963, Betty Friedan published her classic manifesto, *The Feminine Mystique*, which described the oppressive anxieties of unhappy housewives. The victims of a pervasive dissatisfaction, Friedan said, felt that what they did was unimportant; yet the message from the media led them to believe that they were perverse exceptions, if they did not feel "a mysterious fulfillment, waxing the kitchen floor." Friedan explained how the male establishment conspired to deter women from achieving self-fulfillment, and urged them to establish a sense of their own identity through meaningful work; but she cautioned her white, middle-class readers, supported by their husbands, against taking jobs "not equal to their actual capacity," or to "help out at home." Fulfillment, she said, calls for "lifetime interests and goals," and getting paid is a valuable asset because it implies "definite commitment."

The feminist movement that ensued provided those who sought self-fulfillment with a structure—consciousness-raising groups—where they could talk to one another and define the political origins of their personal problems. Thanks to feminism, women not only won extensive legal rights and employment opportunities in the sixties and seventies, but were also able to give themselves permission to move out of the home. Men accepted the new pilgrimage toward the marketplace, provided women continued to perform the majority of housework and childcare activities.

But it was not *The Feminine Mystique,* or even the feminist movement, that caused so many middle-class women to enter the marketplace or changed the emphasis of their participation there from self-fulfillment to earning power. Economic recession and the decline of real wages brought more women into the workforce in the eighties and changed what they wanted from their jobs. The uncertainty of marriage, too, pushed women out of the home: By 1980 the likelihood that a marriage that had endured less than ten years would end in divorce was between 39 percent and 49 percent; even after ten years, 26.8 percent of marriages dissolved.[7] As a result, many women who had expected to be married were divorced, or still single, and responsible for their own financial futures. Those who were married needed a second income in order to meet the rising costs of the American dream as most men's paychecks were no longer sufficient to send children to college, buy suburban homes, or maintain a middle-class urban lifestyle. In 1948 only 10.8 percent of mothers with a child under six worked in the marketplace; by 1992, the percentage had risen to 59.9 percent.[8]

Whereas women college students in the 1950s and '60s studied liberal arts, education, and social work, students in the new, more demanding economic and social climate of the 1980s planned careers that were money-oriented, like law, science, medicine, and business. The feminist who attracted the media spotlight for her marching and bra-burning, however, was not magically reincarnated as the high-earning businesswoman who was chosen to grace the media stage in the money-hungry eighties. Those who graduated in the fifties, sixties, and even early seventies were hard-put to transform their interests and training into the ideal income of later decades.

Meanwhile, the high-earning "superwoman," so often the subject of books, magazine articles, and television talk shows of her era, was held up as an example of what all of us might be able to achieve: She had a family, two homes, a job as a bond trader that she adored, a soaring income (usually not specified), and a "busy schedule" that she adroitly controlled. She looked feminine even in a business suit.

As the media touted the superwoman image, however, it revealed a society's historical ambivalence toward female success. Male-owned and run magazines selected high-earners for portraits, only to subtly de-mask them as inadequate mothers, or lonely and masochistic single women. One not-so-subtle 1984 *Playboy* pictorial "$ucce$$ $torie$: In which Three Bold, Bright, Beautiful Entrepreneurs Show How to Succeed in Business with Out-and-Out Trying," featured three high earners posing for crotch shots. The message: Even successful women will stoop to sexual compromise in order to please men.

By the nineties the superwoman concept was revised, but not dead. Women who seemed to have it all were still featured by women's magazines, which focused more attention on the conflicts between their personal and professional lives. The media also continued to bash female executives who climbed above men on the financial ladder, even as corporate job slots for women disappeared. Movies like *The Last Seduction* and *Disclosure* portrayed high earners as cold, unscrupulous, seductive beauties with no moral values, willing to murder and sexually harass men to get to the top.

As we move into the twenty-first century, most women both need and want to work. A 1995 study by the Families and Work Institute revealed that women had become the "new providers:" 55 percent of employed women earned half or more of their household's income; 18 percent provided all the earnings. Moreover, nearly half the women in the marketplace, the study showed, would want to work even if they did not need the paycheck.[9] At the same time as they affirmed the value of their participation in the marketplace, working women began to reassess the importance of their families, homes, and leisure time; many concluded that they valued personal, spiritual, and social fulfillment more than material wealth.

The messages from society continue to be confusing. Although politicians promote family values, employers are slow to institute work-family programs, which offer women and men flex-time job options that make it possible for parents to take time off for child care. Professional women who make family a priority may find themselves relegated to "The Mommy Track," which denies them important, high-paying positions. And quality child care facilities remain as difficult to find in the United States as in Nigeria or Brazil.

Though women's real lives have altered substantially throughout the decades, the messages that society transmits about women and work have not kept pace. Let us briefly summarize the messages and their changes:

- Your rightful place is in the home, first with your parents, then with your husband and children, and finally caring for elderly parents.
- You may work to support yourself or to help your family or society when they need you. The work you do is most acceptable to us when

it is not work a man would want, because it represents an extension of a woman's "natural" role in the home. If you are very beautiful or talented, however, we will allow you to entertain us.

- You can work if it makes you happy, provided you continue to fulfill your natural role in the home, preferably with the same quality of devotion you have shown for centuries. Change the way you act in the marketplace, but not in the home! We love you and admire you for your traditional role, because it helps us perform our important functions, but we will not pay you for it, or give it a specific economic value. Furthermore, most of us do not really think it is our place to help you do it.

- You can make the money you need, but it is unfeminine to make more than you need, or to see money the way we see it—as a symbol of power—or to compete with us for significant amounts of it. If you are able to turn a profit for us, we will allow some of you to infiltrate our highest echelons and pay you well, but not without extracting a price.

- All right, we admit that we need your participation in the workforce to raise the Gross National Product, and to make sure our middle-class families can live in the style to which we are accustomed. But we won't help you achieve "balance" between home and career, or to succeed, if you dare confess that you value your job as much as your family. Equal pay? Keep in mind the motto of Alexander Liberman, the editorial director of the Condé Nast empire: "Women are cheap labor and always will be."

Unfortunately, most of us have internalized these confusing messages, which have changed not only in the course of our lives, but in the lives of our mothers and grandmothers, too. "Society" is not an outside force, as we have identified it here; we are socialized according to these contradictions, and as a result, we harbor the enemy within. Few ambitious women, then, begin their adult lives with the emotional perspective they need to sort out the contradictions, and decide which parts of the changing messages they can and should incorporate into their lives, and which parts they want to discard or defy. How can they succeed in the marketplace and the domestic sphere—two very different places—at the same time? Some women may adopt one part of the message to the exclusion of the other, and then feel incomplete, condemned to a career that does not satisfy their emotional needs. Others may sacrifice their careers, and feel unrewarded. Still others may plan to put one part of the ideal "balanced" plan on hold, while they devote themselves to the other, and, in the end, have it all in sequence. (This approach is not always successful. Our reproductive biology—often an unknown—dictates how long we can wait before starting a family, and the marketplace often turns away or limits the accomplishments of women who focus on family too long or too soon.)

Since society (and our families) provide no guidelines to tell us how we are supposed to integrate our different needs and goals, we are left to resolve the contradictions ourselves through trial and error. Some women are more successful at this difficult integration job than others: They have been able to distance themselves from the problems long enough to see them objectively, and identify their needs in relation to the difficulty they will have in achieving them. Those who seem to "have it all," on closer inspection have actually sacrificed some less obvious part of it: A traditional homemaking role, a traditional marriage, motherhood, the amount of time and energy they devote to a career, the amount of money they cannot live without, or, in some cases, something less tangible, and yet, valuable to many women—unstructured time for themselves.

Some women's temperaments are also better equipped to handle more of "it all" than others. The most severely wounded casualties of this conflict are women who start battling themselves, and fail to separate their own needs from an image of themselves that they perceive as "ideal." They feel ashamed, confused, and paralyzed. They see the contradictions not as conflicts, but prescriptions for failure. Castigating themselves for their inability to achieve all they believe a "modern woman" is expected to achieve, they feel they have disappointed the world and themselves. These anxiety-ridden women are prime candidates to become money eluders. Unable to identify their financial needs in the bog of mixed messages and other concerns, they can't clarify what they can and cannot do to pursue them. To make matters more difficult, they do not always recognize or comprehend the historical origin of their powerless feelings, and think it is up to them to transcend all problems personally. Money eluders always feel helpless and alone.

The Perils of "The Yellow Brick Road"

Society, then, socialized generations of women to believe that the home was their natural habitat, and the outside world, including the marketplace, represented foreign territory. Many of the popular stories we encountered in childhood dramatized the voyage out of secure and familiar domestic surroundings into the intriguing but perilous "unknown."

One of our favorite myths is the 1939 movie production of *The Wizard of Oz*, starring the ill-fated child prodigy Judy Garland, who herself journeyed too far from home at too early an age. Still popular, this old-fashioned story can be interpreted as a parable about a male-dominated society's traditional attitudes toward women in the marketplace.

Dorothy does not leave home of her own accord; she is blown away by a ferocious tornado from her adoptive parents, who have unjustly rebuked her for misbehavior. In a magical world where good and evil forces, in the guise of witches, vie for control of her destiny, she is frightened, but thrilled, to find herself where she has often longed to be. "Somewhere Over the Rainbow," despite its unknowns, is a more exciting environment than her dull but comfortably familiar Kansas farmhouse. Clad in a pair of magic shoes, she sets out on the "Yellow Brick Road," an image similar to the "streets paved with gold," that nineteenth-century immigrants used to describe the American land of opportunity.

The mood is one of excitement and discovery, but Dorothy is making the hazardous journey only in order to end up back where she started from: She plans to ask "The Wonderful Wizard of Oz" to return her to her home. Skipping, dancing, and singing, she meets three male companions, all of whom are frauds. Together they lack a traditional man's essential qualities: The lion has no courage, the tin man is minus a heart, and the scarecrow does not have a brain. Dorothy, however, has all three, and it is due largely to the encouragement and ingenuity of this bright, assertive little girl that these insufficient and non-rescuing, yet lovable males make it through the trip.

Once in the Land of Oz (also known as "The Emerald City") it is perspicacious Dorothy with the help of her dog, Toto, her alter ego, who discovers that The Wonderful Wizard is bogus. Toto pulls away the curtains concealing the wizard's awesome voice to reveal a tiny, kindhearted old man who governs his city by producing a mechanical illusion of power. The Wizard is able to convince Dorothy's three companions that they do possess the qualities they believe they are lacking. Dorothy herself—the most gifted of the four—is offered the kingdom, but she closes her eyes, repeats intently, "There's no place like home," and finds herself back in Kansas with her beloved Aunt Em, determined never to misbehave again. Her journey, of course, was all a dream—the result of getting conked on the head during the storm—but it has taught the little girl a lesson the author of the screenplay thought she needed to know, and presumably abolished her unrealistic fantasies.

From our point of view, *The Wizard of Oz* is an interesting story, with problems as well as truths. It indicates that a journey outside the home in which a young woman learns that she can use her intelligence and personality skills to overcome danger and achieve is a wonderful adventure, but temporary, the stuff fantasies are made of. It tells us what many adult women already know: That men, too, suffer from the myth that they are all-powerful and invulnerable, and owe much to feminine comfort and support. But what about the glittering Emerald City? Oz reminds us of the modern corporation, which has reportedly left some women who braved great hardship to journey there unhappy, disillusioned, and burned-out. Home is an important place, and wise Dorothy knows it; she does not want to be the first female vice-president of General Motors. Having flexed her talent and courage and seen a bit of the world, she has not lost her original values; she still wants to be with the people she loves, who love her in return.

The problem with the story is that it presents staying at home and going out into the world as an either/or situation, dramatizing society's changing message, which discourages women from trying to do both at the same time. It is unfair that such a strong and talented little girl must choose between the home and the world, because the talents that serve her so well in one place will be wasted in the other. In the world, she is brave, smart, respected, and adored, and in the home, she is supposed to wax kitchen floors, and be loving, obedient, and dependent.

When women describe their career progress, they often use the outdated imagery of *The Wizard of Oz*. They define success as a hazardous journey away from a comfortable, protected environment to an unfamiliar place, where they feel exposed and vulnerable to danger. What are the stop lights, both imaginary and real, that halt women on the yellow brick road, and how can they be recognized and avoided?

1. Fear of Leaving Home or "Risk-Taking"

Many modern women have been working so long that they have forgotten their initial trepidation at setting out for the marketplace. Deanna, a South Carolina mother who put her two daughters in daycare so that she could enroll in college and earn a degree, reminded us of the fear and excitement this initial journey inspires. Because her determination to have a foot in both the home and the marketplace was less common in the rural South than it is in other areas of the country, Deanna's decision to pursue a career subjected her to criticism and her marriage to tremors.

Happily married to a construction worker at twenty-four, Deanna had settled into a rambling farmhouse, intending to be a contented earth mother and earn "pin money" by monogramming at home.

> I thought things were going to be wonderful! I'd stay here, have babies, a garden, and do monogramming, and I'd just love it! Instead, I was bored, the baby was into everything, and the monogramming was stressful, because once it wasn't a nine-to-five job, it seemed like I had a choice not to do it. After my second daughter was born, I thought I'd kill myself if I went on doing what I was doing for the rest of my life.

Although neither of Deanna's parents had graduated from high school, her mother had always worked and her father had pushed his children to excel in school.

> When we were growing up he always told us how horrible his life was working in a factory because that was all he could do. He wanted us to be better.

These family messages allowed Deanna to contemplate the serious option of getting an education that would raise her social and economic class. Once this determined young woman decided to set out for Oz, the sky became the limit!

> I thought about training to be a pilot, which is something I'd always wanted to do. I went out and took an introductory lesson, and I didn't tell Jackie, because I knew he would give me such hell that I never would have done it. I told him after I did it, and he said, "Whaat???" It wasn't fear for my life, I don't think, it was fear for our life. If I'd become a pilot, I might have left him.

Deanna rejected a flying career, not only because it would endanger her marriage, but also because the training program was too long and grueling. Her next move brought her literally back to the ground, and because it was more realistic, it was also more frightening. She began to take courses in soil science at a local community college.

> It was a big deal, a big serious thing, and I thought, Maybe I can't do it. . . . It's bigger than me. It's a big unknown. Oh, everybody is going to be smarter than me. That's how I felt. Now I feel going to college was my greatest achievement. That was one thing I did myself. I went through the agonies myself. Nobody helped me. I feel it was harder for me coming from where I did . . . the things I had to overcome . . . the fears of going out on my own . . . just going into a strange building and feeling my way around. And going to classes! Really putting myself in there! That was harder for me than for people who haven't been so isolated. And following through! And coming to the end!

Deanna describes the process of going to school as a journey to an unknown environment, where she feels her way around, almost like a blind person. More sophisticated urban women, with college well behind them, may experience Deanna's fears when they contemplate career changes or advancements.

What is "comfortable" has different boundary lines for different women at different phases of their careers. A familiar workplace can come to seem like a home, and a new job, with a higher income, represents an unfamiliar territory, demanding new knowledge and personality skills. It is the fear of continuing the journey and finding themselves once again "exposed" that prevents money eluders from making more money.

Sarah, for example, was dissatisfied with her job as an occupational therapist in a rehabilitation department in a New York hospital. When she contemplated quitting the secure position she had had for years, however, and developing a private practice, she saw the move in terms of leaving a home, complete with a loving family.

> One of my friends is going part-time, and the other is quitting to have a baby. That's part of my wanting to leave . . . so many people I like won't be there anymore. I feel like I'm losing my family.

This workplace/home tolerated Sarah's flaws, much as a family tolerates a child's misbehavior:

> There's a basic flaw in me that blossoms at the hospital . . . that part of me that can be careless, or terrific at starting something but not following through. There, nobody knows whether I'm doing it or not; I blend in. But if I was working for a serious business . . . what about those days when I feel like a brainless mush, and I barely function? What will happen when my brain's not turned on, and I'm visible . . . when I'm out there?

Though she feared exposing herself to a more critical audience whose expectations were unknown, Sarah, who felt her income had not kept pace with rising costs and had no savings, chafed at these "family ties," and believed they were self-imposed by a neurotic maladjustment on her part, rather than by an understandable inability to balance cultural messages with her own changing goals.

> The fact that I'm still there and can't leave feels devastating. On my worst days I feel like I'll die at the hospital, but when I feel like leaving, it's like I'm leaving home at the point when my parents are dying.

At any stage of a woman's career, exchanging a known, comfortable job situation for a different or larger venture may seem comparable to leaving home. Molly, a successful New York fashion designer, felt she was abandoning familiar territory when she moved from a small downtown showroom, a walkable distance from her apartment, to larger quarters in midtown Manhattan.

It was shocking! I felt like I was in Chicago when I got off the subway.

This non–money eluder, however, had been able to weigh the comforts of home against the discomfort of losing money.

The showroom in SoHo was very comfortable. However, a recession was coming and budgets were cut, and when out-of-town buyers came in, they only had four days to cover all the showrooms. And the first appointment that got canceled was the one in SoHo, when all the others were in the garment center. After three to six months of this, one day Jan, my partner, and I just said, "Let's move."

Women tend not only to redefine the workplace as home, but to also bring qualities that are effective in their domestic and social lives into the marketplace, sometimes with great success. High-earners in our study told us that they had created a network of important relationships on the job, and used their nurturing abilities and talents for intimacy to develop financially lucrative business relationships. The transformation of marketplace into home, however, can be self-sabotaging when domestic comforts substitute for financially necessary risk-taking activities.

2. Fear of Success

Do women traveling the yellow brick road fear reaching their destination? Many psychologists have theorized that modern women are "afraid of success." The psychologically sophisticated money eluders in our study sometimes cited this much touted terror to explain their income-producing problems. "Fear of success," however, proved to be a convenient catch-all that summarized a number of complex underlying issues.

Jeannie, for example, who was looking for a job, concluded that she hadn't found one because she was afraid of succeeding.

I'll be up against people who are going to compete against me, and I'll be better than they are, or I won't be, and my main fear is that I will be better. I find myself in many situations where I undercut myself in order to shore someone else up. I think it has to do with my not wanting to let out my competitive instincts. I'm very competitive, and I'm terrified of that.

INT.: What would happen if you let the competitiveness out?

J.: I might be terrifically successful.

INT.: And then?

J.: I might make a lot of money, and have a great job, and love my life, and things might be too wonderful!

INT.: And then what?

Jeannie had no answer. She realized it was not really rational to fear "a wonderful life." What did she fear? Why was she afraid of her competitive instincts, if she saw them as a ticket to a positive goal? Her description of her feelings when a male friend got a high-paying job gave us a clue.

My male roommate, whom I like and admire enormously, just got a terrific job which he richly deserves in a field related to my field, but not the same, making $12,000 a year more than he did on his last job. And I was so jealous when I heard about it I was ready to murder him. I could not contain myself. It took three days for me to stop shaking.

According to psychologist Carol Gilligan, author of *In a Different Voice*, women project violence into fantasies of competitive success. Jeannie imagines that when she succeeds others will feel, and direct toward her, the barely controllable envy she experiences when those close to her meet with success. She represses her competitiveness because she unconsciously believes such envy might result in her injury or death, symbolic, if not real.

Women believe that once they are envied, or experience this emotion themselves, they will be cast out of a web of all-important human relationships. Because they fear the envy of others, they find it hard to express their envious feelings, or use them to explore their conflicts about success. Instead, they banish this "unladylike" emotion, or transform it into self-castigation or criticism of those who have achieved.

In order to learn more about the way women deal with envy, we asked the members of our New York money group how they would feel if a woman friend called to announce she had just gotten a great job, contract, or commission that would net her $75,000. Most said they would be envious if the high-earner was an acquaintance, but "happy for her" if she was a closer friend. The envious feelings were strong and violent:

If it's a close friend I'm envious, but I'm still happy for her. God, I wish it would happen to me! If it is an acquaintance it would be.... What! It happened to her! It didn't happen to me! I want that! I know one friend I could actually say that to. I'd say, "I hate your guts!"

Closeness, then, was one criterion of what made it safe, or unsafe, to feel and express envy. Another was the way the success was earned. Friends who were seen as "manipulative," "insincere," or having achieved by using "feminine wiles" in the marketplace were entitled to negative feedback more than those who were hardworking or "deserving." Among the deserving were the Pure in Intent, the Grateful for Support, the Modest Souls Who Remained Good People, and the Passive, Who Did Not Bulldoze Their Way. Those who calculated, or "sold out," or used their talents according to current market values, also merited the (silent) condemnation they got.

> One woman I know is extremely competitive, extremely . . . I would never have the nerve to come out and say to her what I really feel, which is that I'm really jealous. Then I can think of another woman who has a lot of talent, but always puts herself down, and if something wonderful happened to her, I'd think, It's about time.

In other words, our participants expected successful women to earn their success by demonstrating the same qualities in the marketplace that make a "good friend" or a "nice person." Successful men friends, however, were not expected to be quite so accommodating in a work situation. Unfortunately, the rejection of any success that is not "correct" or "pure," according to these stringent criteria, can prevent women from learning valuable lessons from female high achievers. As one woman in our group discovered, envy can be used as a resource.

> I think I've found a way to deal with the feeling of envy, which is not a nice or comfortable feeling; it's very practical. I study these women, who are my friends, and figure out how they did it, how they got what they got, and what traits they have that I can graft onto myself . . . traits that are not totally out of my ken. There are some traits—forget it!—that I can't emulate, and others that I can.

Fear of envy is not an irrational fear. Successful women experience rifts in friendships and may get the "cold shoulder" from still struggling friends. Those who repress envious feelings can manifest their envy in devious ways. We heard one didactic tale about a group of highly motivated career psychologists who gathered to celebrate a friend's book contract with a festive dinner. During the meal many topics were discussed, but the auspicious book contract was not among them. At the end of the evening, the author-to-be's friends went home in pairs, and she found herself sitting at the banquet table alone—hurt and angry. Sometimes those who make it to the Emerald City have to look for new friends who also live there.

Ambitious women who fall prey to the "green monster" are not necessarily neurotic or bad-tempered. They are reacting to an oppressive social and economic fact, which is that the pie to be divided up among women is smaller than the one to be divided among men. When a woman feels that another woman's success has taken something away from her, she is not altogether wrong. Because few women are admitted to the top, there is simply not enough success to go around. Instead of blaming a sexist political economy for the insufficient success supply, however, women blame other women for grabbing their share, or turn the blame inward.

Jamaicans say, "The higher the monkey climbs the tree the more he exposes himself." Women fear that success will expose them not only as enviable, but as different from other women. Because success in the marketplace, particularly in male-dominated professions, is attributed to self-seeking personality traits, such as ruthlessness and competitiveness, women at the top may be perceived as extraordinary, or not typically feminine, and singled out for attention that is not altogether flattering. For this reason, no doubt, Judith Resnick, the second woman in space, who died in the 1986 Challenger explosion, wanted to be known as "just another astronaut, period," and protested tokenism. She once said, "Firsts are only the means to the end of full equality, not the end in itself."[10]

To be seen as "deviant" is particularly threatening. Successful women fear that once they are singled out as "different" or "unfeminine," they will be cast out of the pack and rejected by men as well as by other women. The top can signify loveless isolation. The "top," of course, is relative to the size of the surrounding trees. For a woman who fears the specter of a lonely treetop, even her modest success can be felt as a threat, if those closest to her are clinging to lower branches.

3. Fear of Failure

Money eluders believe that in order to excel they must meet vague, but rigid, ideal standards. They require an exaggerated degree of professional competence of themselves, as well as superior personality skills and a saintly character. The perfectionist who demands that she be totally deserving sabotages herself. She may ask for less money in a salary negotiation because she secretly fears that she could never live up to the higher pay. Jeannie, our money group member who was looking for a job, worried that her imperfection would be detected the minute she stated her salary demands.

> I'm going out on a lot of job interviews, and when they ask me what salary I want, I can't get it out. I'm afraid the interviewer is going to say, "Are you out of your fucking mind? Do you think you're worth that kind of money?" And I think if he said that I would just expire. I've been practicing saying thirty-nine-five and I'm shocked to see them writing it down, as if it's okay.

Fears of proving undeserving, or of seeming aggressively self-seeking, induce women to accept lower salaries than they need, and titles that represent their job descriptions as less important than they are.

Fear of failure inevitably leads to fear of risk-taking. Money eluders project their "inadequacies" onto unfamiliar financial activities or career challenges, and draw back from them. Highly intelligent women may have more confidence in their ability to master the skills that a new job requires than to cope emotionally with change. Selena, a television producer, passed up a chance to buy her building in Manhattan, an investment that would have eventually allowed her to quit her job and pursue her real goal—making independent film documentaries.

> The fear was that I would be overwhelmed by that kind of responsibility, that it would take something away from my private life. I didn't make a decision in a rational frame of mind. There were some rational things, like how managing the building would interfere with my time, but there were irrational things like, God, what if they call me up and tell me the boiler is broken? As though I couldn't cope with that! And yet, I knew perfectly well that I could. I felt that as soon as that would happen I would panic; I would turn into a terrified woman. And if I had bought it, I'd be in great shape; I would have so much money it would be ridiculous. At the time, I had no ability to see that vision.

We asked Selena if she hadn't projected some other "terrified woman" into her fantasy of owning the building.

> Down the line it was my mother, there's no question about that. She laid that trip on me totally. She didn't believe in risk-taking!

Many women, like Selena, learned fear of risk-taking from their hearthbound mothers. For some, fortunately, this message was modified by their fathers, who taught them how to go into the marketplace. Some fathers, however, were inadequate instructors. Women in our study with serious money eluding problems had fathers who achieved far below the level of their talents. These fathers, also money eluders, were exploited by others, or dutifully supported their families, but were not financially ambitious; they, too, placed boundaries on the amount of money they allowed themselves to earn.

Detecting Money Eluders: The Six-Figure Fantasy

Success is an elusive word until one attaches a price tag to it. An unquantified financial fantasy can be material for dreams or nightmares, a source of pleasure as well as self-reproach. A woman who is unable to calculate the dollar value of success also finds it difficult to calculate what must be done to achieve it. Since she is also incapable of imagining the effect that more money will have on her time and relationships, she never confronts secret fears. Once "success" has a price tag, however, the reasons for failure become clearer, or so we discovered when we asked the women in our money study to fantasize an opportunity to earn a very high salary.

In our Six-Figure Fantasy game, we asked each woman we interviewed to imagine that she had been invited to a chic dinner party and found herself seated next to a successful woman who was earning a lot of money in her own field. Next, we asked the participant to describe this woman and their conversation. How did the successful woman relate to her? After we heard the imaginary give-and-take, we had the rich and powerful female tycoon make our interviewee a once-in-a-lifetime offer—the job opportunity of her wildest dreams. We tailored the job to fit what we felt was the ultimate career goal of the participant, based on her questionnaire and what she had already told us in the interview. Artists were offered mural commissions; those in the social services were given their own clinics and consulting firms, and so on. The salary that came with this job was always far more than our participant was currently earning; in some cases, it matched the salary she had named as "ideal." Usually, we offered her the sum fantasies are made of—$100,000! How did she reply? Did she accept the offer? If she took the job, we asked her what she would do with the money, and how earning it would affect her relationships with the man in her life, with men in general, women friends, and family.

The fantasy material proved to be an excellent resource for our research. Money Phobic symptoms that the rest of the interview had failed to uncover came into focus, as did rewarding reflections on the interviewee's business and personal relationships. Fears of risk-taking, envy, and loss of femininity appeared like invisible ink under a revealing light. The Six-Figure Fantasy was especially useful in helping us pinpoint exactly what was holding our money eluding participants back from earning more and establishing their financial identities. Here is a summary of what "stopped" our ambitious women from seizing an opportunity to make the high salaries they told us they wanted.

1. Stopped by the Successful Woman at the Dinner Party

A number of our participants were stopped at the start of the fantasy by the successful woman herself, who was seen, according to time-honored social stereotypes, as being cold, severe, evil, or unfeminine.

Dana, a video writer reluctantly working in another field, found it difficult—with some justification—to believe that a woman who was enormously successful in the visual media even existed. Once convinced, she described her dinner table companion like this:

> She's wearing black and pearls. Extremely plain and kind of severe, with a thin, slightly drawn face. I can't relate to her at all. She feels that I'm some underling that might want something from her that she doesn't want to give. I'm very reserved! I don't initiate anything! I will take an opportunity to respond to something she says and show myself as well as I can, but the idea of pushing myself on this person and saying, "Hey, I'm a talented writer, you really ought to meet me, blah, blah, blah. Have you got any work?" I would never in a million years do that.

Women like Dana, who could not make a positive identification with a successful female, and who expected her to be forbidding and unpleasant, have placed unconscious boundaries on the amount of success they feel they, as women, can safely achieve. They cannot envision themselves as very successful, because they fear success will transform them into hard or unfeminine creatures. They reject the self-made woman, not only in the fantasy, but in themselves, and instead, angrily accuse her of rejecting them at first sight. They may also cherish unexplored feelings of competitiveness with other women. These women find it hard to see other successful women as resources or as models for achievement.

Some of the participants were envious of the tycoon or tried to "disarm" her by uncovering her "human" side; one very low-earner said she would draw her out, and get her to confide her "abortions" and "the other tragedies in her life." Although those who failed to see the tycoon as a resource accepted the high-paying job she offered them with alacrity, they had already revealed the unconscious blocks that were preventing them from taking the necessary steps to find a high-paying job on their own initiative.

Even big-earners rejected the successful woman. Georgette had already made more than $100,000 a year in the world of finance; for her, we had to up the ante to $500,000. She described the high roller at the dinner party like this:

> She'd probably be awful. She'd be very cold, very driven, not very nice, and very snotty. I would be uncomfortable because I would feel that . . . there would be an axe coming my way at some point and it would be coming from this woman. I've always traditionally done my worst when I've had a woman in a superior position over me. They just hate me and I hate them. Once I was being interviewed for a vice-president's job—a big job—but I saw through the interviews that there would be friction with the woman boss. And I have more trouble with women like that than I do with men with the exact same attributes. I think it has something to do with my mother.

Though Georgette's distrust of successful women is based partly on experience, her unquestioning acceptance of a negative stereotype suggested that she had trouble internalizing her own success and integrating her concept of her own femininity with her income-producing powers. A fantasy is a good place to examine stereotypes, as this woman did:

> She looks happy. There's no tension in her face. My initial reaction was to make her into a stereotype, but my mind is saying it doesn't have to be that way. My mind says no to a business suit, cropped hair, and a hard-looking, unfeminine woman.

2. Stopped By Feelings of Low Self-Esteem

Some of our participants were awed by the successful woman and felt their own failings more acutely in her presence. What they said to her revealed that they didn't think much of themselves. Deanna, the South Carolina mother who had overcome her fear of risk-taking to go to college, had grown up in a poor family with a "bad reputation." Soon to graduate, she had decided that she would look for a job in pharmaceutical sales. Appropriately, we seated her next to the owner of a pharmaceutical company.

> She's well-dressed and you can tell she is rich. I feel I am not as good as she is. She would have to start the conversation because I would be shy. I can't do a thing when I first meet people like that.
>
> INT.: What do you say when she asks you what you do?
>
> D.[embarrassed laughter]: I'd say the usual stuff . . . that I'm going to school.

When the pharmaceutical executive offered Deanna the coveted job, her answer came not from her present courageous self but from the insecure child who had felt demeaned by her family status.

> I'd say yes! That would be ideal. I'd be thrilled. Then I wouldn't have to go out and find someone who would say that to me. Or beg for it!

Our fantasy alerted Deanna to a potential dilemma she faced when she left college (by now a comfortable home) and continued her journey toward the marketplace. She would have to be aware of the ways her feelings of inferiority could prevent her from projecting the self-confident attitude that would convince an employer to hire her.

The women in our study were surprisingly eager to confess their lack of accomplishments to a more successful woman. Some seemed to feel she would understand and sympathize with their frightened feelings as a mother would. Claire, our money denying set designer from the previous chapter, told the female producer of a Broadway hit all about her inadequacies.

> I'm such a goof, I'd probably say, "Oh, I wish I could do something like that! That's fabulous!" I don't really push, and I'm not a hustler, and I wish I had a little more of that."
>
> INT.: So you downplay yourself right away?
>
> C.: Yeah, probably.
>
> INT.: Well, what if she says, "You're a set designer? How interesting! What have you done?"
>
> C.[in comically melodramatic voice]: Oh, a little show on off-off-off-off Broadway.

We doubted the women in our study would have presented themselves in quite so unflattering a light if a real opportunity with the elements of our fantasy dinner had existed. We wondered, however, how much their unquestioning acceptance of their low self-esteem caused them to crumble in an intimidating situation without a fight. Were they alert to the presence of potential resources and cognizant of the politics of the "networking game," or did they let promising possibilities slip through their fingers? A fantasy, we thought, is a good place to prepare oneself to overcome psychic stopgaps with positive, not negative, visualizations.

Sharon, an artist, was also insecure about her accomplishments, but was able to treat the fantasy as a chance to deal with the difference between how she felt and how she should act. She saw the rich collector at her dinner table as an opportunity and acted accordingly.

> She relates to me with reserved interest, assuming I'm where I am, and I relate to her, mixed, according to my emotional mood. Inside I feel nervous and scared, but increasingly confident, because my work has gotten better and I've gotten good responses. It's like a game. She's buying and I'm selling, so I can't act too eager, and yet I have to act confident. She would probably ask, "What kind of work do you do?" There would be chitchat and I would tell her, and I would try to be my wonderful, most intelligent self.

3. Stopped by the Job

If our participants could not get past the female fat cat, or their own low self-esteem, the rest of the fantasy was a rhetorical exercise, imaginary indeed. Yet most of those who did not pass "Go" were eager to take the job and collect their six figures, and did not foresee that having the money would cause major problems. Some, who met the successful woman with relative equanimity, were stopped by the job and its expectations. One money denier was all set to take her wad and head straight for a Caribbean paradise for an extended vacation, until we reminded her that she now had a job with demanding obligations. The large amount of money elicited fears of risk-taking and failure in women who had been able to overcome such fears in relation to less impressive opportunities in their real work history.

Penny, for example, who had developed new skills in order to design computer programs for doctors on a freelance basis, was stymied when offered a six-figure job running a large business of this kind.

> That's when you get to my core. Can I do this? That's something I'm struggling with now. I'd have to make her [the successful tycoon] understand and honestly know what my capabilities are. I don't want to be in a situation where she believes I can do something I know nothing about.

Penny, like many women, believes she needs to know the skills a new job requires before she accepts it. According to Margaret Hennig and Anne Jardim, authors of *The Managerial Woman*, men take on new career challenges, confident that they will learn on the job.

Rene, offered a consulting business in her field, measured her skills against vague, self-imposed perfectionist standards she attributed to the wealthy entrepreneur.

> My first reaction is, "Can I live up to that expectation?" She has expectations about what kind of work she's going to get for $100,000. I would have to produce X amount of work of a certain standard that comes out of another person's head.

Others, with a history of performance problems, feared they could not work hard enough to succeed on the new job.

> I'm scared shitless. About proving that I can do it. About having to work so hard. I don't want to work so hard. I don't want to get myself in a situation where I'm expected to work twelve hours a day, which is what my boss, a woman like the one we're talking about, tells me she works. I would probably start by saying I have a child, and I can't work that hard. Is it possible to do it given my limitations?

It may well be that this woman's high-powered job will require long, grueling hours that will interfere with other priorities—a good reason to turn it down—but she presented her limitations and assumed the worst before asking the potential employer for a job description. She leaves the responsibility of deciding whether she "can do it" up to the boss, indicating she wants to be reassured and taken care of. In effect, this money eluder has fired herself before she is hired, and revealed much about the inner disturbances that might communicate themselves to a perceptive employer when she applies for a real job.

4. Stopped by the Money

Money squeamish women were stopped by the "filthy lucre" itself or by the female tycoon, because she had it. Before Sue, a social worker, would even talk to the tycoon, she wanted to know how she had gotten so rich.

> She's got way too much money. You don't get that much money by doing right. Somebody is getting fucked over for her to have that much money. I mean, nobody should have that much money. Nobody is worth that much. Nobody deserves it, or works that hard.

For Candace, who warred with genteel poverty in chapter 3, we had to lower the salary to $50,000, and even that was too much:

> I'm just not the sort of person who was meant to have half of six figures.

She was so eager to disabuse herself of her newfound wealth that her expenses exceeded her total intake. First, she bought a new home, then rented a vacation house in Mexico, and invited her parents to visit. She had plans to make charitable donations, too.

> I'd endow a number of benches in Denver for people who are waiting for buses to sit on. Yes, there's now a memorial bench or two with my name on it. I like the idea of having money so I can take my friends out for dinner, send a little to my brother . . . hand it around. I'd send some to an old boyfriend's wife who's been reduced to selling falafel on the street. It's an opportunity!

The money blind rejected the high salary because they were unwilling to look at its impact on their financial situation. Ann-Marie, married to a doctor, turned down the $75,000 salary we offered her to administer the restoration of the pre-revolutionary buildings in her town because it would "put the IRS on her back."

A.M.: I would say I'm very interested in that, but don't pay me $75,000, because the IRS will take it all. Pay me a stipend, and put the rest back into the restoration.

INT.: Wait a minute! Seventy-five grand is a lot of money! It's not $20,000. You're going to come out with something.

A.M.: If she insisted on paying me $75,000, I guess I'd have to talk to the accountant and see what he could do.

Modest salary desires may be noble, but they are not always productive. Women can be rejected for high-powered business jobs because they ask for salaries that are too small to convince the employer that they intend to "earn their keep" by aggressively turning over a profit for the company. For better or worse, if a woman rejects the idea of making money, it is difficult for her to be "successful" in American terms. There are, however, other, more personal measures of success a woman must consider when she weighs her financial needs against other goals.

5. *Stopped by the Effect of the Money on Their Personal Relationships*

Women who could not imagine themselves taking advantage of an opportunity to earn a high salary did not think money would affect their relationships with men or friends. Those who could were able to see potential problems. The artist who sailed through the dinner table "interview" enjoyed the job and used the money wisely, but she was stopped when she contemplated the effect of the huge fee she earned for painting a mural on her love life. She saw earning a lot as a way of undermining her boyfriend's masculinity.

I think he would be proud of me, and feel good about it. He would be supportive, but he would feel some anxiety. It would represent a pressure. The image that comes to my mind is "stealing his thunder." I would be the victor, who would take away the prize—which would be a lot more money— and he would slink off in the bushes. Money is erotic. Visually, I see the $100,000 as a triumphant erection of money, which I would have.

While some who played our fantasy game feared the imaginary windfall would introduce elements of competition and envy into relationships, others saw money as a means of separating from loved ones who had strangleholds over their lives. Simone, in a troubled marriage, relished the idea of the job, but saw the salary as a specter of freedom, both tempting and terrifying.

I think Pete could live with it; it wouldn't be threatening to him. The feelings of difficulty are that the money would make it easier for me to leave. Right now our relationship is about the worst it's been. If I were economically independent, I would be more likely to say, "Fuck this!" Having the money introduces an element of choice. I would have it, and he could just leave, and I wouldn't have to have any more contact with him over money. I wouldn't have to "work it out."

Toni, twenty-four, thought the high salary would change her relationship to her parents in a "scary" way. She said she would use the money to pay her upper-middle-class family back for her college education.

I love my parents so much, but I think I'm a little too dependent. I don't think I've broken away from them in that I've never really done something I wanted to do badly, even though I knew they didn't want me to do it. That hasn't happened yet, and when that happens, I'll be independent.

For Toni, who knew her parents did not expect or want repayment for her education, offering them a large sum of money symbolized "buying" her freedom, without severing the important tie. Though financial independence facilitates the complex process of separation from the family, true emotional separation is not a commodity that can be bought. Toni, we felt, would have to look more deeply into her relationship with her parents, particularly with her successful mother, who had influenced her career choices, in order to become less dependent.

Overcoming Money Eluding:
The "Right Answer" to the Six-Figure Fantasy

One participant called after her interview to say she had been disturbed by the fantasy; she felt there had been a "right answer" and she hadn't "gotten it." There was no "right answer" to the fantasy from the therapeutic point of view, as each "wrong answer" gave us, and hopefully the participant, valuable insights into the fears that were holding her back from articulating and realizing financial goals. Non–money eluders, however, played our game quite differently.

Barbara, thirty-nine, an advertising copywriter who earned between $35,000 and $50,000 a year, with additional income from wise investments, was seated next to a well-known woman who ran a public relations firm that represented superstars and rich people. What was she like?

She's got elements of the Queen Bee, as well as a fluffy Helen Gurley Brown. Like most successful women, she's patronizing to some extent, letting the conversation focus on me rather than on her. I've already read about her in all these magazines, right, so we'll talk about this "little girl who's on her way up in the world." If it seems like she's genuinely into the questions she asks, and interested in me, I'll open up a little more.

Barbara has an idea of what the tycoon is like, but her definition is flexible. She does not see her as threatening or masculine, and believes her most obvious flaw, her patronizing attitude, can be put in service to her own advantage. She believes the Queen Bee will be interested in her and is therefore approachable.

We then had The Bee offer Barbara a $100,000 a year job, helping to create "personal images" for the wealthy people she represented. Barbara was interested but reserved, weighing her desire to make money with her current needs and personal goals.

When you first started to talk about it, I got turned off, because my reaction was that this was going to be a lot of hard work. But then, the more you described it, it sounded right up my alley, and if it's right up my alley, it isn't hard work anymore, because it's something I could do fairly easily. Hard work is when you're faking it, and you really have to sweat through a project because you don't know what you're doing.

Confident of her abilities to brave even an unknown job situation, Barbara did not want to "sweat" for money as she had in the past, because she had just gotten out of an oppressive marriage and valued her "fun time" and social life. She knew making a lot of money would prove demanding.

My idea is to find a sinecure that pays me a hundred grand a year, and I have my weekends off! That's my ideal, but the real world doesn't work like that.

She is able to fantasize how the new job will affect not only her bank account but her social life.

In a job like that my personal life would become the job, because I might start dating people involved—a high-powered jet set life. If that happened, it would all blend together and I wouldn't have a separate life. If I wanted a sex life, I guess I'd have to change my attitude about not getting involved with rich men. I've had my chances with guys who are rich and it frightens the hell out of me, because to me, money is power, and these guys have a lot of power, and if they turn it on me, I don't know what's going to happen.

As she weighs the advantages and disadvantages of the new job, Barbara takes her need for a "sex life" into account. Because she is aware of her conflicts between sex, money, and power, they do not paralyze her. Barbara is clear about her desire for money. She prepares to hedge her bets with the Queen Bee and make a deal that will offer her maximum financial security.

> I might ease my way into it by doing it half time, and keeping my own freelance contacts until I'm sure it's going to work out. I'd try to make that part of the deal. I want to make sure we can work together. I have other work that pays the bills, and I don't want to give it up and just drop myself into her lap.

Once she has thought about her options, planned her "deal," and decided to go for the job, Barbara turns the table on the patronizing Queen and invites her to lunch.

> I'd say, "Let's talk about it." I might do something amusing like, "How about I take you to lunch?" And I'd pick not Lutece, but a pretty nice place. It would amuse me that I'm taking this woman who's worth millions to lunch.

Barbara was the only participant who added a scene to our fantasy script. She was able to play with the deadly serious prospect of a job interview, letting her future employer know that she considers herself an equal, despite the financial disparity between them. She fantasizes herself in an active, creative role, instead of a passive, or defensive, position.

Once she is making more than double her current income, Barbara plans to find a female financial adviser whom she trusts and ask her to make "conservative investments that will help me save on my tax bill."

> I probably wouldn't do anything terribly radical about buying a lot of things.

Did Barbara expect her friends to be envious? Having already been a victim of the Green Monster, she was realistically pessimistic.

> They couldn't be any worse about this than they were about my getting married. They were really bad about that!

Almost no one is totally non–Money Phobic, and Barbara was no exception. She was money paranoid, a common trait in successful women. Because she had one friend who often borrowed money, she planned to keep her high-earnings "under wraps" so the borrower would not know she had it. Since she was not planning to "flaunt her wealth" she did not think the men she was currently dating would "know much about it" either. Barbara's low-grade Money Phobia, however, did not include money eluding. She ran most of the bases: She saw the successful woman as a resource, appraised her own ability to handle the job positively, and weighed her financial needs against other, personal goals. She was not afraid of risk, failure, envy, or having more money. Her money paranoia, however, might prevent her from enjoying her new wealth or recognizing its effect on her relationships with men.

How can a woman transform herself from a money eluder who doubts her own abilities and fears the multi-dimensions of success or failure, into a Barbara, who approaches the concept of making money with a positive, confident outlook? Pop psychology primers galore have tackled this problem, indicating that the way to eradicate a "poverty mentality" is to simply stop doing the wrongheaded things that we do and take other tactics. These primers give us the "right" ways to define our career goals, sharpen our resumes, deal with job interviews and negotiations, behave on the job, and finally, manage and invest our newfound wealth. Many of these well-meaning, sometimes helpful manuals scold us for our negative attitudes, and emphasize the power of positive thinking; if we can envision ourselves as successful, they say, we have already taken an important step toward financial improvement.

We say, "Easier said than done!" For money eluders, the gap between hearing good advice and putting it into action can be equivalent to crossing the English Channel once someone has told you how to swim. Before a money eluder can take good advice about how to make money, she has to pinpoint exactly what is stopping her from hearing it. It is hard for her to envision herself as "successful" when the world has offered her so many unsuccessful images of her sex and condemned those who were successful in ways so subtly brutal we may never quite comprehend them. Before she can succeed, then, a woman must understand how her emotional blocks conspire with a sexist political economy to put up stop lights on her yellow brick "freeway." Once the fears and confusions, as well as the harsh realities that prevent us from making more money, are accounted for, we have the knowledge we need to make self-aware choices about how much we want to earn, and what we are willing to sacrifice to earn it. We may find ourselves more willing to reexamine our financial needs, utilize our resources differently, and redefine success in terms of our own individuality. With a clear perception of what we want—as opposed to an impossible ideal of what we are supposed to have—we can set out for the Emerald City if we choose to do so, less at the mercy of evil forces.

Chapter Six

The Pleasure of Spending: Reviewing Money Folly

So far we have looked at the personal and social problems that inhibit modern women from seeing money clearly, and the cultural messages, which once internalized, prevent them from creating a lifelong financial plan. In the next two chapters, we will turn our attention to the question of spending: What are the obstacles inside and outside ourselves that keep us from enjoying our money and using it wisely?

The non–Money Phobic woman strikes a comfortable balance between squandering and hoarding her financial resources. She decides what she wants, why she wants it, and enjoys buying it. The money folly victim, on the other hand, can not make rational or informed decisions about what she wants to do with her money, but spends in order to achieve emotional goals. Because she buys to resolve emotional problems instead of to obtain goods and services, her concept of money is subjective. Depending on her mood, she views her resources as inexhaustible or insufficient, and is unable to calculate how much real money she has to spend. She may think of money as "play money."

Women with money folly, like the money blind and the money denying, live in a financial present. They do not see that their everyday expenditures are part of an overall financial identity, formed by the way they earn and use money not only today but in the future and past. A common symptom of Money Phobia, money folly plagued most of the women in our study at least some of the time. Divorced women often commit money folly, spending their settlements on luxuries in order to compensate themselves for the emotional trials of a marriage gone bad, or overspending on their children, to make up for the absent father. Single women, who fantasize that a rescuer or windfall will arrive tomorrow, are liable to overspend today. Widows are prone to money folly, too: A study, conducted by an insurance company, determined that within eighteen months 80 percent of newly widowed women had none of their deceased husband's insurance money left to spend. Some had lost it to dubious investments, but many had quickly squandered it all.

The average over-spender is simply unaware of how much money she spends and what she spends it on. A hundred dollars a week for lunch vanishes involuntarily from her pocketbook. She buys goods and services she unquestionably regards as "necessities," and loathes the idea of keeping track of expenses. She "forgets" how much she has charged to the credit cards bursting her wallet's seams and what their various interest rates are. Wanton spenders see budgeting not as an effective method of taking charge of their financial lives but as a submission to outside forces that, like punitive parents, conspire to deprive them of gratification. If you want to insult an overspender call her "cheap," an epithet she readily applies to savers. Even as she falls into debt, she may continue her unconscious spending.

Those who commit money folly are not necessarily financial underdogs: Women are more apt to fall into debt as their income rises, and credit opportunities present themselves. (For better or worse, the days when a woman couldn't get a credit card without her husband's signature are history.) Marcia Clark, for example, the prosecutor in the celebrated O. J. Simpson trial, had installment debts and living expenses that exceeded her $96,829 annual salary by $1,380 a month in 1995.[1]

Though money folly women may feel nervous about their lack of nest egg, or "strapped" by the way their precarious financial edge limits their mobility, they still find it difficult to take a critical look at the way they use money, or to ask themselves crucial questions such as: Are there other kinds of financial behavior my spending helps me safely avoid, like taking risks on the job market? Have I sacrificed my quality of life because I've acquired the American Dream—a new car or home? Are my "necessities" really consolations? Am I spending profusely on small, inexpensive items because I don't feel I will ever earn enough to buy anything big? And last but not least, am I spending all of my money because I eventually hope to live on someone else's pile?

Women with money folly can also suffer from too much of a generous spirit. Generosity, of course, is a traditional feminine virtue, and most women, whether they are generous or not, would like to believe it is one of their qualities. Four times as many women in our money study defined themselves as "generous" as opposed to "cheap," and most said others saw them that way as well. Since society encourages us to give gifts, generosity easily becomes an acceptable financial behavior we find difficult to identify as part of a destructive tendency to overspend. Gifts, like purchases for oneself, however, can have inappropriate emotional goals. Some Lady Bountifuls lessen uneasy feelings they have about relationships or attempt to manipulate others with presents. They may also sabotage the family's financial health by being overgenerous with children. One divorced mother realized that her generosity was inspired by guilt:

> My boyfriend says I should install an ATM machine in my kitchen, because on weekends it's "I need money for this, and I need money for that." I've let them try every class and every piece of equipment they wanted, and sent them to expensive art camps. I am very strong with them on their creative interests, because I feel I was shortchanged that way by my parents, and I feel guilty because I'm divorced and my children don't have a nuclear family. Now I think that I've done to them what my parents did to me in a different way—that is, I haven't been particularly honest with them about life's financial deal. My daughter wants to be a photographer and has no interest in earning money. She thinks Mommy will always be around to give it to her.

Those who commit money folly can also be bingers, submitting to uncontrollable urges to spend. Unlike the woman who knows what she needs and why, and sets out for the marketplace to buy it, the money binger has a less concrete goal—to spend and keep spending. Her closets overflow with clothes she seldom wears; she buys Gucci luggage for trips she cannot afford to take after she buys it, and antiques she can barely squeeze into her jammed studio apartment. Shopping is a necessary and often pleasurable activity, but the overspender does not really enjoy either the process or the purchases. Once in a store, she feels that she is at the mercy of dictatorial forces, and she emerges package-laden, frightened, and guilty. An extreme money binger in our study described one of her emotionally draining "rampages" like this:

> A couple of weeks ago I had a really bad day. I was in a total rage. I work across the street from Bloomingdale's, which is an unfortunate place to be situated when you're somebody like me. I ran in there and breezed through the place, grabbing things like a maniac in the Anne Klein department. I was so completely loaded down I could barely walk. I handed it all over to the saleswoman and said, "Send it!" I was feeling kind of tired, so I went back to my office. Then I thought, I have to go back there! I have to get some more! So I raced back to the same department and started grabbing. I didn't even know what I bought. This time I took the package with me. A few days

later the UPS parcel arrived. When I hung up the clothes I noticed that I had two Anne Klein skirts—$150 each, side by side, and they were exactly the same! The same color, the same style. I was freaked. Even for me, buying the same skirt twice on the same day was going a bit far.

Bingers like this one are actually addicts, sometimes called "shopaholics." Although we tend to think of an addict as someone who is hooked on a drug, experts say that any substance or behavior habitually used to alter a negative mood can be regarded as an addiction. A woman addicted to overeating learns that putting something in her mouth at a stressful moment makes her feel less anxious; the overspender buys satin pajamas and gets the same transcendent feeling of relaxation. When she finds herself having to spend more money more often to get the good feeling she craves, her diversion has become an addictive habit. When she goes into debt and keeps on spending, her addiction is out of control. Surprisingly, some who succumb to "impulsive" buying may profess that they "hate to shop," but once in a store, lose control over their purse strings, and spend too much. Many money bingers, we learned, can be binge eaters, too, who suffer from unshakable debts as well as pounds.

Some with money folly binge on bargains, attempting to control the marketplace, even as they lose control of themselves. The bargain hunter will never pay full price for anything, but may spend a great deal more by buying dozens of reduced items she does not really want or need. More than other shoppers, she is susceptible to the allure of the Almighty Brand Name: Norma Kamali, Manolo Blannik, and Ralph Lauren are Holy Grails, and she both undermines and enhances their status by her much-prized ability to outwit the system and obtain them for less than their "real" value. She can recognize her fashion icons even without their identifying tags, and scoop incredible "steal deals" from flea markets and thrift shop tables. Her house and closets may bulge with junk she eventually returns to the Salvation Army. The bargain hunter does not decide what she wants, but bases her desires on the relationship of the label to the price. The time and money she wastes, however, get undervalued in her obsessive wheeling and dealing.

According to consumer trend analysts, women spend most of their money on themselves and their homes. Those who overspend on clothes, make-up, and beauty treatments, traditional enhancers of female sexuality, may use a sexual term to describe the overspending experience—blowing it! The money blower does perform a vital service for the American economy, for without the insatiable female consumer, multimillion-dollar industries would fall to the wayside, among them cosmetics, fashion, diet centers, perfume, exercise studios, beauty salons, home furnishings, and cosmetic plastic surgery. It is in society's interest, then, to perpetuate female money folly and wage advertising campaigns that convince women of the necessity to purchase an endless stream of products.

Advertisers never hesitate to play dirty pool: They insist that editorial copy reflect their products, and indicate that without their goods we will be unfeminine, subtly preying on our fears of ending up alone. A 1995 issue of *Mirabella*, a magazine that purports to be "a busy woman's guide to the good life," offers us a product to buy on every page and features an article by a popular novelist titled "Yes, Please, and One of Those: The Irrefutable Case for Irresponsible, Out-Of-Control Spur-Of-The-Moment Spending." A Bill Blass ad for a new perfume, to cite one among billions of possible examples, shows the ruggedly handsome designer posing between lists of "What he likes and doesn't like so much in a woman." Among his dislikes are "A woman who talks about money all the time" and "A woman who won't spend her last few bucks on perfume." The advertising message, like society's, is mixed, offering us conflicting fantasies of what material goods we need to be "real women" at any given moment. One season we are offered the dress-for-success man-tailored look and the next, poufed skirts for "a return to femininity"; sometimes both fashion options are promoted at once.

Unlike some feminist writers, we do not believe that women are necessarily victimized by this fashion game, provided that they also spend money on freedom and security. If we remain conscious of the forces that influence our purchases, shopping for "femininity" can be an enjoyable pastime with its own rewards. Many of the industries we support with our shopping, moreover, are owned by or employ women (although not always in the most influential slots). It is when the shopping game, and the nearsighted intensity with which we play it, begins to sap our financial strength and becomes a joyless obsession, limiting other, important life options or preventing us from dealing with our real deprivations and fears, that it becomes a dangerous symptom of Money Phobia.

The Money Folly Myth

This is the age of money folly, and plenty of men suffer from it, too. As money bingers rack up debt on ever more available credit cards, the national debt threatens the nation's economic health. Throughout the last third of the twentieth century, the individual predilection for money folly has mirrored the upswing in government spending; between 1980 and 1990, when the deficit was soaring, consumer debt also rose—from $350.3 billion to $794.4 billion. Although debt levels rise and fall, most Americans buy now and pay later; today, virtually every marketplace good can be captured with plastic, including groceries, with free frequent flier miles thrown in with the charge. Easy credit makes it convenient to forget rainy days. In 1992

University of Minnesota researchers found that 6 percent of Americans, or 15 million, may be compulsive shoppers who run up debts with the mistaken notion that they will later find money to finance their addictive shopping behavior.[2] Few, experts say, put aside enough for retirement, and some may be blowing the pensions that their employers have saved. In 1995 the *Wall Street Journal* reported that retirees, offered the opportunity to take their pensions in lump sums before they retired, were blowing their nest eggs on spending sprees.[3]

The decline in real income—or what our salaries can actually buy—is, in part, responsible for our desire to concentrate our cash in consumer goods and services instead of banks. Since the end of the Second World War, the middle class has been defined by its ability to own one's own home, educate one's children, and afford amenities such as family vacations. Today, the price of the middle-class family's lifestyle is increasing, while the share of the national wealth it receives grows smaller. As the value of money shrinks in the marketplace, it shrinks in our regard, and we want to exchange it for things that do not alter their worth, or "treats" that give us immediate gratification. Women, who earn less "real" money than men, and have traditionally spent it on "little things," suffer even more from this syndrome, and, experts say, are more inclined to be shopaholics than men.

Women with money folly did not learn it from previous generations of women. During the Depression and postwar years, it was women's astute management skills that got their families through lean times. Mothers who worked in the home in the 1930s and '40s let down hems, made pound cakes with only one egg, and transformed Sunday's leftovers into Monday's lunch. They knew where to find two cans of tomato sauce for under a dime. It was thanks to these thrifty wives, who budgeted for education, that many of their daughters were able to go to college and become independent professionals.

These careful money managers of the past, however, bought things they could touch, cook and see; they did not engage in speculative or abstract economic activities, like investing, unless it was to switch the family savings account from one bank to another in order to get the free toaster oven. Moreover, their careful spending symbolized their fundamental economic powerlessness and dependent state. Although they often controlled the family resources, the money they managed was not their own, nor did they get paid for the hours of work they did to conserve it. Traditional fathers, who worked outside the home, took responsibility for major financial decisions.

Contemporary women inherited some spending lessons from their mothers and grandmothers, but rejected others. They learned what women spend money on, and that shopping can be fun. Some were taught the art of bargain-hunting, and others found out that luxuries can provide rewards or consolations. While they learned to control money they made themselves, what they did not learn (or want to learn) was how to invest, budget, and save. Those who did have working mothers, and grew up in the liberal economic climates of the sixties, seventies, and eighties, did not identify with the deprivations that past Great Depressions imposed, or foresee the shrinking job markets of the future. While some women witnessed their parents' struggles during recessions, or survived the downswing of a mother's divorce, they continued to believe that their own financial futures were limitless horizons, and did not dream of curtailing desires for the American Dream of material wealth. For those who grew up in an atmosphere where money was scarce, or handled carefully, penny-pinching messages may have represented a depressing, colorless wasteland—a financial and emotional claustrophobia—they wanted only to flee.

Whether our childhood financial scenarios were pinched or prosperous, as we came of age and began earning our own money, we wanted to spend in a way that conveyed the journey we had taken—or hoped to take—to govern our own lives. As we hurdled high barriers in order to achieve financial independence, sometimes at great cost, we did not want barriers around our ability to spend. We saw the things that money could buy as tangible proof of our success and as rewards for our struggles. It was in a spirit of positive exploration, then, that some of us progressed from the pleasure of spending our own money on ourselves to the perils of money folly. What began as financial behavior that expressed our positive feelings about ourselves became an expression of what we felt we were lacking.

Society provides those with the tendency to overspend with legions of role models, endlessly celebrated by the media—the heiresses, daughters, and wives of rich men, famous models, and glamorous stars of the stage and screen. These women have always received attention for spending as if there were no tomorrow, and their money folly is part of the mythology of American wealth.

The money folly legend began when the daughters of the robber barons, who made millions by building railroads with exploited labor after the Civil War, helped "launder" their fathers' disreputable earnings by marrying impoverished European aristocrats, and raising conspicuous consumption to a high art form. Barbara Hutton, the Woolworth heiress, one of the last of this line, was perhaps the most famous money blower of all. In 1924 she inherited $28 million (worth more than twenty times as much in today's currency), which her father doubled with astute investments that were able to survive the stock market crash. While bread lines formed during the Great Depression, Barbara incurred the national rage (and also envy) by throwing extravagant parties, buying the jewels of deposed princesses, villas, palaces, Cadillacs galore, and European ne'er-do-well princes and barons. Throughout her life, Barbara, who was wed seven times, used her capital to purchase good sex. When she got tired of men she paid them fabulous sums to quietly decamp, knowing her huge fortune would soon draw another. Her fifth husband, Dominican playboy and renowned superstud, Profiro Rubirosa, collected approximately $2 million in gifts and $2.5 million in cash in their fifty-three-day marriage.[4]

Barbara is by no means the only goddess in our money blowing mythology. The money folly of prominent women is inevitably a major feature of their publicity profiles. The press eagerly pries into the closets and jewelry boxes of the rich and famous: It tells us about Elizabeth Taylor's robin's egg sized diamonds, and Dolly Parton's 2,400 pairs of shoes, and 410 wigs. Jewelry designer Elsa Peretti, we learned, once tossed a $35,000 sable coat into a fireplace in the heat of an argument. Mae West, actually a smart investor, is more renowned for her swansdown-marabou stoles.

Female money folly is rampant on a grand international scale, as well. Spendthrift wives of foreign dictators have helped topple their husbands' corrupt regimes. After Ferdinand Marcos was forced out of power in the Philippines, journalists and poverty-stricken peasants were led through the Malacanang palace to marvel at his wife Imelda's loft-sized closets, trunks of girdles, and shelves of unused Gucci bags. We know less about the way power-hungry dictators themselves spend their filthy lucre; they seem to invest it in real estate, or salt it away in discrete Swiss banks. In fact, we seldom know the intimate details of how rich or powerful men dispose of their discretionary cash. We almost never see what they have in their closets! When it was disclosed that President Bill Clinton sprung for pricey designer haircuts on a jet tarmac, his money folly was hailed with derision and rage.

Female money blowers, then, embody a popular American fantasy—unlimited wealth—and their excessive spending remains part of an ongoing legend about what women do when they have money to burn. Wealthy women who use their money wisely or donate it to worthy causes, like Sallie Bingham and Peg Yorkin, who sponsored important women's foundations, are scarcely household names. Good sense, it seems, makes bad copy. We may despise the way infamous money blowers misuse their wealth, but we cannot help imagining ourselves with equal sums at our disposal.

Most of our own lives are defined and controlled by financial boundaries, which often seem to restrict our emotional freedom and creativity. In fact, it is when we feel financial restrictions limiting our options that we are most tempted to imitate women who live what we perceive as glamorous, romantic existences. Unfortunately, we are rarely offered intriguing prototypes of working women who both manage wisely and enjoy their money.

It is easy to forget that the majority of classic money blowers, with enviable unlimited options, are not in the same financial position that most of us are. They are not self-made or independent. They were either catapulted to wealth through fame, or are the beneficiaries or wives of powerful men. Many are not responsible for their financial futures, and many do not manage their own resources, but are controlled by powerful family males, condescending lawyers, and corrupt trustees.[5]

Some, like Barbara Hutton, never worked a day in their lives. The women in the money folly pantheon, moreover, are seldom happy or well-adjusted. Barbara Hutton was one of the least happy. Placed in boarding schools after her mother killed herself, she was a lonely child, ignored by her father and shunned by schoolmates who envied her money. When the girls at Miss Shin's School told Barbara that people would always hate her because she was so rich, she asked her aunt if she could give her money away. After her aunt said no, Barbara proceeded to cut up all her clothes with a pair of scissors. Her deprived childhood condemned her to repeat this destructive act throughout her life, which she passed with no higher purpose than trying to prove she could give her money away, or destroy her resources. She died alone and almost penniless, addicted to alcohol and drugs.

Detecting Money Folly: The Little Match Girl
Who Earned Six Figures

Modern money blowers may strive for money and fame to compensate for a lack of love and attention in troubled childhoods. It is often when a woman has struggled up the ladder of success, and finally has money to burn, however, that her real anxieties are illuminated. When time-consuming efforts to overcome financial difficulties are no longer necessary, she may find herself falling apart.

At first, Tiffany did not seem Money Phobic; at twenty-four she was an all-American beauty with a heart-shaped face, blue eyes, and curly blonde hair. She had a boyfriend who was understandably crazy about her. Not only was she beautiful and adored, she was also successful: Her ingenue role in a television comedy series netted her $100,000 a year. We were not surprised to find that she radiated self-confidence and charm.

We had asked Tiffany to volunteer for an interview because her questionnaire indicated big financial trouble brewing beneath her enviable exterior. Though she earned much more than our other participants under thirty, she had no savings, and owned no stocks, bonds, or real estate. She indicated that her inability to save was an "emotional anxiety."

> Now that I am at the point I've worked so hard for, I know I have to start thinking smarter and learn to invest. I find if I have money saved I can be a completely happy person. And saving money for me is rare. Some people are born just plain spoiled, and I will always spoil myself if I can.

Why did a simple financial activity like saving represent a happiness this high-earner felt unable to achieve? Spoiled can mean both "destroyed" and "damaged by overindulgence." Was Tiffany unconsciously trying to ruin herself, and if so, why? What had she learned about the meaning of money in her family? We discovered that the smiling, gracious young actress who had worked her way from a Miami nightclub to New York City's brightest lights, had a persona she often referred to as you, as if she was somebody else, while the real Tiffany was a deprived little girl who saw herself as a bag lady from a fairy tale.

Tiffany's rise had been meteoric. By the time she was a senior in high school, she was completely self-supporting and living in an apartment of her own. She was going to school, and dancing in a local nightclub on weekends. A year later she was discovered by a Hollywood agent, and moved to the West Coast. After going to drama school, Tiffany was soon earning $800 a day playing small parts in TV shows, sometimes written in especially for her. Eventually she was offered the important role in the New York-based series. When we met her, she had been making six figures for almost a year and was due for a raise. What was she doing with all this money?

It was not easy to find out. Like many spending addicts, Tiffany hid her habit, even from herself. She did not want to look at, or talk about, the way she managed her money. She rejected investment advice from her manager and boyfriend, and felt humiliated by our questions about her spending. She said they made her feel as if she was on "the gynecologist's table," where, she said,

You just pretend you are somebody else.

She denied she was a "shopaholic":

I spend a lot of money on myself, but nothing big. I don't have a lot to show for it. I think I treat myself fairly okay. Anytime I want to get some things I do. Play things. Um . . . gifts for friends. Whenever I'm out, if I see something someone would like I grab it . . . things . . . you know, a new pair of sneakers . . . whatever. I don't like to feel deprived. I was never the type to leave $100 sitting in the bank. If I saw a wonderful new red jacket that I had to have . . . well, I would have to have it.

We pressed Tiffany for details on how much all these "little things" cost:

INT.: How much a month do you spend on clothes, would you say?

T.: Not that much—$500.

INT.: You keep track then?

T.: No. . . .

INT.: So you spend about $6,000 a year on clothes?

T.: More than that.

Tiffany "grabbed" anything that caught her eye, showered her boyfriends with fabulous carpets and costly exotic plants, and indulged in "nice dinners" at trendy restaurants. She did manage to save for a trip to Europe; she told us she needed $2,000 "just to shop."

> I got a nice paisley silk jacket . . . no, two silk jackets. I got some luggage, real nice luggage that was very expensive, and, of course, makeup and perfume of every scent . . . lots of things like that. Outfits and shoes, lots of shoes.

Did all these new presents give Tiffany pleasure? Like most money bingers, she wasn't sure.

> I had fun, but now these things are all thrown about, and I can't even enjoy them. [Tentatively] Of course I had fun. . . .

The reason Tiffany had no place to put her purchases, we learned, was because she did not have her own apartment. Although she had been in New York for more than nine months, her reckless spending had prevented her from accumulating enough cash to pay a broker's fee, deposit, and first month's rent on a "decent place." Feeling "thrown about" (like her purchases), she had lived at a hotel for six months, then moved to a sublet when she fell behind in the bills. When we interviewed her, she was staying in a "little rathole" someone had loaned her.

A home was extremely important to Tiffany, despite the fact she had not yet managed to find one. She told us that once she had a desk, and a place to organize her checks and bills—a "center"—she could begin to manage her money better. Home also represented a center of emotional tranquility.

> For what I do, for how I get my work done, it calls for a whole lot of concentration. I need a home, and to know that my desk is there, and the TV, and the VCR, so I can sit down for hours upon hours and study my part.

If home was such an important place, why had Tiffany invested in homelessness? Like a modern Dorothy, Tiffany had gotten stranded in Oz and could not find her way back up the yellow brick road to Kansas.

As she began to open up and reveal her real self instead of her starlet persona, we realized that home had never been a place where Tiffany felt cared for or secure. Her childhood home had been "broken" by her parents' divorce when she was seven. Her father was an unreliable gambler, who cardsharped the rent money away.

> He's a high roller. He never had a job in his life.

Although Tiffany and her two sisters visited him every summer, he never paid regular child support. It fell upon her mother to take care of her family by working as a secretary until she remarried four years later.

> She did it on her own. She's a very tough lady.

After she remarried, Tiffany's mother continued to work. She raised her daughters to believe that they would be responsible for their own support.

> I had a very strong mother, and I watched her all those years, working really hard. She said, "I want you to do well, to do what you want to do." The trick of it is knowing that you can't depend on someone else.

From her hardworking mother, then, Tiffany learned how to go out into the world and become an independent risk-taker. Unfortunately, she was taught this important lesson at a high emotional cost. Her father was not there, and her mother had little time to spend with her children.

> It was hard being away from her during the day, and having to do all the things she had no time to do. She was tired on the weekend.

Tiffany, then, felt neglected by her mother, who had no choice but to work during her children's formative years. When her mother remarried, home became a threatening place. Tiffany confided that her mother's second husband, her stepfather, was abusive and beat her mother when he was drunk.

> He wasn't too cheery to be in a household with. I always saw my mother staying with him because she couldn't keep doing it on her own.

When Tiffany talked about her stepfather, her voice dropped to a distracted whisper. We wondered if he had abused Tiffany, too. She also told us that homelessness went back a generation in her family. Her mother had been placed in a Catholic home by her mother, who said she could not afford to keep her. Tiffany, a sensitive child who loved her mother and identified strongly with her, suffered for her as well as for herself. Deprived of the attention and sense of security a child needs to feel loved, Tiffany learned that money could be used to buy consolation or communicate emotions.

> After she remarried my mother's income was really play money for us girls. I think it was my mom's way of saying that she was sorry she was away all day. Or that she had been poor and she wanted us to have all the things she didn't have. Even though my family didn't have a lot of money, my sister and I always looked like a million bucks. We always had new clothes, makeup, and all the things that make it fun to be a girl. So I found out that having new things made me feel good. If you don't want to wake up in the morning, but you have a pretty new sweater (in bright red) to put on, you are out of bed in two seconds, looking at the sunshine.

The real Tiffany, then, missed having loving, responsive parents. But the Tiffany persona could put on a new costume in a color that did not express the way she felt inside, and become someone else—sunny and confident. She began her adulthood, then, with all the psychological ingredients to become an ambitious high-earner, unafraid of risk or success, who binged and blew the money she made in order to block out deeply rooted feelings of deprivation.

Though she had no home of her own, Tiffany's fantasies were all about houses. She wanted to buy a house for her mother. She planned to donate money to a home for abused children, with whom she also identified, when and if she could put a halt to her compulsive spending. She fantasized about homes of her own—villas in the South of France and California, and apartments, reminiscent of the luxury palaces of thirties' screen stars.

> In California I was struggling and working for something, and when I got it, I expected it to be glorious. A penthouse, you know, with white carpets and a white marble fireplace. To be living somewhere fabulous! That didn't happen. The opposite happened.

For Tiffany, a home was a fantasy that she expected success would make real. It symbolized the emotional security she so desperately needed and did not have. This young actress, earning more money in one year than most women her age could earn in four, told us:

> I feel just like the Little Match Girl.

Tiffany had chosen a homeless character from the saddest of Hans Christian Andersen's fairy tales to identify as herself. The Little Match Girl, who is also beautiful and abused, wanders the street barefoot on a freezing New Year's Eve, afraid to go home, because she knows her father will beat her for failing to sell her matches. In order to warm her fingers, blue with cold, she begins to light match after match. In the brief glow of each, she sees a tempting fantasy of holiday cheer in a warm, secure home—a roast goose, a Christmas tree with thousands of lighted candles gleaming under its branches. When the match goes out, this youthful bag lady's fantasy fades with it. Finally her dead grandmother, who loved her, appears in the glow, lifts the little girl up in her arms, where they soar in a halo of light and joy, far above the earth's cold, hunger, and pain.

> In the cold morning light the poor little girl sat there in the corner between the houses, with rosy cheeks and a smile on her face—dead. Frozen to death on the last night of the old year . . . with the ends of burnt-out matches in her hand.[6]

Home, for the Match Girl, is more than a place; it represents a positive emotional state where one feels loved and secure. Ironically, those who get insufficient love in childhood may continue to deprive themselves of the people who could give them love, or not be able to take it in, because they want it from those who denied it in the past. Tiffany dramatizes her internal plight by depriving herself of the place that symbolizes emotional contentment. Like her poignant fairy tale role model, she burns her inventory, forgetting that it may be limited, as she fantasizes secure and comfortable homes.

Unlike the Match Girl, however, Tiffany has the financial resources to get what she needs. She spends on "little things" in order not to feel pain, but material consolations fail to console her. In order to give herself a "home," she must unite the two Tiffanies and face the neglected child, frozen at the center of the beautiful and successful actress. She cannot change her childhood, but with the help of psychotherapy, she can explore its deprivations, mourn for herself, and then accept them. She can learn to provide a good mother and a warm hearth for the sad little vagabond she harbors within.

Money Folly Fantasies

Though few money bingers are as emotionally deprived (or as successful) as Tiffany, all spend in order to experience brief, glowing fantasies. All see visions of a different, better, or more interesting life as they spend. Though women commit money folly in numerous ways, including buying houses they can't afford, it is easiest to pinpoint their anxieties and fantasies when they spend on jewelry, household items and clothes—props for their imaginary drama.

Shoppers and bargain hunters set out for the stores in response to anxious feelings. Usually the shopper defines them, if at all, as anger, boredom, or restlessness. The shopping, like any addictive habit, momentarily relieves the troubled emotions and prevents the shopper from exploring them further. The more compulsive and destructive the habit, it seems, the more deeply buried are its emotional causes and the less able the shopper is to see them. Little Match Girls, like Tiffany, with debilitating out-of-control spending addictions, are expressing feelings of deprivation and emptiness that began in childhood. Other, more moderate money blowers may be responding to the frustrations of their adult lives. As they shop, the anxieties give way to pleasurable fantasies, which offer a real, if brief sensation of relief. If these women remain alert to their feelings while shopping, they can learn much about their real emotional needs.

Clothes furnish costumes for a woman's fantasy life and also deck out her fantasy persona—the different self she might like to be. A working mother told us:

> I have this dress I bought a while ago, thinking of a slinky image. It was a beautiful champagne knit with a V front. . . . And I pictured myself walking into a room . . . sexy . . . I never took the tags off because it's not me . . . I'm not sexy, I'm not slinky, I'm your basic. . . .

Shopping can also provide transportation from a demanding modern life, where a woman is responsible for her own support, to a more romantic era, where her rescue fantasies would be fulfilled. One single corporation executive who hedged her shopping habit by buying collectibles she could resell at a profit, said:

> When I'm feeling depressed I'll go on a shopping binge. My passion is antique jewelry. When I look at these beautiful things, done in such detail, so feminine, so delicate, I kind of get away from my reality into the Victorian era. Then I have to own it. It takes me out of a rotten, painful life into a soothing world, and gets me out of my depression temporarily.

Sometimes it is the relationship of buyer to seller that offers emotional relief. One harassed mother, raising a two-year-old, while nursing an ailing relative, and maintaining a large suburban home, as well as working part-time, shopped for attention and help.

I have trouble with sizes, so I find myself in a specialty store where someone will help me. I enjoy having somebody help me.... "Oh, try this! Try that!" That last paycheck I blew at Ms. Bazaar ... what intrigued me there was this little girl who kept pulling things off the rack and who knew by looking at me what would look good. If it looks good, I'll buy it, and if it comes in three different colors, I'll buy three.

These shoppers are using money to solve problems through illusion; with imagination and a willingness to change a pleasure-giving habit, they might use their resources to provide real solutions. The mother who bought the slinky dress she never wore might save for a glamorous cruise for herself and her husband; the corporation executive in need of stress relief might start a therapeutic English garden; the harassed mother might "blow" her paycheck on a part-time housekeeper.

Shopping habits, we learned, are not always ultimately destructive. Sometimes shopping can put women in touch with buried skills, as well as problems. For one of the participants in our suburban money group, bargain-hunting was a way of using familiar behavior to recognize and develop latent abilities. Kit, forty-three, had been a high school teacher since college graduation and was thinking of changing professions—for her, a major step.

My parents wanted me to be a teacher. They felt it was a respectable occupation for a woman with a family. Where I came from, you listened to your parents. Now, I'm burned out. I've been a successful teacher for twenty years, and I'd like to try something new.

In our group meeting, Kit confessed she was an avid bargain hunter.

I want to die next to a clothes rack. I'm serious. I love it. I just love to shop.

One of the reasons that Kit loved shopping is that when she hit the stores she used business skills that she'd had no opportunity to employ in her teaching job. She hunted for clothes with the same high-powered intensity with which Wall Street brokers hunt for undervalued stocks, researching the market before she bought.

I like to go to Loehmann's, but before I go there I want to check out Macy's, Bloomingdale's, and a couple of others, so I know the quality of what I'm getting when I hit Loehmann's. It's not like I go there and don't know what I'm buying. I know the inventory.

She used her shopping time with maximum efficiency; like the frenzied broker, she grabbed a quick lunch on the job.

I can set out in the morning, plan my day, and hit five different places. Sometimes I pack lunch and eat it in the car, so I don't waste any time.

Like any successful businesswoman, Kit prided herself on her astute eye for value.

If I don't get it on sale, I feel like I've betrayed myself, that someone's putting one over on me. The other day, I found the same designer jeans I'd seen at Macy's for $68 at Clothing Town for $27.90. I wanted to shout, "Look what I found!" I mean, I felt great!

Sometimes she left the domestic market to invest in international stocks.

Last year I went to London, determined to get a good-quality camel suit. A Jaeger suit. And I don't know what the hell I paid for it. I think I paid 90 pounds for the skirt alone. I have to admit I went to England mainly to shop. I could have cared less about the crown jewels.

Like stocks and bonds, bargains have seasonal ups and downs, and Kit accommodates.

There are seasons when I have a low period—when nothing's on sale, and I know I can't wear the stuff I'm seeing in the stores for a couple more months.

Though Kit is proud of her shopping expertise, she guiltily smuggles her purchases into the house.

I bring them home and slither them into the closet. I feel, Why get my husband all upset? Why aggravate him? There's no need for this. And eventually he might see it on me, and he might say, "Gee, when did you get that?" and I'll say, "This? Oh, I've had it for awhile."

On her questionnaire, Kit had confided that her husband was jealous when she went to New York for a job interview.

I could sense the jealousy in my husband. I know that if I do change my profession, he will feel threatened.

Kit's husband's jealousy gives her ambivalent feelings. On the one hand, it confirms her own success, and on the other, it threatens their relationship. Her husband, she told us, would not object to her spending the money she earned on clothes. Why, then, does she hide her bargains from him? We felt that what she was hiding was not the clothes, but her ability to match wits with the marketplace, and her desire to turn her consumer savvy into income-producing power. It may have been the fear of transgressing career boundaries, imposed first by her relationship with her parents, then by the one with her husband, that kept this talented, assertive woman in a profession that had ceased to challenge her for so many years.

Kit drove us home after the money group meeting and told us a secret. She had just been offered a new job as a sales representative for a large office furniture company and was considering quitting her teaching job to work partly on a commission basis. We suspected that shopping would become less of a preoccupation once Kit gave herself the opportunity to exercise the skills she had shown as a consumer in a seller's marketplace. Kit was using shopping as a training program: As she hunted for bargains she expressed and enjoyed abilities that had not been encouraged in her career-planning years. Traditional feminine behavior was helping her pinpoint her career fantasies and develop the confidence she needed to take new risks.

Overcoming Money Folly: The Moneywatch

Stopping money folly, like stopping overeating, calls for a twofold approach. First, money folly victims must step outside their spending behavior long enough to review the way they are using money, and label the anxieties and fantasies they bring to the process. If they are money bingers, once they see that what they are shopping for is love, comfort, or self-esteem, and not a red sweater, they have taken the first step toward limiting the addiction's control. Those who dribble money away on unaccounted for purchases must also examine the emotions that influence their spending. Most important, any woman prone to money folly must develop "moneywatching" techniques in order to observe when, and under what conditions, she is inclined to spend, and how much money passes from her hand to commercial establishment. Organizations like Debtors Anonymous and Consumer Credit Counseling Services give overspenders group support and specific methods to help them halt their rampages. Some will even negotiate with creditors.

The overspender in search of a cure must prepare herself to experience what will at first seem like deprivation as she trades in her habitual patterns for a higher goal—getting a grip on her financial life. Some, like this Los Angeles woman, resort to unique and drastic measures to curb their money follies:

I took my credit cards, put them in an ice cube tray, and froze them. Since I don't have a microwave, I'll have to think for quite a while before I use them.

A spending plan, like an eating plan that restricts the intake of food, is most likely to become a permanent way of life when it feels like a positive expansion of the entire self, rather than a temporary or one-dimensional punitive act. Overspenders in our money group who went on the "money-watch" and wrote down their daily expenses in a notebook, reported that not only did their expenditures drop, but they also learned interesting facts about themselves and other people. (For details about the "Money Watch" see Tool #6 in chapter 10, "Tools for Overcoming Money Phobia")

Andrea, who wanted to save so that she could buy her apartment and travel, saw that she could exploit others when she was not exploiting herself—a character trait she found "disturbing."

I wrote down so much for subway, so much for drinks, and so much for this and that. I told all my friends I was doing this. I didn't stop going out for drinks at first, but I'd bring ten dollars, and that's all I'd bring, so I wouldn't spend more than that. I have one male friend, whom I sense wouldn't mind being more. He's an easy prey in a way; I know him well enough to know that he has a thing about taking care of women. When he said, "Have another drink" and I said, "I can't, I don't have the money," he'd say, "Oh, that's okay. I have money." I discovered a willingness in myself to let someone else pay, to take advantage . . . a feeling that if he wanted to throw his money away on me, let him do it. That made me feel uncomfortable. This guy isn't rich; in fact, he makes slightly less than I do. To be a real friend to him would have been to say, "Don't do this! You shouldn't be spending your money either."

Another participant on the "moneywatch" began to see a man she was dating in a different light.

When I looked up the year my ex-husband's maintenance payments end, and began keeping a mental record of my expenses, I realized that Dave has terrible money problems, too. The minute he has it, he blows it all, and then he's broke again. I liked it when he spent on me, but I asked myself, "Do I need a man with my bingeing problem?"

Reviewing money folly does not imply a life devoid of the pleasures of spending. Women who learn to control their spending really enjoy the things that they buy; they make consumer decisions, instead of responding to hidden anxieties. Ilona, a Wyoming psychoanalyst, decided to celebrate her graduation from an analytic institute by buying herself an expensive concha belt to replace a piece of heirloom jewelry that had been stolen while on a trip to Denver. She budgeted between $900 and $1200 for the belt, and made a special pilgrimage to a fine Native American jewelry shop in a ski resort. She promptly ran afoul of seller sexism. When she hesitated over one belt and asked to see more, the salesman suggested, "Why don't you come back with your husband?"

> The idea was that I hesitated because I needed my husband to approve of the belt, aesthetically as well as financially. I said, "Sir, there is no husband, and it is high time you realized that women are buying their own jewelry and paying for it with their own money." I walked out of that store and felt great, like I was flying down the icy street.

Ilona is not shopping for love, but for an expensive piece of turquoise jewelry. She is not blowing money; she has decided to spend it in order to reward herself for a significant accomplishment. With this clear purpose in mind, she is not about to allow anyone to deter her from the full pleasure of spending on herself. For her, spending symbolizes the control she has over her life, not the lack of it. A sexist salesman would most likely have made a money folly victim in a similar situation feel guilty and alone.

When a woman cures herself of money folly, saving, as well as spending, becomes a source of satisfaction. While earning and spending are an integral part of our financial present and past, savings determine our financial future. Savings also increase our wealth, because investing—an important facet of the earning process—cannot be undertaken without an initial sum of saved money to invest.

As women become less Money Phobic, they tend to look in the future direction, and translate savings into financial goals with a place and a name. When they can do this, "putting money away" seems less like a deprivation. Time often helps women to see the necessity to save, but if they have been big-time spenders, they have to help themselves modify their financial behavior. Let's look at one money blower as she begins the painful process of starting to save.

Molly, a New York fashion designer, who worked hard to develop her lucrative career after she was divorced, now earns more than $50,000. Until she was forty-one, however, she spent every cent she made on herself and her two children.

> What gave me the desire to be ambitious and make money was the desire to spend it. I feel like I can now look at my house and see the things that I bought and that feels good to me. I don't want to wear jeans anymore. And when I

take the kids out to dinner, instead of taking them to McDonald's and spending fifteen dollars, I take them to Hamburger Harry's and spend thirty-five dollars. That's the way I've always been. I'm not cautious about money, and spend pretty much whatever I have.

As Molly starts to save, the new experience is uncomfortable, like a diet.

I don't like it that I have to take the money I've really worked hard for and put it away instead of spending it, so I'll have money when I'm sixty-five or seventy. But if I don't do it, there's not going to be anything there. When I turned forty, I started to think about some of this stuff.

Her new financial experience makes her question her rescue fantasies, often at the bottom of money folly.

I've recently given myself a budget for the first time in my life. The reason I never had a savings account was partly because I was afraid that if I had one I would really save. It was that part of me that says, "Why do I have to do it all? Why doesn't someone come along and take care of me?" There's not much there yet, but I like having the savings.

Though Molly is about to marry a man she loves, as she puts money in the bank, she realizes that taking full financial responsibility for herself is satisfying as well as necessary. She begins to see her savings account more positively.

I would like to have investments . . . I would like to own property, and have a house in the country. I want to buy art . . . stocks!

As her savings begin to represent exciting images of resources that will make her future life more enjoyable, as well as more secure, this ambitious and successful high-earner joins the ranks of the modern, liberated women who are finally Money Phobia–free.

Chapter Seven

The Pleasure of Saving: Comprehending Money Paranoia

Women who are not Money Phobic know that money in the bank is able to transform their lives. They intuit when it is appropriate to spend—on themselves and others—and when it is wise to squirrel money away. A penny saved, they understand, instead of spent, ultimately earns important intangibles, like security, comfort, freedom, opportunity, and time. It is savers, not spenders, who find it comfortable to retire, educate their children, and invest; to take personal and marketplace risks, and time off from the job.

Some women, however, save too much, or they use money to control others and punish themselves. To them, rising and falling bank statements are barometers of their feelings, and symbolize conflicts that make loved ones blow hot and cold. These money paranoid women believe others will rip them off, or that by overspending, they will rip themselves off. They use their money to build protective fortresses that make them feel invulnerable. When they become paranoia-free they can use investments and savings to hedge their financial futures, and seek other solutions for emotional insecurity.

The money paranoid may be money holders—female Scrooges who are obsessive savers. This lady skinflint is seldom generous with others or with herself. Friends term her "cheap," and she fears exploitation. It is hard for her to distinguish between dollars and pennies, or to part with her "secret stash." She may sock away money for a specific goal, denying herself creature comforts she can well afford, but she never buys or does what she is saving for. Sometimes she spends freely on one thing, then withholds on another, buying an expensive dress, then castigating herself by making chicken soup with backs and necks for dinner. She equalizes assets and debits to keep her fortress strong, and her cheapness creates conflict with those she regards as "spenders."

Not all money paranoid women are cheap, however; some fear others more than themselves. They are afraid that friends and threatening strangers are plotting to borrow or steal their money, lean on them, live off them, or "suck them dry." These Fortress Women can spend, but they may do so in the wrong places, on the wrong people, or at the wrong times, making their rip-off fears a self-fulfilling prophecy. As irony will have it, they do get ripped off, often by the men in their lives.

The money paranoid may be obsessive savers who salt away modest salaries (some of the women in our study with significant assets earned much less than those with money folly, who spent it all), but usually they are successful, with highly developed financial identities. Unlike the money blind, they understand the power of money, and focus on faraway financial horizons. Though the most paranoid are hush-hush about finances, because they do not want potential exploiters to get wind of how much they have, many speak frankly about the subject that occupies a central role in their thoughts and feelings. Unlike eluders and the money confused, the paranoid are good at earning, managing, and especially negotiating; they know how to fend for their financial rights. These future-oriented women never imagine that anyone will rescue them—quite the contrary! In many ways, the money paranoid appear a step ahead of most Money Phobic women, and have accomplished some important financial goals. But they use money to sabotage themselves emotionally.

Money paranoid women cherish deep feelings of insecurity about their future well-being and often suffer from low self-esteem. Even if they are successful, they may not have internalized their success or identified themselves with it. They feel the slightest wrong move will topple their fortress, which for them is illusory, like an image of Oz. A vice-president of a financial firm who earned six figures told us:

It's one step from the shithouse to the penthouse, and vice versa.

Because they have little faith in the fortress's foundations, the money paranoid do their utmost to increase the thickness of its walls. They try to accumulate as many assets as possible, and their insecurity may be mistaken for greed. One real estate broker said she felt that her success was "luck with a marshmallow."

> What is enough? I need to make a million dollars in the next five years. With a million dollars I will feel that I have achieved something. My worry is that if I do get there I won't be able to stop. When one deal goes down and I don't have another to jump into I feel horrible about myself. When does it end? When do I stop? That's what I ask myself.

Women with the broker's problem invest the dollar sign with magical powers and believe money will take care of their emotional needs.

Because they feel their position is precarious, it becomes important for the money paranoid to control others and their own desires instead of their lives. They see money—a symbol of power and security—as a mechanism of control. While bingers and blowers succumb to uncontrollable urges to spend in order to feel good, the money paranoid solve emotional dilemmas by maintaining financial control at any cost. Some save, controlling their wants, and others spend (or do not spend) to control those whom they fear may exploit them.

The financial behavior of the money paranoid woman tends to be rigid. Instead of seizing opportunities to vary her financial modus operandi according to her needs, she sticks to narrowly defined ideas of how, why, and when she should use money. She can live behind the unyielding walls she constructs with her gold and feel more or less in control, but the minute a crack appears, or someone arrives who might tear the wall down, she panics and becomes even more inflexible. She puts so much energy into fighting off the enemy—and the enemy can be within—that she loses touch with what her well-being requires.

Ann, one of the withholders in our study, for example, felt too guilty about spending on a new hairstyle to enjoy it.

> I went to Bendel's and blew a wad on a haircut and perm. Afterwards, I was so guilt-stricken I couldn't sleep, and woke up at night for a week thinking about it. Even though I'm looking for work, and feel more confident with curly hair, I thought I could have done something cheaper to make it look better. I got no pleasure from it. I couldn't decide whether I liked it or not. I've been feeling like a failure lately, and I don't feel like I deserve anything. I only feel I deserve to reward myself when I'm working hard . . . killing myself!

Ann also told us that she was considering delving into her savings to upgrade her laptop computer, but was afraid that once she started spending, she would never stop. She feels she lacks control over her life, and tries to restore law and order by refraining from spending.

The money paranoid may recognize their behavior as inhibiting and try to eradicate it. However, they tend to do so in a way that confirms their suspicions that others are trying to rip them off, and their fears distort their true instincts and perceptions. One Fortress Woman loaned $300 to a boyfriend who had never been reliable.

> Originally I offered to loan him $100, but he asked me for more. I agonized over the decision. I knew that he—and a lot of my friends—think I'm a tightwad. We were getting back together and I wanted to show him I could be there for him. I thought, He needs me to express my feelings with money; am I capable of giving him what he needs? Secretly, I thought that if he realized I cared about him enough to loan him money—a big move for me—maybe he'd respond by being a better boyfriend. When I thought about it, $300 didn't seem like so much. I thought I could afford to lose it. I only saw him once after the loan; he disappeared and never paid me back, and never contacted me about the money. The three hundred began to seem like three million. I couldn't forgive myself. I decided I'd never loan money to anyone again.

This woman had attempted to control a man who had already proven untrustworthy. Now, armed with evidence that others will indeed try to rip her off, she can justify her desire to remain a "tightwad" and close herself off to the possibility for change.

The most severe cases of money paranoia, however, never made it into our study. These women inevitably expressed more than passing interest in our subject, and enthusiastically offered help and information. Naturally, we contacted them and asked them to fill out the questionnaire—our prerequisite for an in-depth interview. Suddenly, we encountered serious resistance. A twenty-seven-year-old Texas entrepreneur sent us names of experts on the money question, told us about money seminars in her state, and described her job developing real estate with a new lover. She graciously offered to "share her knowledge about money with us." We sent her two questionnaires, at her request, but never received either of them. A Boston woman sent the questionnaire back blank with a letter criticizing our "scientific method." Later, she confided to the mutual friend who had given us her name that the idea of revealing information about her financial behavior had evoked anxieties. These women were in positions of control, and they wanted to stay there. Opening up about their personal relationship with money would have made them feel vulnerable and exposed.

The Case of "The Yellow Duck"

It was not money per se that elicited fear in the money paranoid, but the way money was entangled in their emotional lives. We approached one friend, a high-earning New York cosmetics executive whose question we had not yet received, and said we hoped she would soon find time complete it. Somewhat precipitously, we told her that we wanted to interview her about her experience supporting a man for fifteen years. She panicked; she did not want to talk about that—she did not like it, but had had no choice—and she hoped our questionnaire didn't ask questions about that! She would, however, be delighted to share the reasons why her moneymaking goals had become more concrete in her thirties. We said that rules were rules and before we could interview her, we needed the questionnaire. She retorted that no woman in her right mind would provide personal financial information and sign her name to it! What if the IRS saw this "paper trail?" Anonymity was guaranteed, we explained, and respondents were welcome to eliminate any question that made them uncomfortable, (provided they said why), including those that asked for details about salary and assets. She allowed that maybe she would fill out the questionnaire, but she would never sign it with her real name. "I'll use a pseudonym like . . . Yellow Duck!" she told us.

We thought Yellow stood for "chicken" more than for "duck," and that Duck was for "ducking out." By telling this powerful woman that we wanted to discuss an aspect of her financial behavior over which she felt she had lost control, we had obviously blundered into a touchy emotional area and deprived ourselves of a valuable case history.

Why Women Are Money Paranoid

No discussion of money paranoia could exclude Sigmund Freud, who linked frugality and parsimony with the anal stage of human development. According to Freud's famous theory of infant sexuality, the infant sees his feces as his most treasured possession, and its elimination gives him erotic pleasure. During the toilet-training process, he comes to view what to him is precious, and to his parents "filth," as a gift, or an object to hoard—a symbol of the power struggle between himself and his parents. Money eventually takes the place of excrement, Freud said, and in the adult mind may evoke the same responses and symbolize the same conflicts.

If the infant is toilet trained gently and persuasively at the appropriate time (that is, when he is physiologically and emotionally ready), he learns that he can have control over himself as well as his parents' approval. If he is trained too early and punitively, before he is able to perform this important developmental task, he experiences shame and self-doubt, which he brings to the next stage of his development. He may grow up with an exaggerated sense of the importance of control, not trusting himself or others to "let go" and resenting submission to authority. In a society that values money, he

as a symbol of control, and may use it to control himself
...y believe that people are conspiring to take his money
...other took away his feces, and as a result, he hoards and

...; in the Freudian theory leads us to believe that girls are
...rshly toilet trained than boys, most of the money holders
we know from life and literature are male. Dickens's Serooge had to be visited
by groaning ghosts on Christmas Eve before be could dig into his coffers
to help crippled Tiny Tim. Howard Hughes, despite his fathomless wealth,
borrowed tuxedos, packed his possessions in cardboard boxes, and never
picked up a tab if be could help it. John Paul Getty, another rich and famous
miser, once installed a pay phone in his mansion, and John D. Rockefeller,
charged for two chickens instead of one in a restaurant, demanded that the
bones be reassembled as proof before he would pay.

Perhaps history provides more examples of money paranoid men because
men have always had more money to fear losing. Before women earned
money of their own to withhold, they practiced the principles of money
holding in their housekeeping roles. Traditionally, a good housewife was
frugal; mending, cleaning, and repairing to stretch money, and controlling
the family's day-to-day expenditures. Often she had a "secret stash," saved
from her housekeeping money, which her husband knew nothing about.
(Many married women still "stash" money in private accounts today.)

Female misers are viewed in a negative light because our culture expects
women to be generous, open, and trusting. When women earn or inherit
money of their own, however, money paranoia grips them just as it does
their successful male counterparts. But our money paranoia does not
necessarily hark back to toilet training; fears of exploitation accurately
reflect the traditional social and economic status of women. In the booming
1980s, a *Working Woman* magazine survey revealed that one out of two
affluent, well-educated women feared ending up destitute and suffered
from "bag lady" nightmares.[1] Bag lady nightmares continue to unnerve
women today.

Unfortunately, a woman's fear of ending up alone and poor is not
irrational: In 1994 one half of elderly women living alone in this country
had incomes of less than $9,500 per year; more than a third are expected
to be poor in the year 2020.[2] Why should women with employer-provided
retirement plans (only 9 percent) and substantial assets continue to fear
eventual destitution? Older women in our society are not only poor but
socially devalued, passed over for important jobs, sometimes cast aside by
husbands, and deemed "undesirable" by men. A bag lady is a useless,
discarded, lonely, isolated, unattractive outcast! Women with money who
are afraid of becoming homeless and carrying their belongings around in

bags are reacting to the emotional state that the bag lady symbolizes. Given the harsh realities that confront American women as they get older (including those who are not bag ladies), it is a wonder that more women do not believe a storehouse of money will combat emotional as well as financial vulnerability.

The First of the Big-Time Women Withholders: Hetty Green

Hetty Green, "The Witch of Wall Street," was one of America's most notorious money paranoid woman. Born to a wealthy New Bedford whaling family in 1835, Hetty grew up reading stock market quotations on her father's knee and following him about town as he conducted his business. She had little positive feminine influence: Her mother, whose own sizable fortune had been removed from her hands by her husband, took to her bed after the death of her infant son and stayed there. Hetty's aunt, also rich, was bedridden, too, and bequeathed much of her fortune to a manipulative doctor.

When Hetty grew up, she continued to follow in her father's footsteps, amassing a personal fortune of $7 million by 1900. (At that time, the national average income was $490, and the tab for a nine-course meal at Delmonico's was less than 75 cents.) By 1908, her real estate holdings, stocks, railroads, and other properties had increased in value to $150 million.

Hetty, however, did not enjoy her wealth; she merely accumulated it and fought off those she believed were conspiring to take it away. Throughout her life she dressed in dingy rags, did not bathe, and lived in cheap, working-class boarding houses in Hoboken instead of in the mansions she could well afford. She dined on cold oatmeal, which she heated on the radiator of her Wall Street office. (In 1888 her weekly expenses were estimated at $9.) She sacrificed health, as well as comfort, to her money paranoid fears. Her son Ned's infected leg was eventually amputated because his penny-pinching mother dragged him from clinic to clinic, pretending to be a poor immigrant, in hopes of obtaining free medical care. Hetty herself suffered from an enormous hernia for twenty years rather than pay a surgeon to remove it.

Stories about her cheapness are endless. She once spent half a night searching for a misplaced two-cent stamp. She was not beyond shady dealings to save and obtain either. She forged a false will in order to garner more than her share of her dead aunt's fortune, and evaded taxes by moving furtively from state to state. When she died in 1916, the richest and most detested woman in America, she left not a single penny to charity. Her withholding tendencies, however, were partly responsible for her legendary wealth. When others panicked and sold in stock market recessions, Hetty tenaciously held on; the properties she saved eventually became worth millions of dollars.

Unfortunately, Hetty's money paranoia undermines her accomplishments as a financial pioneer. This original "Supermom" was one of the first women to invade and conquer the all-male Wall Street domain. Being a "first," however, was part of her problem. Like many women at the top of their fields today, Hetty had no role models to teach her how she could preserve the positive traits of her sex and still pursue her professional interests. Having seen her neurasthenic female relatives succumb to illness and financial control, she grew up disassociating femininity from her ambitious drive and fearing male dominance. As a result, she forged her personal, primitive financial style, which included denying herself and her family. Determined to out-man the men in a male capitalist world, she evolved into an iconoclastic "economic animal" who played by her own unique rules. Though few women are as withholding—or as wealthy—as Hetty, the same forces that shaped this nineteenth century tycoon shape money paranoid women today.[3]

Detecting Money Paranoia

Money paranoid women were difficult to detect on the basis of their questionnaires. Often they appeared to be earning high salaries and have clear financial goals. In our money groups they were regarded as being "together" about money, and provided constructive advice to the money eluders and deniers. In our two-hour personal interview, however, the Fortress Women were easy to detect. The "rip-off" theme entered the interview in the first five minutes and was repeated throughout. Usually they told a story involving exploitation (of themselves or somebody else) immediately. Some who feared exploitation tried to break the rules and rob others before they could be robbed; others tried to gain power by making the rules work to their advantage. For all, money was magic, an almighty power that, if worshipped devoutly, could control and protect. And yet, money magic had failed them; they had all been exploited at one time or another.

Money paranoid women, we learned, had some common factors in their backgrounds. They grew up believing that they were responsible for their own support, and although they cherished vague hopes of finding a man who would at least share expenses, they did not really believe that marriage would make them feel financially secure or enrich them. Most had a male ne'er-do-well (often an alcoholic) in the family and a female relative who had been left impoverished by her relationship with him. Though this "bag lady" may have been a remote cousin or aunt, her misfortune became part of the family myth, cited as a reason that women should be financially independent. Sometimes family hardship had made the money paranoid woman fear poverty or dependence on others. As a result, she grew up with the belief that she could control her own life and shield herself from unpredictable male behavior by having her own money. Often her parents were "cheap" or gave her money on an inconsistent basis, although they may have also encouraged and helped her use her abilities to produce income. Most were financially independent at an early age and earned while they went to college. The amount of money they had or were earning was their most important measure of career success.

"The Horst Syndrome": How One Fortress Woman Ripped Herself Off

Gabrielle, thirty-nine, had no practical problems with money: She had developed a highly successful direct-mail advertising company, and earned more than $75,000 a year writing and designing promotional brochures. Her company promoted many products, ranging from quartz watches to Caribbean vacations. She had invested her money wisely in a Long Island house (which doubled as her office), as well as in bonds and aggressive growth mutual funds. She said money was "very important to her," and that she saw it as a "security blanket."

Gabrielle's anxieties seemed centered on men, but we soon learned that money was part of what troubled all of her relationships. When we interviewed her, she had just extricated herself from a traumatic, ten-year marriage to an abusive alcoholic, and her lawyer was warring with her husband's lawyer over the divorce settlement. Her husband, it seemed, was claiming a portion of her business, in which he had never been involved, and refused to sign divorce papers until she paid him his share of it.

While Gabrielle waited for the divorce to come through, she was dating two men: A Hoboken artist who worked as a carpenter and was bitter about his sporadic success, and an Italian antiques dealer, whom she had met on vacation and saw whenever one of them could make the transatlantic trip. She was already worried that the painter was also a rip-off artist: She had paid him for one of his lithographs, and after two months, he had neither produced the work or returned the money. Gaby was confused. Why did she always choose "roller-coaster guys"—men who were poorer than she was or financially unstable?

> It could be that because I'm steadier making money, I feel a sense of power with them. I feel I can deal with men better when I have a source of power that they have traditionally had. A man with money might think that what I was making was chickenshit, and want me to give up what I'm doing and play all the time. I feel more in control of guys who are very up and down with money.

Gabrielle was money paranoid. Money was instrumental in her desire to control men and to maintain her own autonomy, but her focus on money kept her from focusing on her emotions. She told us that she was good at "fooling herself" and often felt "numb":

> But I don't feel numb when I'm making money.

Uncomfortable feelings of emotional numbness had led her to wed the man she was in the process of divorcing. At twenty-nine, Gaby had succumbed to her mother's pressures to marry and have a child.

> When I went home for Christmas, my cousin, who's my age, was pregnant. I thought, Jesus, I'm almost thirty. If I ever want to get pregnant and have a kid, I'd better find myself a husband. That's step number one.

Like many women, Gaby found it difficult to integrate her own ambitions with her mother's traditional script for her life. Cut off from her own feelings, she chose the wrong man.

> I knew him about nine months before we got married. It was a stormy courtship; we fought all the time. He did bizarre things, but I swept them under the rug and forgot about them. If you knew what they were, you'd think I was crazy for not dumping this guy immediately. Living alone, I'd started to feel numb. My emotions ran the gamut from A to B. He came along and he was like fire all of a sudden. Even though a lot of the feelings were negative feelings, at least I was feeling. And one of the reasons I got out of the marriage was because I had become totally numb again. The only way I could deal with his tirades and tantrums was to just block them out. In a way, I have him to thank for my success, because I blocked him out by locking myself in my room and working really hard.

Once in a difficult marriage to a man she did not trust, Gaby used money to protect herself. Like many money paranoid women, she was excellent at devising "systems" for sharing expenses.

> For the first six months he just sort of paid for things. That created a lot of friction. I think I was the one who hit on the system that we finally used: There would be certain things that would be joint expenses, like rent, and others that would be separate, like clothes. And we would write all of our joint expenses down in a book with a column for him and a column for me. At the end of the month we'd total everything up and figure out who owed whom.

At the time, Gaby's husband was earning a good salary, and she was copywriting on a freelance basis for publicists. Her career had not taken off, and she was barely earning a living wage. Gaby feared her husband would exploit her because she earned little and constructed her system so that it would work to her advantage.

> I thought because he was older, a man, and had more experience, he would always be earning more. This is where I outmaneuvered myself. I said, "The only fair way to do this is for whoever makes more at the end of the year to pay more of the expenses. Let's say you make a third more than I do. Then you have to cover a third more of the expenses, and vice versa." Shortly after that he got fired, and from then on it was practically always vice versa, and I would end up giving him money at the end of the year.

Later, when Gaby started earning high fees working for prestigious clients, she feared her husband would exploit her because she had much more than he did. She bought land in another state so he could not spend her money.

> As time went on it became clearer and clearer he couldn't be trusted. He thought I was paranoid about the money, but all I could see was that here was a man who hated women, and he was going to get me. He knew that money was important to me, and that's what he'd go after if he could.

Her divorce problems, too, were due to financial maneuvers in which she had outsmarted herself. At one point her husband had suggested that she apply for a $20,000 bank loan to get her direct-mail business off the ground. Afraid that he would spend the money, and she would be responsible for repaying the loan, Gaby made her husband sign a partnership agreement, stating that he had invested $5,000 to capitalize the business and owned a percentage of it. That way he, too, would be responsible for repayment.

> We never got the bank loan, but he's got his name on this piece of paper. He now believes he actually put $5,000 into my business. He can't come up with a canceled check because there isn't any.

After a separation Gaby came back to her husband, on condition that he sign an agreement stating that if they split up, neither of them would have to pay the other any money.

> So when I wanted to get out of the marriage, the only thing he had to hang his hat on was his so-called stake in the business. He's still got the general

partnership agreement saying be owns a percent of it and that he put money into it, which he never did.

Gabrielle, then, married an untrustworthy man and tried to make the relationship safe by establishing complicated and rigid financial arrangements. Her belief in the magical powers of money led her to give money a job money cannot do—protect her from a husband's abuse and take care of her emotionally. Since her husband's abuses were not only financial, and she had other reasons to distrust him, her arrangements did not save her from pain. By becoming "numb," she managed to stay in the doomed relationship. Gaby's systems failed to offer even financial protection; because they were inflexible, they rapidly outmoded themselves. Nevertheless, she continued to put her faith in money, working hard to earn as much as possible; but money could not give her the supportive relationship she wanted and needed.

Why did Gaby choose "roller-coaster guys" and let money stand between her and the closeness she craved? Her family background, we learned, provided fertile soil for money paranoia to grow. Her parents were married during the war and divorced soon thereafter. Her father, angry with her mother, paid almost no child support, and her mother abandoned her nursing career to run a small nursery in her home, so that she could keep her infant daughter with her while she earned a living. When Gaby was five, her mother married a stable man, but did not make Gaby feel part of the secure new household. Instead, she told her that her stepfather supported her out of the "goodness of his heart."

> She emphasized that my father was behind in his payments, and that my stepfather was paying for things he shouldn't have to pay for. She said the only things she could ask him to provide were the food on the table and the roof over our head. When she sent me to dancing school she made a big deal about how she was paying for that out of her own money, and how it was her money that was going to put me through college. I was made to feel that my circumstances were different than my stepsister's. She just complained that my parents were tight.

Gaby, then, grew up feeling insecure about her financial well-being and source of support. She learned early on that she would soon have to take care of herself.

> My mother made it clear that I was going to get an education out of her, and that's all I was going to get. Then you're on your own, baby.

Though her mother forced her to be aware of financial realities, she sheltered her emotionally.

> She thinks children shouldn't know what goes on in the world, about evil things, like sex. Money is practical; you can know about that.

Gaby also learned that men were not to be trusted. Not only her father, but also her uncle, left women "high and dry."

> My aunt was a secretary who got screwed financially by her husband. He went bankrupt and she had to go back to being a secretary.

Her stepsister, too, suffered from what the family now jokingly calls "The Horst Syndrome."

> Every woman in the family so far has managed to come up with a man who's a bum. And that includes me. My stepsister married this German guy who has absolutely no responsibility about money. His name is Horst. So we refer to it as "The Horst Syndrome." The reason it didn't get labeled "The Jack Syndrome" is because my husband at least felt guilty about not making money. Whereas Horst never felt guilty about it at all.

In the clutches of a family myth, which stressed that men were financially unstable, and with unique feelings of personal insecurity, Gaby grew up yearning for closeness, yet afraid that men would rip her off. She also learned money paranoid defenses, which helped her to become a high-earner and protect her financial interests, but she did not learn to let her emotions decide whom she could trust. Ironically, as an adult, she chooses men who give her a reason to maintain the strong defenses that have helped her survive and function in the world. These men confirm her worst fears and validate her mistrust. Since her defense system includes a lucrative career and financial autonomy, Gaby is afraid that a responsible man who also makes money would sabotage this important and positive aspect of her identity.

Gaby desperately wants to break this vicious circle. But money paranoia is not easy to shake. Some time after our interview, she told the money group she joined that she had spent a month with her Italian boyfriend and was planning to marry him. He would live with her and look for a job in the States. Since he had less money than she did, she wanted to ask him to sign a prenuptial agreement stating that if the marriage did not work, each partner would leave with only the assets he came in with.

I thought, If you've ever met a man you could trust it's this man. So why are you putting him through this little exercise? And I finally decided that the reason I'm doing it is to make me feel more comfortable.

Though it is reasonably self-protective to ask a fiancé to sign a prenuptial agreement, Gaby felt her request symbolized mistrust and guiltily tried to compensate. The agreement, she revealed, would apply only to the money each partner brought into the marriage, and would state that after marriage they would "share the pot." The group reacted strongly to this information: What if her new husband, a newcomer to America, failed to earn any money at all? Gaby's career was thriving. Wouldn't the agreement entitle him to half of all the money she earned after they were married? But Gaby still believed in the power of money, and was now using it to convey positive emotions:

How I felt about money when I married Jack was symbolic of how much I distrusted him. And the symbolism now is that it's really time to trust somebody. Because money is so important to me, I'll let money be the thing that says, "Okay, I trust you, and this is a symbol of my trust."

Gaby believes that money talks, but she has to learn to speak for herself and to hear the replies. She is relying on a purely external criterion to express trust and mistrust. How does she know what money means to her fiancé? Does it symbolize the same emotions? Before she tries to control him with financial agreements, she might enter into a dialogue and find out in what language money speaks to him.

In order to find a trustworthy man, Gaby must be able to trust herself to choose one—difficult, because she was raised to mistrust men. As long as she believes in the magical powers of money to protect her, she will cut herself off from the emotional messages that are telling her whether to trust or not, and in hopes of outmaneuvering the untrustworthy, outmaneuver herself.

Overcoming Money Paranoia

Money paranoia is difficult to overcome. Because the money paranoid woman believes in money and the way she uses it, she feels anxious when she defines her financial behavior as a problem. She may feel as if she is disavowing her faith in God; changes might jeopardize her lifestyle and future well-being. Her problem is compounded by society's tendency to reward the money paranoid. Women who are focused on money and know the rules of the marketplace game look at money with clear eyes, value its importance, and negotiate deals. As a result, they accumulate cash and assets, which our materialistic culture commends. In fact, we believe a mild case of money paranoia is good for women!

What the severely money paranoid do not understand is that marketplace rules do not apply to more intimate arenas, and when practiced there, can sabotage their personal lives. It is only when a Fortress Woman becomes aware that money is coming between herself and her emotional goals that she can take a critical look into her money mirror and examine the way she uses money to solve problems that have nothing to do with money.

The Sixty-Nine Cent Breakfast Special: How One Withholder Learned to Spend

Money paranoid women who are capable of spending tend to focus their suspicious fears on individuals; withholders, however, believe in an almost cosmic conspiracy to rip them off. These are misers in the Hetty Green tradition, who try to outwit the marketplace by keeping their money far away from it. They, too, use money protectively.

Sheilah, like Gabrielle, was raised in a climate perfect for the cultivation of money paranoia. Her parents, first-generation immigrants, had lived through hard times, and become confirmed withholders.

> They didn't have much money, and they were very careful about spending it. In my entire childhood we never ate out in a restaurant—that was absolutely a waste of money. To save ten cents we would walk several miles to the subway instead of taking the bus. My mother still buys reduced rotting vegetables on sale and cheese ends and ham ends.

Like many withholders, Sheilah's parents saved for goals they never accomplished.

> My father's dream was to make a great trip around the world, because he really was a geographer by training, but he ended up working for the telephone company for forty-five years. He wanted to travel someday, and do it really big, but he also never wanted to be poor again. My mother is too afraid and generally not strong enough to make such a trip. So they accumulated all of this money, which they saved all their lives, but they really haven't done anything with it. After my father retired, they finally bought a house and paid for it in cash, so their expenses are minimal.

Sheilah got lessons in low self-esteem as well as withholding. Her parents, themselves insecure, told her that she wasn't attractive and that "nobody would want her." She grew up believing she would never marry and would have to take care of herself. The family myth was that she was untalented as well.

> When I was about fourteen my mother was told I had a low IQ and was an overachiever, a thought which she shared with me shortly thereafter. I've always thought of myself as an overachiever who isn't very bright. They did spend money to counterbalance my natural deficiencies. I was given every kind of lesson possible, and I had orthodontic work done for seven years. So they made choices as to what was important to them, and they spent money on those things very generously. It was just a question of where the choices were made.

Despite her "deficiencies" Sheilah had achieved a great deal. She had earned a graduate degree in biology and had done laboratory research at a university hospital for fifteen years. She was an excellent musician, a competent photographer, and lived out her father's dream by traveling extensively. She did not, however, manage to overturn the family money holding pattern and followed her parents' financial footsteps, saving, and making rigid choices about how money should and should not be spent. She spent freely on travel, but exactly like her parents, refused to spend on restaurants or local transportation.

> I stashed away everything I made, and had a lot of trouble—and am sure I still have—parting with nickels, dimes, and quarters. There's a part of me that would still rather walk to the subway. I'm comfortable doing it. I'd never take a cab! In psychological terms I was anal retentive. I just wanted to hold on to it all.

Her inflexible holding created "loads and loads" of problems between herself and friends.

> I tended to spend much less than anyone I knew, so it prevented me from eating out a lot as a social activity. I would back off or express a lack of interest. When I was dating in my twenties men tended to pay most of the time anyway, but I had trouble accepting covering my own expenses. If a man wanted to go out to dinner, my feeling was, I wouldn't go out to dinner if I wasn't with you, so therefore you should pay. They paid, even graciously, but I was always uncomfortable. My parents said, "Don't be a gold digger. If you go out and someone pays for you, be sure you always take the cheapest thing on the menu." All these goofy things with money—a real source of tension.

Sheilah sought help with her money holding when it broke up an important relationship.

What finally split us up and drove me into therapy was we were visiting Washington and he found a place where they had a $1.99 breakfast special, and I knew a mile down the road there was a 69 cent special, and I insisted I wasn't going to eat at the $1.99 place. We had this incredible battle scene about it. He decided that I was a bit too much for him on this kind of thing, and I decided to go into therapy to try to sort some of this out. Money had not been an issue in other relationships because I usually went out with very poor people who couldn't spend.

In therapy, Sheilah learned that her childhood feelings of low self esteem had not been diminished by her many accomplishments. Her fears of ending up alone, coupled with an inherited money-holding pattern, had led her to use money to protect herself emotionally, as well as financially.

I wanted to make sure I was covered for all kinds of contingencies.

As she began to understand that her focus on her own fears had prevented her from understanding others' needs, or empathizing with them, she saw the financial aspect of her most recent relationship in another light.

When we went to a play, and he wanted to sit in the orchestra and I wanted to sit in the balcony, I would get totally crazy and torn and wracked with upset because I didn't want to spend so much. I'd be hostile and guilty. He said, "Look, one play we'll sit in the orchestra and the next we'll sit in the balcony." I was not feeling that this was a reasonable compromise, but shit, you're forcing me to spend every other time on something I don't want to spend on. I wasn't looking at it from the point of view that I was forcing him to sit in the balcony and be uncomfortable half the time.

When Sheilah was asked to vacate her rental apartment and realized it would be economically smarter to buy a condominium than to rent, she was faced with a major spending dilemma. Her impending investment seemed to signify the onslaught of the lonely vulnerability she had been saving to avoid and created an emotional crisis.

I needed a place to live; it made a lot of economic sense and would give me a lot of freedom to buy. But it was an immense commitment. Here I am, buying a house alone! It meant that in some way I was an absolute failure. I remember throwing myself on the floor of the therapist's office, crying hysterically. I really had it in me that single women don't buy, and if you were to buy a house, that was an admission that you would never get married.

Her therapist helped her to see that buying the condo was an accomplishment rather than a failure, and Sheilah began to understand that she could take care of both emotional and financial needs in ways other than saving. Owning the condo gave her personal as well as financial satisfaction when it rapidly doubled, then tripled in value. Gradually, Sheilah was learning to spend.

> Now I wouldn't risk a relationship over $1.99 bacon and eggs. When I first started to spend, I wouldn't have risked it because I would have realized it was crazy, but I would have still been unhappy about spending the money. In the last few years, something has snapped that makes it easier.

Sheilah found that in many ways her compulsive saving had paid off. She had turned a modest salary into more than a half million dollars worth of assets. She had a pension, a valuable home, and was drawing a full-time salary, as well as interest on long-term CDs and money market accounts.

> I looked at what I had and thought, It doesn't make sense to be crazy over money at this point. I have so much coming in regularly that I can't begin to spend it; I can get more comfortable with it. My knee collapsed a couple of years ago, and I spent a lot of time in the hospital. I also watched two friends die, and I realized time was passing all too rapidly. I began to look more and more at how other people spent money, and how they lived.

With these revelations, Sheilah could loosen her rigid criteria about when and how money should be used, and spend it in new ways:

> I did a three-week African safari for $3,000. I've never done anything like that in my life. I do very easily pick up and tootle off to Mexico for a month now without worrying how much the trip is going to cost. I bought a $100 sweater last year that was on sale from $200. Never would I have dreamed of doing that before.

Sheilah had come a long way, but the family money holding legacy continues to plague her. She had seen an expensive piece of camera equipment she wanted, but had been unable to buy it. She asked, "How do you get yourself to spend when you know you have the money?" Ironically, her condo had replaced her savings account as a secure fortress, and was standing between her and the love relationship she wanted.

Having a really super place of my own has made me feel real good about a lot of things. But the package, in some way, seems to have removed me even more from the average male, because I have—at least in material terms—gathered so much together, and built myself such a strong little world, my feeling is that it would be overwhelming to an unput-together male. I feel that me, plus everything I have around me, is such a strong statement that if ever I was to live with someone, we couldn't live here, because it's so strongly me. There's no way anyone could come into my space.

When Sheilah takes the next step, and sees that her condo, like her savings account, symbolizes the protective fortress she has built inside, she will be able to open the door and invite a man in.

Chapter Eight

The Negotiating Game: Clarifying Money Confusion

Negotiating for her financial well-being is a game that the money aware woman is ready to play. She knows that money matters—from a salary raise, to making an investment, to what percentage of bills each partner in a relationship will pay—involve an essential dialogue. As she warms up for the confrontation, she hopes to create a win-win situation, productive for both teams, but realizes that some games—like a sex discrimination suit—are, by definition, ferocious battles, and that her adversary, not her, may post top gains. Sometimes she is willing to sacrifice one goal to attain another, or to leave an unfair playing field behind. Whether or not she pulls out ahead, she sees a financial negotiation, important or small, as a confrontation she must hurdle, not tiptoe around: She prepares her own strategy, second guesses her opponent's tactics, and defines and keeps her focus on the prize.

When a woman who is afraid of money enters a negotiation, money confusion strikes. Unable to see money clearly, or feeling that talking about it is crass or wanting it is greedy, or believing that someone else should take care of her, she flounders in a process that she doesn't see as a game. Whether the negotiation is minor (Who pays for what on a date?) or one that may affect her total well-being, the money confused woman is unable to separate money from pressing emotional issues and messages about negotiation that she has received from her family and culture.

Like the fairy tale heroine, she hopes to be rewarded for being good, hard working, feminine, or even needy, and neglects to strategize. Instead of arming herself with information and support in a systematic way, as she would for any other event she recognizes as important (a charity benefit, or planning a wedding), she tends to hope the negotiation will "turn out all right." With her focus fixed on her own and others' emotions, she does not formulate definite financial goals. When negotiating, she tries to cooperate and make the process comfortable for her adversary. Because she wants to emerge from the confrontation certain she has not compromised herself or her ideals, she tends to take a passive position and let others assume responsibility for the outcome. The chronically Money Phobic may avoid negotiating at all.

Although she may not have been sufficiently self-protective during the negotiation process, the money confused woman takes a failure too hard: She castigates herself for getting "screwed," and dwells on her ineptitude, instead of analyzing the game to learn what wrong moves she made and why. Unfortunately, our society, with its tradition of male winners, does not always help money confused women obtain financial justice. They must help themselves, and their confusion prevents them.

Why Women Are Money Confused

Few of us learned the important art of negotiation at home. In the traditional American middle-class family, women did not negotiate because they did not work for pay. Full-time homemakers earned their keep by doing a demanding twenty-four-hour-a-day job, cleaning, cooking, sewing, nursing, childcare, and managing the household money. These arduous and necessary tasks were not regarded as income producing or assigned a monetary value, nor was the maintenance the "housewife" received regarded as "pay." Since her job had no description, her responsibilities were unlimited, and she was often overworked. She got no raises, overtime, unemployment benefits, or Social Security plan for being a homemaker.

Although wives who were supported by their husbands' salaries earned their keep, the myth was that they worked for spiritual or emotional reasons and were valued, not for their labor, but for gloriously representing the institution of motherhood. As mothers and wives they were both above and beneath the baseness of the marketplace. On the one hand, their work in the home was "priceless," too great to be measured in monetary terms, and on the other, economically valueless—worth nothing at all. Since their work was not perceived as a job, but as a kind of voluntary activity, inspired by love or a sense of duty, there was no objective measure to evaluate or reward their success. Hardworking wives received gifts, chosen at their husbands' discretion ("Promise her anything, but give her Arpege"), doled out, not as bonuses for a job well done, as in the corporation, but for admirable personality and character traits, such as loyalty, lovability, and self-sacrifice.

Their wives' labor, however, enabled men, whose basic domestic needs were taken care of, to pursue successful careers. Yet, no matter how skillfully and devotedly a woman filled her homemaker position, she could still be "let go" without any notice when a younger employee applied for the job and legally deprived of an equitable portion of her husband's wealth.

Although most middle-class women work outside the home today, they are still expected to moonlight as mothers and housekeepers with limited help from their husbands: Studies show that women still do 70 percent of the housework and childcare.[1] Even women who earn more than their spouses do most of the housework.[2] The value of this unpaid work is high: According to John Kenneth Galbraith, the U.S. gross national product—the total value of the nation's annual output of goods and services—would rise by 26 percent if the homemakers' labor was included at replacement cost.[3]

How did the traditional homemaker, who worked in the home for no pay, play the negotiation game? Because the work she did was important in so far as it provided emotional satisfaction for herself and others, she also bargained in emotional terms. A housewife who wanted something from her husband often resorted to tactics such as nagging, complaining, pleading, martyrdom, or clever manipulation; sometimes she mastered the art of making her husband believe that he had decided to give her what she wanted of his own accord. The breadwinner, however, did not have to negotiate if he did not want to. He could make unilateral decisions about how his money would be spent, and give or withhold as he saw fit. Not all fathers, of course, chose not to negotiate, but those who did humiliated their wives and taught their daughters that unheeded requests for money were associated with shame or blame. A woman in our Boston money group described her family's negotiating game like this:

> My father gave my mother a budget and an allowance. Decisions about money were made by him, and he decided what was a reasonable amount. The amount he gave her was actually unreasonable. As prices went up, he became very anxious, and he compensated by not giving my mother a raise. They would fight all the time because she fell short. She would argue that there just wasn't enough, and he would say, "You must have blown it; you must have done something wrong." It really did affect her self-esteem.

Mothers who were unable to negotiate at home often felt helpless when they had to negotiate with the outside world. (Women who did work in low-paid, sex-stereotyped jobs, discovered that they had more clout when they bargained collectively in unions or powerful political groups.) Some developed negotiating skills, but used them to earn money, not for themselves, but for charitable organizations. A New York woman with a history of negotiating problems described the lesson in "selflessness" she learned from her mother:

> My mother runs everything and talks all the time. She handles the books. She's always complaining, "How we managed on what your father was making, I don't know." She was real active outside the home, but not for money. Everything was for the Good Will. She was president of the woman's club, president of the library, and raised more than anyone had ever raised to build a new one. She knows a lot of very important people. For years she's been talking about getting a frozen yogurt franchise or a car wash franchise. I say, "Go do it! Get the money from your rich friends . . ." But no. She's a tycoon for everyone else, but not for herself.

The daughters of middle-class homemakers, then, learned that negotiation involved trading positive personality traits and selfless devotion for an undefined amount of material support, hardly a good lesson to bring to the marketplace. Instead of seeing negotiation as a means to obtain a specific amount of money for a specific amount of work, they saw it as a vague process, involving not only money but their own self worth and the emotional well-being of others. Given lessons in selflessness, some found it easier to negotiate for others than for themselves, or to win a negotiating game when they didn't really want what they were negotiating for. Playing "hard ball," or divorcing their emotions from money in a negotiation, felt like a sacrifice of their feminine identity and made them anxious. Today, as women enter the marketplace intending to stay there, essentials their mothers never demanded—maternity leaves, child care, and an harassment-free environment—make the negotiating game's rules logistically and emotionally more complex.

How Parents Deprive Children of Negotiation Skills

Some parents prevent their children from mastering the negotiation game by the way they handle their requests. When a parent greets a child's demands with a non-negotiable "yes" or "no," the child does not learn how to bargain effectively. A woman with a father who said no, for example, found it difficult to negotiate with men in both her personal and professional life.

> I have a lot more trouble negotiating with men than with women, and that's because my father always said "no," whereas my mother would mostly say "yes" if it was within her means.

If the parent made the child feel guilty for asking, indicating that her needs were inconsiderate, greedy, or burdensome, a woman may bring the same guilt, as well as a sense that she is undeserving, to adult negotiations. She may feel she has to work harder than others to merit a salary or a raise. A Massachusetts woman told us:

> I saw my father sweating over the checkbook. I had a sense that I had to watch to know what it was okay to ask for. I remember asking for a bike, and my father telling me how many loaves of bread he would have to sell in his grocery for me to have it. That was when I stopped asking. I learned to baby-sit, and from that moment on, I bought my own clothes.

When a daughter associates asking for what she wants with family economic distress, she is likely to go off on her own and take care of her needs—the first step toward forming an independent financial identity. Going off on one's own, instead of negotiating, however, is not always possible or effective in the marketplace or in personal relationships that demand the power to stay and persuade.

On the other hand, if the girl is given whatever she asks for, with no negotiation involved, because her parents feel guilty about their divorce, or don't want to deprive their children in ways that they were deprived, she may also not learn the art of bargaining to accomplish goals.

Detecting Money Confusion

Personalizing Money

Money confused women may not give their best performance in a negotiating game because they personalize money, that is, attribute human or animal traits to cash. Some project their feelings about the context in which they earned it onto their pay and spend it accordingly. A Washington architect told us she "cared more" about the money she got for projects she believed were worthwhile:

> The money I got for designing a museum almost embarrassed me, and I felt calm and sober about the check. But the money I earned for doing a McDonald's inspired immediate visions of a leather jacket and red boots.

A woman physician personalized the debt she had incurred for her medical education. She could not take in her financial planner's sensible advice not to clear the debt, which she had incurred in the mid-seventies, but to pay only the interest, which was then tax deductible. The planner argued that since the value of the loaned money had decreased, she would actually be paying back less than she had borrowed (not true of debts incurred now). This economic truth, however, fell on deaf ears. The doctor saw her debt as a kind of vicious wild animal, and wanted to "get rid of it."

> I want to clear my debts. Every time I clear one, it's like striking a piece of my past away, getting rid of another reminder of how hard I had to work, how little I had to work with. It's worse to know the debt is sitting there, ready to leap on me and eat me alive.

The personalization of money can also extend to the people and places that handle it, and women may develop transferential relationships to financial advisers and institutions. Some feel "comfortable" with a bank and leave their money in a low-interest passbook account. Others develop affection for a mutual fund, loyally holding on to its shares, even when they fall in value. Women may give a financial adviser too much power, maintaining a "little girl" relationship, or remain ambivalent, refusing to trust the broker in charge of their account. Stormy relationships with financial institutions, reminiscent of the kind a rebellious adolescent daughter has with her parents, may develop, too.

A woman in our study threw tantrums in a "horrible" bank she "hated and despised" because she regarded it as having an uncooperative staff. When it was suggested that she close her account and open a savings account elsewhere, she told us she "didn't know why" but she "couldn't do it." Instead, she formed a passive-aggressive relationship with the bank and got even with it by removing her money little by little, spiting the bad institution, while maintaining her power over it. Needless to say, personalizing money and its institutions makes it difficult to accomplish objective financial goals.

Unconscious Bartering Behavior

During feudal times money was not an important means of exchange. Instead, people bartered goods for goods, services for goods, and services for services in a network of ongoing complex relationships. The development of a monetary system allowed for more mobility and flexibility (a trader no longer had to carry his bushels of wheat), but short-circuited personal contacts between seller and buyer. When used consciously, bartering is still an effective form of negotiation. In the corporation's good old boy or good old girl networks, important favors, leading to increased income, are routinely exchanged. Networking, in which career information is traded, is also an effective form of bartering. For an equitable barter to take place, however, each party must know what he is giving and getting in exchange, and the goods and services traded must have equal and measurable value.

Money confused women, however, tend to exchange services that have monetary value for emotional assets, such as affection, loyalty, or respect. Because the terms of the barter are never established, and the participants are unaware that a barter is taking place, one party may feel ripped off.

A working mother told us that her boyfriend, who earns half of what she does, vacuums and does laundry instead of contributing his share of household costs. Though this is theoretically an equitable barter, since his housework spares her the expense of hiring a cleaning lady, she feels it would be bitchy and aggressive (or destroy closeness) to set specific times for him to do these tasks, and the unvacuumed floor and dirty laundry still occupy her long list of anxiety-producing responsibilities. By keeping the terms of the barter unclear, she is preserving what she regards as important feminine qualities (gentleness and understanding), and trading her anxiety for closeness.

Succumbing to Money Confusion: The Sad Saga of Meredith Vieira, Who Let Inner Conflicts Win Her Negotiating Game with CBS

Meredith Vieira, a gifted television reporter, who believed she had a right to a family and career, was the youngest child and only daughter of an emotionally cold, absent father, and a "too available," but frustrated mother. Although Meredith's mother "hovered" and her own life appeared to revolve around her children, she advised her daughter to make career a priority; "Never rely on anyone. You need to be self-sufficient," she said. Her own gifts, intense drive, and broadcast opportunities that the Equal Employment Opportunity Act of 1972 made available to women enabled Meredith to fulfill her own—and her mother's—ambitions. At thirty-five she was a respected reporter for CBS's trendy "West 57th Street" show.

Meredith, like many successful women, wanted to have children, too. Her mother did not support this plan, fearing it might interfere with her daughter's high-powered career. When her fourth pregnancy was a go, after three wrenching miscarriages, Meredith planned to take advantage of the six-month maternity leave offered by CBS:

> When she became pregnant she thought she had worked it out better than her mother. She could spend time with her child, and have a job. She wasn't going to be trapped.

Although she planned to return to work, she looked forward to going home, having her baby, and putting her dynamic career on a brief hold. However, as she was slipping out of the office to go into labor, a network executive made her an offer she couldn't refuse—the job she had dreamed of since college days. Would she like to "do" "60 Minutes" when she returned?

Meredith felt torn. "60 Minutes" would offer a rare opportunity for serious, sensitive reporting about social problems on commercial television. But she was concerned about the many days of travel and passionate commitment her dream job would require, and determined not to neglect her much-wanted child. After weeks of agonizing, she hit upon a viable solution: She would negotiate with the network for a half-time job.

Initially an astute negotiator, Meredith played "hard to get," involved an attorney, and successfully bargained for the half-time position with the brash, hard-driving "60 Minutes" producer, Don Hewitt. Known to demand total devotion from his correspondents, who, with the exception of Diane Sawyer, had always been men, Hewitt was determined to add the talented young woman reporter to his aging male staff; he agreed to let Meredith travel only twice a month and work at home with producers. He failed to flinch when she defiantly brought her newborn son to their power lunch to let him know how important he was to her. There was one hitch: After a year of the part-time position, which would pay her $450,000, Meredith agreed to replace Harry Reasoner, about to retire, and work full-time.

> Near the end of the lunch, Meredith voiced a reservation. "You know, I might have to come back a year later and say this is not working," she said. . . . She felt uneasy as she left the restaurant. Hewitt had agreed to everything she asked. But was she writing off her child for her own ambitions? She hadn't even mentioned that she wanted more children. How would she fit that in?

Meredith embarked on a stressful year, walking a fraying tight-rope between a traditional concept of motherhood and a ball-busting career. Despite her vow to stay at home with her son, she found herself in the office before the end of her maternity leave, and later incurred Hewitt's wrath when she honored their agreement by working at home. Ironically, Meredith became the "hovering" caretaker her own mother had been; she found it wrenching to delegate parenting responsibilities either to her husband, editing a TV documentary and playing "Mr. Mom," or to a full-time babysitter that, unlike most working mothers, she could easily afford. When her job forced her to leave her son, as it did more often than she had thought it would, she wept uncontrollably, sure that he would reject her when she returned.

> She wanted to be the emotional nucleus of the family, the primary nurturer. That was the way it was supposed to be. . . . She had finally found someone who was going to love her unconditionally in a way she had never experienced.

Despite their huge income, Meredith and her husband lived unpretentious lifestyles. After her husband, who suffered from a mild case of MS, was hospitalized for a week, she worried that she might eventually become the family's only earner, and feared losing her CBS contract. Conflicts with Hewitt over her casual dress, time out of the office, and her reportorial style aggravated her increasing anxieties.

When Meredith became pregnant again at thirty-seven—before the end of her first year with "60 Minutes"—she refused to fly or to report a story at a toxic waste site for fear of miscarrying, which infuriated her boss. Still determined to hold on to her dream job, she attempted to "buy time" by renegotiating her half-time position for another year. If she could hold out part-time for awhile, she reasoned, it wouldn't be long before her children were in school. When she confronted Hewitt with her proposition, to her surprise, he seemed acquiescent. Another woman reporter, Lesley Stahl, wanted a part-time position, too, he noted, and he might be able to "make it work." Although Meredith was unaware that her boss had been talking to another woman reporter—a bad omen—she was relieved. Then she blew the negotiation.

> Hewitt asked when she planned to stop having children. Reading the question as a friendly one, she laughed. "I might be kidding myself. I might want another in a year," she said, letting down her guard without thinking about the self-destructive consequences of her candor. A one-year extension might not be enough, she added. . . . Meredith left the office feeling great. . . . she felt she had pulled through on this one.

It wasn't "candor," but confusion that provoked this savvy and experienced negotiator to "let down her guard" and sabotage herself by revealing too much information to a hostile employer. Too stressed and anguished by her difficult balancing act to look deeply into her money mirror, she had brought her unresolved conflicts about motherhood, marriage, and career, as well as her relationship with her parents, to the negotiating table, where they didn't belong, and let them speak for her. Although she knew her employer's needs were not the same as hers, she ignored the fact that he was an adversary, and trusted him to take care of her, even as they both vied for gains.

Hewitt, faced with a reporter who had revealed, to his mind, that "her primary interest was having babies," and wanting a correspondent who gave her all to the show, reneged and offered an ultimatum: Meredith had to work for "60 Minutes" full time or not at all.

All she could see was that the career she had spent fifteen years building was slipping away.

Could Meredith have negotiated with Hewitt successfully? Perhaps. First, she needed to negotiate with herself, looking inward to find the emotional flexibility and resilience to integrate her modern, multi-faceted definition of a satisfying life. She needed to make room for her childhood dream of the perfect job, room for her marriage, for her children, and for herself, getting older. Instead, she adhered to rigid, traditional definitions of her desires, thinking that by keeping them in separate compartments, she could have all of them at the same time.

Subsequent negotiations with her attorney present, and public accusations that CBS was practicing sexual discrimination by firing Vieira, did not change Hewitt's mind. Meredith, who had hoped to be a "trailblazer" for women who wanted both family and career, was replaced by Stahl. Because she was still on contract, she didn't lose income, and accepted a morning newscaster slot on an early morning show—a dull job that proved almost as stressful as the one she really wanted—and soon became pregnant with her third child.[4]

Overcoming Money Confusion: Winning the Negotiating Game

Let us now analyze three important negotiation games that affect women's lives and identify their obstacles: (1) negotiating for pay; (2) negotiating with a partner over money issues; and (3) negotiating a divorce settlement.

Negotiating for Pay

SOCIETY'S OBSTACLES: Working women do not make as much money as men do and never have. Pay gaps vary, depending on the field, who is calculating the difference, when and how. (In 1988, for example, the Census Bureau artificially inflated women's earnings by using weekly instead of the standard yearly wages, exaggerating the salary of many part-time workers, who aren't employed all year.)[5] Some statistics—those that fail to get media attention—reveal that the pay gap is widening, not shrinking, in many occupations, including some to which ambitious women aspire, like corporate management. Although the Census Bureau reports that women's wages have crept up one penny a year since 1981, closing the pay gap by one percent per year, in 1991 they backslid two cents. In fact, by the mid-eighties, supposedly a boom time, women were back to where they started in 1955, earning 63.9 percent of what a man was making.[6] By the end of that decade, 80 to 95 percent of women said they suffered from job discrimination and unequal pay.[7] In the mid-nineties, when women's pay appears to be catching up to men's, analysts say the figures are skewed because men's wages are falling.

Although the GNP has risen, thanks to our increased participation in the labor market, laws designed to protect women's paychecks, like the 1963 Equal Pay Act, fraught with loopholes for employers, are enforced less and less.

Some women receive lower salaries because they work in professions dominated by their sex. (Historically, when women begin to dominate a field that men have dominated before, the pay goes down along with the prestige associated with the job.)[8] Pay scales for jobs that employ mostly women have not been rising as have those for sex-integrated jobs. Experts say that low-paying service jobs, often filled by women, are expected to increase, not decrease, in the future, which means that unless pay differentials are equalized, women will continue to receive lower pay.

Unfortunately, women often unwittingly collaborate with a system that conspires to pay them less than men. Uninformed about salary differences, or comparing themselves to other women, instead of to men who earn more, they unconsciously accept and perpetuate the status quo. Alison Estabrook, for example, a prominent breast cancer surgeon at Columbia Presbyterian Medical Center in New York, discovered after years on the job that she was receiving $40,000 less than male surgeons who had been hired at the same time; she had assumed, without asking, that equal pay in her field was a fact.[9]

Companies prevent women from evaluating their objective economic worth by encouraging all workers to keep wages confidential. This practice allows the employer to negotiate salaries with new employees on the basis of their credentials and experience, and to give merit raises without causing dissension. Salary secrets also permit companies to violate the Equal Pay Act with impunity. Money confused women keep their salaries a secret, however, because disclosing the amount they earn seems a question of establishing personal trust, instead of necessary strategizing to meet mutual goals. A woman who had worked for a large publishing conglomerate told us:

> A colleague who did an identical job and I were going to tell each other what we made. At the time we related to each other as kindred spirits, which turned out not to be true at all. (Since then, she has gone on to a very big job in a totally dollar-oriented field.) But there was this moment when we agreed to trust each other that much. It became this huge big deal. And something happened and we never did it. It was so frightening to ask, "What did they offer you? What did you come in at?"

Needless to say, in a salary negotiation game lack of knowledge about what one's services are worth is a handicap. Other marketplace realities—

general workplace harassment, sexual harassment, and ongoing sex discrimination against women—also keep a woman's ability to protest pay inequities and request higher salaries in check.

THE OBSTACLES WITHIN: The marketplace, as we have described it, is an ideal backdrop for money confusion. In a discriminatory and sometimes violent atmosphere it is easy for women to confuse the goods and services they have to offer with traditional definitions of their female role. What forms does money confusion take in a negotiation for pay?

First, those who do not understand that negotiation is a game may be naively unaware of its most basic rule—no expert player ever asks for the amount of money she expects to win:

> The guy before me was making more than forty-five. So I go in there, and I figure I don't have the experience he had and they're not going to pay me what they were paying him, but they should give me at least forty. He said to me, "How's forty?" and I said, "Fine." Then he turned around and said, "Well, the big boss won't give it to you; he'll probably say thirty-eight with a raise in six months." I was hot and tired and I agreed. Later I thought, What a jerk I am! Stupid! Idiot! I should have known he would screw me down right away. So I got thirty-eight and every time I went back to him for more money he'd say I wasn't doing a good enough job.

Women who have seen their mothers working for free may find it difficult to distinguish time for which they ought to be paid from time devoted to caring for other people's needs. A computer programmer who designed studies for private clients, became money confused when asked to evaluate a study for a potential customer—a task that proved more time-consuming than she had thought it would be.

> I went home and looked at the data. The study was ridiculous—terribly set up. I wasn't responsible for the study, only for telling him what I thought of it at that point. So what is the price I should put on this? Finally, my husband asked, "What's it worth for you to be sitting in your house on a nice day, trying to make sense of it?" What is my time worth? That was the question. I had to get real angry and tell myself, This is set up wrong, not me, before I could decide to charge him twenty-five dollars an hour for the evaluation.

Money confused women, who view their salaries as a symbol of their total self-worth, may be unable to negotiate on days when they feel insecure, or when they are troubled by personal problems. They may also confuse employer-employee relationships with friendship.

Patricia, a magazine editor who had recently been fired from her job, undersold herself when a friend, the publisher of an industry house organ, asked her to work on a per-diem basis. Before she offered Patricia the per-diem job, she had given her a writing assignment. The research had been difficult, and Patricia felt that she had written a piece that was not quite what the publisher wanted. She was prepared to be "open and honest" with her employer-friend, instead of fending for her own self-interest.

> I was going to tell her that it wasn't so good, but my husband said, "Then you'll be putting it in her mind that you didn't do a great job. Just give it to her."

Feeling nervous about the article she had written, doubting her competence because she had been fired from a job, and worried about outstanding bills as well as her appearance, Patricia blew a negotiation that took her off-guard.

> So I was thinking, Oh God, this piece is going to be killed. I'm never going to get the money, or be able to pay my sheriff's fine for overdue parking tickets. And I felt fat, and my stomach hurt because I had cramps. I was dressed nicely, but not like I was going for a job. I turned in my assignment and she said, "Come and see me before you leave." When I went into her office she said, "I'm ready to start work on those projects I mentioned. Can you come in?" And I said, "Sure." She asked, "What's your rate?" I said, "I don't know," like a fifteen-year-old dope. Then I told her $150, and I should have said $175. I was so excited, I just didn't think. I wanted to work with her. I wish I had said, "I want to think about it. I'll let you know tomorrow."

Any negotiation is a contest between adversaries, even if the two parties were friends before it, and go on being friends after it is over. Money confused women, however, may feel estranged from their femininity when they have to take an aggressive role and fight a winning battle.

A law student in our Boston money group, who had left a low-paying social work job to train for a law career, described winning a large settlement in a mock negotiation assignment as "devastating."

> I was defending an imaginary plaintiff who had gotten injured from a wrongful discharge. We researched the case for two months, and I finally sat down at the table with the other lawyer to try to settle out of court. I came away with a very large amount of money—higher than anybody in my group, and way above average. In a real case, I would have gotten to keep a third of the settlement. So I exactly fulfilled what I wanted to happen. And I went home and felt devastated. The other lawyer was a man, younger than me,

and very nice. I felt like I'd been cruel to him . . . a monster. It felt lonely to know that I couldn't be friends with him. In my previous job, I had made little money helping people. I had never been an adversary.

As an adversary who won by being more aggressive than her male opponent, the law student felt cut off from a network of all-important human relationships. Fortunately, she was able to put herself back into a supportive, personal context by discussing her feelings with a female teaching assistant:

> Everybody was buzzing about the negotiation and asking me, "You made that much?" I took her aside and said, "I really feel guilty and really stupid for having such an inappropriate reaction to my success." She told me she'd had the exact same feelings the first time she'd negotiated a very high settlement. It was validating to know a woman associate who had similar issues doesn't have them anymore.

Women who do not play the negotiation game to win, or try to help the other player, may underprice their goods and services. An artist who had sold a drawing to a friend for less than it was worth, told us:

> When he wanted to buy it, well, he was a friend, he was in school, and I know he doesn't make that much money. He was surprised it was so cheap. I think I should have charged him fifty dollars more, but when I sell to friends, I always deduct at least ten dollars so that it's more personal.

On the one hand, the money confused artist made herself feel comfortable by making the sale "more personal"; but since she had done so by putting a lower price on her drawing, she felt she had "cheapened" herself and her work. Though the amount she had undercharged her friend was minimal, it symbolized painful self-betrayal.

> I went as low as I could go for my self-respect. I think I should have sold it to him for what it was worth. I was too emotional. I was thinking for the work, and for him—I was doing everybody's job.

Some money confused women, then, try to take care of their opponents. Others, who bring their traditional feminine personas into the negotiation game may expect their adversaries to take care of them. They want their opponent to provide them with information about how much money they should bargain for. Instead of researching pay scales for their particular area of expertise, they wait for the other team to hand them the ball.

If someone says, "Come to me with a price," I'm always stymied. I indicate that they should give me a guideline, and they won't tell me anything. I don't find it difficult to negotiate if what I'm offered isn't enough, but to name a figure? . . . I go through such anxiety. Somebody once suggested I could ask a crucial question like, "What ballpark are we talking about?"

The slang commonly used to describe failure in a negotiation process—"fucked over" or "screwed"—has a special meaning for women. It signifies a financial rape by a sexist system in which they cooperated. One woman who failed to negotiate an appropriate salary for a new job, described her feelings in these sexual terms:

I felt like I'd just slept with someone I shouldn't have slept with.

Losing a negotiation game, however, is not necessarily the same as "getting screwed." Money confused women may not understand that risk is an inevitable part of every negotiation. Those who associate the outcome with their total self-worth may feel ashamed and humiliated when they do not win.

OVERCOMING OBSTACLES: GETTING WHAT YOU'RE WORTH: These examples of women who played the negotiation game, and did not win, partly because of inner obstacles, offer some important suggestions. The computer programmer and editor both asked their husbands for advice. Some men, who associate self-worth with the amount of money they make, know how to play the game and can be good coaches; but it is important to choose men who do not see themselves as competitors to play this role. The lawyer who won a mock negotiation was able to play her game on a practice court, and in the process, became aware of emotional "injuries" that might occur when the game was for real. Her sympathetic woman adviser provided reassurance and understanding, and let her know that her feelings were neither unique nor inappropriate, but predictable responses to her socialization. Mock negotiations and women mentors, who have already conquered the hardships of the game, help us win and enjoy success.

Most important, all of the women were able to look back at a failed negotiation and analyze what went wrong; their self-reproach did not stop them from considering new strategies to bring to the next negotiating tournament. As they reviewed the "plays" and examined their feelings, they were able to take a step toward depersonalizing this important process and acting in their own financial self-interest.

Personal Negotiation

THE OBSTACLES: Other symptoms of Money Phobia prevent women from negotiating equitable financial arrangements with those they love. Money squeamish women feel it is "petty" or "not nice" to discuss money, or to demand their financial rights in the context of a relationship. Struggling to integrate their traditional "ladylike" side with their quest for modern independent selfhood, even those who desire equitable financial relationships may feel confused. One money squeamish woman described her difficulty negotiating with the man she lives with like this:

> I am very squeamish dealing with Lionel about specific amounts of dollars and cents. I look at the phone bill and check his long distance calls, and then I don't say anything to him. I feel it's not nice to say, "You owe me $1.50." I feel guilty about making an issue about such a small amount—like I'm moneygrubbing.

Women who believe they ought to be generous may feel it is "selfish" to keep track of expenses in a love relationship, and may become money blind in order to avoid feeling "ripped off."

> He's very generous, and I'm very generous, and we get to the point where we're out-generousing each other. And then I ask myself, "What actually went down there?" and I get uncomfortable thinking about it. He plays right into my discomfort by teasing me and saying, "Don't worry, it will all come out even in the end." It may be that I'm spending $2,000 a year more than he is on our relationship, but I'd never know, because I have no idea how much I earn and spend in a year.

Money deniers, who secretly want a man to take care of them, may feel angry and resentful when asked to pay their share on a date. When they get involved in nominally equitable relationships, they believe a loving partner is by nature just and fair, and will fend for their financial interests; they do not think they should have to negotiate.

> It annoys and bothers me that I have to ask him to contribute groceries or rent money, but it bothers me more that he can't, or isn't more compelled to offer.

"Systems" for dividing expenses, or keeping them separate, may symbolize an emotional separation to the Money Phobic woman. When inequalities develop, however, she feels "ripped off," furious at the man for creating them and at herself for failing to seek redress. A Boston woman, unable to negotiate with her husband to have her name put on joint assets, felt angry and powerless:

> There's a whole lot I do as a human being in this marriage that should give me more say as to how the money is spent and how it is earned. I should have as much leverage with the property equity as he does, so I can go to the bank and say, "I'm going to take out a $50,000 loan so I can go to school," and not have to check with anybody. My husband doesn't have to come to me and say, "I'm going to sink $150,000 of our income into my business." He just does it. It's mine—as much as his.

This woman, who associated negotiation with emotional manipulation and futile tantrums, found it difficult to imagine the language she would use to bargain for her financial rights.

> If I imagine asking I hear this very bitchy voice that doesn't sound competent. One must be able to ask in a civilized, rational way. If I go in screaming like a banshee, I won't get what I want either.

Inequitable financial arrangements can also occur when a woman uses money to barter for power. Some women may reverse the old formula, in fact, and take care of men. Forty-two of the 123 women in our money study had at one time supported a husband or lover—a surprisingly large number. Some (who did not believe in financial equality) did an about-face and married another man who supported them; others felt they had been exploited and swore they would never support a man again. For most, the inequitable arrangement had proved unsatisfying, possibly because they had never accurately defined what it was they were "buying" with their money.

One of the women we interviewed was aware that she had traded economic inequality for a position of control—a barter that backfired.

> I supported us. It wasn't a decision. It sort of evolved. Part of it was the philosophy of the hippie era—what's yours is mine and what's mine is yours—and the traditional applications of the male-female roles were smothered. I didn't think about it. When I look at it in retrospect I think our arrangement emasculated him from my point of view and from his point of view. Our sex life went down and became nonexistent. I think he looked at me as a mother, and I acted like one. I would never support a man—or anyone—again, now or ever. It gave me a kind of power, but it became a double bind, because I had the power and then I lost it.

This woman is now married to a man with whom she adamantly shares all expenses, even when it feels "uncomfortable"; in fact, the night he proposed in a candlelit restaurant, they split the bill.

OVERCOMING PERSONAL NEGOTIATION OBSTACLES: In order to negotiate successfully in a relationship, a couple must establish a tradition of discussing money. According to Philip Blumstein and Pepper Schwartz, two sociologists who studied 12,000 couples for their book *American Couples: Money, Work, Sex*, most of the financial disputes between couples involve quarrels about when, how much, how, and on what money should be spent, differences in spending and saving styles, problems with record keeping, and unclear property titles. Almost all of these issues could have been avoided or settled peacefully if the couple had evolved a diplomatic financial style early in their relationship and learned to negotiate flexible "deals."

Blumstein and Schwartz, who blame the failure of interpersonal financial arrangements on money squeamishness, observed that courting couples discuss prior sex lives, but ignore mutual economic histories, because "it is not very romantic or interesting to talk about net worth or projections of income or one's indebtedness." Money, say Blumstein and Schwartz, becomes the "last frontier" of self-disclosure, even though each partner may hold strong feelings about the ways money should be dealt with.[10]

Once a couple institutes a solid bargaining tradition, individual transactions do not seem "petty," nor does each partner have to break an unacknowledged code of secrecy about money matters in order to discuss them. (Both parties may benefit from completing and discussing Tool #2 "The Family Money Tree" in chapter 10, "Tools for Overcoming Money Phobia.")

To talk about money with any loved one, however, a woman has to let him or her know that the topic is important, and find her negotiating voice— harder in a personal relationship than in the marketplace. To find her voice, she must become aware of issues that silenced her in the past.

Andrea, in our New York money group, was able to negotiate with her sisters for a larger portion of an inheritance once she realized that her peacemaking role in the family had kept her from asking for what she wanted in the past. Andy's mother had died nine years before and left a bank account to be divided between her four daughters, with the lion's share going to the one who had cared for her in the months before her death. A younger sister contested the will and then died, too. Andrea, who needed money to buy her co-op apartment, had to examine her relationship with her two surviving sisters before she could speak in her own behalf.

My older sister called and said, "Now about that account." I began to do what I recognized as my typical number in the family, which was to say, "Oh, anything, just so long as we don't have fights. Anything you want." And what she wanted was essentially to grab the biggest hunk.

Weighing her financial goals against her traditional emotional role in the family, Andrea hung up the phone and thought, No, this is not okay. Her first attempt to reopen the issue with her sister, however, failed; she wrote a hesitant, conciliatory letter that began, "I'll never mention this again, but. . . ." Her sister, of course, ignored this self-effacing plea, and Andy realized that a one-sided statement was not an effective bargaining strategy; she would have to confront both her sisters and play the negotiating game. For all successful negotiations-in the marketplace or personal sphere—the timing must be right. Andy took advantage of her sister's personal happiness to make her first move.

> Very conveniently, my older sister got married, and as I was flying to the wedding, I thought, "Well, this is your opportunity. If you're going to con-front this, you have to do it now, or you're going to hate yourself." At one point the three of us were alone in the hotel suite, happy and gay and drinking champagne. I thought, "Now or never," and I plunged right in. I caught my older sister at the right moment, because she's in a marriage and she's happy. I knew my younger sister would go along with what the two of us decided. I said that what I wanted was to be given my dead sister's portion of the account. That way, neither of them would get a penny less, and I would get a little more. They're both married and they both have two incomes, whereas I am self-supporting and live in New York alone—and I have to deal with that. But I didn't say all this at first. I just laid out what I wanted. And they both said, "That's okay with me."

Since Andy's relationship to her sisters was based on an emotional tie, she did not feel that she had achieved her goal until she brought the negotiation back into a personal framework. She used an expression of positive feeling after she had won the game to reinforce her relationship with her sisters and make them feel good about her victory:

> I sat there for a moment, still feeling like a sulky kid, and then I thought, "This is really important to you, Andy—let them know this." I hugged my one sister and then I started sobbing, "I've just begun to realize I have to take care of myself. . . ." I felt she understood, because she's a loving person. So we hugged and cried, and then I went to my other sister, and we hugged and cried. And it was this incredible moment of true intimacy between us. It was wonderful, and yet, it was one of the hardest things I ever had to do.

Andrea, then, was able to separate the personal aspect of the negotiation with her sisters from the strategies necessary to win the game. In retrospect, she realized that she had mastered new skills she had never been taught and altered her traditional family role. She understood that she had taken a risk and won, but that her self-worth would have been damaged more if she had not negotiated at all than if she had lost. She learned that assertiveness is an essential component of self-esteem.

> I was terrified. The only way I got myself to do it was to have a stern talk with myself. "Andy, if you don't do it you're going to be really disappointed in yourself. What are you afraid of? That maybe they'll say no? What if they do? It's a learning experience. You'll live through it. It's not going to kill you, and you'll feel a lot better for having done it."

Her new knowledge of negotiation is one Andy should be able to transfer to the marketplace, as well as to other personal relationships.

Negotiating A Divorce Settlement

THE LEGAL OBSTACLES: "No fault" divorce laws, enacted in the 1970s, were designed to help women get equitable settlements; yet courts continue to discriminate against women when parting couples litigate to divide the wealth. Several studies have shown that divorced women initially suffer a reduction in their standard of living while living standards for husbands improve. The sharpest drops are suffered by unemployed women with young children, and older women, who may enter the marketplace in their fifties or sixties, or remain there, instead of retiring, because they need the income to survive.

Until the 1970s the majority of states gave ownership and control of property and income to the spouse who had acquired them and whose name was on the assets. Under these outdated laws, if the savings account and other properties were in the husband's name, they were his, no matter how much his wife had contributed to the marriage. Patriarchal judges, however, assumed wives were dependent on their husbands, and usually awarded them the family home and sometimes alimony as well as child-support payments, provided the wife was not seen as the "guilty party" in the dissolution of the marriage. In 1970, California passed the first no-fault divorce law, which allowed divorce on the grounds of "irreconcilable differences." In the next ten years, forty-four other states adopted some version of these reforms.

In a no-fault divorce, marital property is theoretically divided on the basis of need and the ability to pay. A judge who applies equitable distribution laws is supposed to distribute the family assets "equitably" (which is not the same as "equally"), taking the ages of both divorcing partners and their future prospects into account. Decisions about child custody, as well as property division, are made with the assumption that men and women are social equals. With this in mind, alimony payments have been replaced by temporary maintenance awards to help women who have been dependent on husbands become self-supporting.

Though equitable distribution laws were expected to help women, the results have proved disappointing. The new divorce laws are less sexist, but the judges who interpret them, and the husbands who defy court orders, are not. They tend to disregard marketplace sexism, and assume that a woman who has had a career as a homemaker, or who has worked part-time, will be able to get a high-paying job and support herself. As a result, they grant short-term maintenance awards, which are taxable, or nothing. In deciding who has a right to marital property, they continue to undervalue non-monetary contributions to the marriage by the wife as a spouse, parent, and homemaker, and bestow the larger chunk of the goods on the husband whose income acquired them. Surveys in several states have shown that judges were misinterpreting the statutes to mean that women should get one third, not one half, of assets from the marriage.[11]

In unsettling new developments on the divorce front, judges are awarding maintenance payments to husbands of women who earn substantial salaries, and settlements to those who claim to have supported and developed their wives' careers. When Marisa Berenson divorced a wealthy lawyer in 1988, the court ruled that the "increase in value" of Berenson's career as a model and actress was joint marital property, and awarded her husband an undisclosed amount.[12]

Under the new laws, the burden of proof rests upon the woman, especially if she has not been working outside the home. If she does not hold title to property, she must prove that she deserves it, and hire accountants, appraisers, tax pension specialists, and a first rate lawyer to help her. The husband, on the other hand, often benefits from hiding income, and divulging as little information as possible, for which he, too, requires expensive professional help. As a result, the cost of contesting a divorce has skyrocketed, and may be financially prohibitive to a woman who emerges from a marriage with insufficient capital to fight for her rights.

Equitable custody laws have also given husbands another weapon. Because judges often assign children to the man in a contested proceeding, some fathers now raise the possibility of fighting for custody as a bargaining tool. They use "custody blackmail" to intimidate their wives, terrified of losing their children, into accepting lower settlements and child-support payments.

A woman who has been working part-time, or in a low-paying job, may be awarded little or no maintenance or child support. If she has a demanding or lucrative job, she may be deemed an "uncommitted mother," and not only lose custody, but may be required by the court to pay child support to her husband.

THE INNER OBSTACLES: Divorcing women, then, face a complicated and unfamiliar legal process that still favors husbands, despite changes in the law. Their money confusion may make it difficult for them to separate the legal and financial aspects of the divorce from its intense emotional ramifications. Whereas women who are left by their mates may be too shell-shocked to strategize, those who are leaving may feel too guilt-ridden to fight for their rights. The divorced women in our study whom we were able to interview had left their husbands, or had parted by mutual agreement. They, too, felt desperate and confused. Said Darlene, who divorced her husband in the 1980s:

> I knew I had to leave to survive, but I couldn't really face what I was doing. I had to have blinders on everything. Everybody's life, it seemed, was crumbling because of what I was doing, and I had no way of supporting myself. I couldn't look. I had to shut my eyes, and nothing seemed real.

The first mistake a money confused woman makes is to choose the wrong matrimonial lawyer. Feeling helpless and frightened in the face of an uncertain future, she may look for a lawyer who will comfort or take care of her—a father figure. Darlene, who "had blinders on everything," said she was "looking for a savior, not a lawyer," but chose one who insulted her with his patronizing attitude:

> When I asked about the settlement he patted me on the head and said, "Don't worry. If it wasn't for divorced women we wouldn't have waitresses." And I ended up using him, even though I didn't like him. I had all my signals off because I was so confused and scared about what I was doing.

Whatever the reason for the divorce, women tend to feel guilty and responsible. Their guilt makes it difficult for them to see their husbands as legal adversaries, and they may choose a lawyer who reinforces their feelings of failure and low self-esteem, or one who will help them take care of husbands they believe they have wronged.

Divorcing husbands, too, experience deep emotional trauma. They are more adept, however, at separating the financial from the emotional issues and bringing marketplace games into the interpersonal drama. When Rebecca, a New York woman in our study, felt that her marriage was falling apart, she gave her "macho" husband an ultimatum: Either he went into therapy or she would file for divorce. He did not go to a therapist, but immediately started hiding income and removing money from joint accounts. When litigation began, her husband, vice president of a large corporation, changed lawyers and reneged on verbal agreements—excellent strategizing, which prolonged the proceedings—and wore Rebecca down with his "tremendous stamina."

> We would sit down and go over all the costs, and he would say, "I don't want to hurt you," and there would be all this tenderness. Then we'd meet with the lawyers and he'd say, "I only discussed that; I didn't agree to anything." He kept bringing in new legal blood, whereas my lawyer had already done the work (and raised his fees for new clients), and didn't really care about my case anymore. I couldn't afford to get a new lawyer.

While this husband wheeled and dealed to his own advantage, Rebecca continued to confuse her caretaking and adversarial role.

> My husband kept saying, "You're taking my family away." He was a macho guy and that part of him was breaking down. I felt caring about him. At one point I even interviewed a men's rights lawyer, thinking we could have joint custody. I didn't hate him yet, or want to destroy him. Why I ever thought I might have the power to do that, I now don't know. I wanted to believe the best, and couldn't believe what he ended up doing to me. And I still can't believe it, because I know he really did love me. When I look back I realize I should have gone to court. I shouldn't have been so honest; I shouldn't have given him the house—all these "I should haves" which make me sick.

Many divorcing women eventually "give up" and accept unfair settlements because they find it too emotionally painful to go on fighting aggressively. Beth, who did not review the divorce laws in her state before consulting a lawyer, gave the husband she was leaving half the worth of a house she had paid for with her earnings:

> The house was in both our names, and I was referred to as *et ux* (and wife) on the deed. At the time, I remember feeling furious about the *et ux*, but I was unaware of what it would mean. He really shouldn't have gotten any part of the house, but my lawyer said, "Equitable Division of Proceeds. . . ." He said we couldn't fight it, but now that I think about it, I don't think the lawyer particularly wanted to fight it. I don't think I wanted to fight it, or had the strength to fight it, because all I really wanted to do was get out of the marriage. So I left him the car, the dog, and the house and took my freedom and independence.

Getting "screwed" in a divorce, as in any important negotiation, leaves a wake of low self-esteem and bitter chagrin. For this reason, many women choose to deny that the negotiation failed or that they made mistakes. Beth still feels she had "no choice" than to give up half of her house without fighting for it. A larger settlement, however, would have increased, not decreased, her newfound freedom.

OVERCOMING OBSTACLES: A divorce settlement usually reflects the way the "business" of a marriage has been conducted. If a couple's financial arrangements have been equitable and flexible, the divorce settlement will tend to be the same. If financial roles within the marriage have been rigid and traditional, the husband will fight to preserve his control during the divorce, and his wife may not have either the emotional or economic wherewithal to change the balance of power. Couples who both earn and keep property separate or equal, or who have flexible systems that enable them to share financial power, are more likely to emerge with a mutually satisfactory settlement.

If a woman learns to negotiate for her financial rights within the context of her marriage, she will be better able to obtain them in the event of a divorce. Many women, however, believe that to negotiate a prenuptial agreement, or make self-protective financial arrangements, indicates a lack of faith in the future of the marriage. To confuse the emotional and financial clauses of the marriage contract may be to set oneself up for a fall if the marriage fails. Though no one who marries "plans" for a divorce, learning and practicing personal negotiation about money matters is excellent preparation should one occur. Couples with a history of discussing money and creating equitable financial arrangements are more likely to benefit from divorce mediation—a social service that offers a non-adversarial, much less expensive method of making divorce and separation agreements outside the court.

Once a divorce is in process—or a settlement has been made—a woman can accomplish her financial goals by keeping business issues between herself and her ex-husband clear. Molly, who felt she had gotten an unfavorable settlement because she chose a mild-mannered lawyer, found divorce an incentive to earn. After experimenting with various careers, she finally started a fashion design company. Once she was experienced in business negotiations, Molly was able to apply marketplace concepts to her divorce settlement. Her ex-husband rarely sent her child-support check on time.

We played this game which was that I called him and said in a cute, wheedling voice, "Oh, hi, Justin, how are you? Could I please have my child-support check this month?" And he'd put it in the mail. Then I decided I really hated doing that. Why should I have to ask him for the money? So now I have this new system, which is that I call his secretary and say, Tell Justin I'm sending a messenger tomorrow." My business pays for the messenger service to go to his office and pick up the check, and there's always an envelope with the money in it waiting.

By using a business-like approach to collect her child-support check, Molly lets her ex-husband know that she understands that the money he must pay her is not a favor or gift. When a woman clarifies the difference between "business" and "personal" in her life as well as in the marketplace, she ceases to be money confused.

Chapter Nine

Healthy, Wealthy, and Wise: Life Without Money Phobia

The time has come to stop analyzing our problems with money, and to describe the happy woman who does not have them. How does a woman with a healthy financial identity live her life and relate to money? The non–Money Phobic woman, it may surprise some to learn, is not necessarily rushing off to a high-salary job with briefcase in hand. She is, however, getting paid what she is worth for the work that she does, and making the amount of money she considers necessary for a meaningful lifestyle, future security, and flexibility. She adapts her financial behavior to her age, to changes in her own economic status and goals, and to upswings and downswings in her country's economy. Taking advantage of financial opportunities, she works hard, and uses her resources wisely—spending neither too much nor too little to satisfy her needs.

If she is sharing her goals with a partner she still sees herself as a financial individual, with power over her own economic life. Most important, she understands the meaning of money; she has gazed into her money mirror and is aware of how her parents, and people close to her, have influenced her financial life style, beginning in childhood. As a result, she neither fails to acknowledge money, nor overemphasizes its importance. She has learned how much is enough for her, and does not strive for more. Sometimes she realizes that she may have to earn less to get the qualities of life that she values—time for tranquility, love, and creativity. Her realistic appraisal of the value of money, however, allows her to handle a windfall (an inheritance) or a crash (a stock market correction) with aplomb.

We found that women with well-formed financial identities enjoy money, what it means, and what it can do. The non–Money Phobic women in our study took pleasure in earning, spending, and investing, and delighted in their financial independence. These women—admittedly, few—were happy women, who communicated feelings of overall satisfaction. Because money in our society spells power—a power women have historically been denied—those who had learned to deal with money effectively radiated an aura of assertive self-confidence. What gave these financially healthy women such high self-esteem, we felt, was that they had feminized the meaning of money in a positive way. They understood how to integrate their desire for money and financial independence with activities that have traditionally held meaning for women. They had not sacrificed their relationships with others to become driven workaholics, like many high-earning men.

Although our non–Money Phobic case histories were not earning what a powerful man would call "Money!" all enjoyed rewarding relationships with other people and active sex lives. For women, we found, there was a definite connection between a healthy financial identity and a healthy sexuality. Those in our study who were "good" with money, as we have defined that, tended to have good relationships, too.

The relationship between economic power and sexual satisfaction has also been noted by other researchers. In a study that measured women's sense of "well being," Grace Baruch, Rosalind Barnett, and Caryl Rivers, authors of *Lifeprints: New Patterns of Love and Work for Today's Woman*, said that the money a woman contributed to her family's income had a strong impact on her sexual satisfaction. According to these psychologists, sexual satisfaction was part of a feeling of "mastery"—that is, self-esteem and a sense of control. Contrary to stereotypes that indicate high-earners may "emasculate" men, women with extra large salaries seem to enjoy good sex lives, too. Studies have shown that even in two-income couples where women earn more than their husbands (29 percent), both partners express more satisfaction with their sex lives than do other couples.[1]

Why should non–Money Phobic women enjoy good sexual relationships? According to money sociologist Pepper Schwartz, a strong self-concept and high self-esteem—the same traits that project women into important jobs—make for better sex lives. A healthy sexuality, like a healthy financial identity, also requires the ability to create flexible and practical options to satisfy one's needs. Modern women who enjoy sex as well as money not only have a strong sense of self-esteem, but of freedom, and control over their destinies. They have been able to negotiate relationships that they find personally meaningful, instead of succumbing to passive fantasies of an ideal romance or subscribing to traditional definitions of women's sexual role. In other words, they are successful sexually for the same reason that they are successful financially—because they have taken care of their desires.

The definition of a satisfying sex life, like a satisfying financial life, of course, varies from woman to woman. The healthy, wealthy, and wise women in our study had evolved different sexual as well as financial styles. Some were involved in a traditional monogamous marriage or lived with partners, and one, who had not rejected the Sexual Revolution's battle cry, enjoyed a number of lovers simultaneously. All, however, had in some way altered the original "script" society and parents had drafted for their lives. And all were equally emphatic about their sense of independence in the context of the relationship, and defined that independence partly in economic terms.

The Queen of Non–Money Phobia: Mae West

One of America's all-time most outrageous stage and screen personalities is an excellent example of the joys of non–Money Phobia. Known for her famous one-liners and physical charms ("My measurements are the same as Venus De Milo's, only I got arms"), Mae West was also a financial whiz. From her early days as a child vaudeville star, she earned, negotiated, and managed wisely, eventually becoming the wealthiest self-made woman of her generation. She also led a full, if extravagant, emotional life, and, by the end of it, claimed to have had an orgasm a day for most of her eighty-seven years.

> Sometimes it seems to me I've known so many men that the FBI ought to come to me first to compare fingerprints.

From childhood she knew what she wanted and was determined to get it. Mae's mother, who recognized that her daughter was unusual, indulged her whims, and never held her back from accomplishing her ambitions or suggested more traditional goals. By the time she was in the third grade, the rising star had quit school, and was performing suggestive dances and singing songs, mimicking the accents of New York's immigrants to the delight of the audience of the vaudeville stage.

Even as a little girl, she was aware that show business was indeed a business. In her autobiography, *Goodness Had Nothing to Do with It*, published when Mae was sixty-six, she remembers and notes the amount she received for each of her first performances. She had an instinctive knowledge of the negotiation process, and refused to pick up money that was thrown on stage, as was the vaudeville custom, knowing that "stooping for money" was not an effective posture in the negotiating game. Later, an agent treated Mae and her dancing partners contemptuously, offering them a trial gig in

South Norwalk for no remuneration, except ten dollars in traveling expenses. Mae refused this pittance, knocking the agent's hat down over his eyes before she exited from his office. Outside, her partner protested, "Gee, Mae, maybe we should have taken the ten dollars," and Mae replied, "Don't worry, that ten dollars will get us more from Mr. Bohm." The act was a huge success and the agent was soon groveling, as Mae had predicted he would be.

Her prodigious awareness of the value of money led Mae to make a timely move from Broadway to Hollywood. Sentenced to ten days in a New York jail in 1927 for her obscene language and "coochie dance" in her own play, *Sex*, she took the opportunity to ponder economics. Mae read reports of Hollywood films' high earnings in her cell.

> In 1925 Paramount reported earnings of $21,000,000; Metro $16,000,000; and First National $11,000,000. Nice, solid, round figures that I liked. I gave some real thought to motion pictures and how they could use my style and personality.

Once in Hollywood, Mae, who proved adept at studio politics, convinced conservative producers to do her kind of film. Eventually she earned $300,000 a picture—the highest salary paid to a star until then—portraying a lusty woman who knew what she wanted and always got it, and was never dependent on or at the mercy of men. She was soon involved in writing and helping to produce her own films, in which she also starred, delivering unforgettable lines like, "Is that a gun in your pocket or are you just glad to see me?" She also learned judo, how to fire a six-shooter, and insisted on entering the lion's cage herself when a stunt man got sick during the filming of *I'm No Angel*, which grossed $85,000 in the first week of its New York run.

In 1935 the flamboyant blonde earned $480,833. Only William Randolph Hearst, who earned $500,000, made more. The wealthy newspaper publisher wrote vindictive anti-West editorials. Mae, who recognized the forces of sexism but was not affected by them, took an indulgent view:

> He hated to see a woman in his class. I didn't hold it against him.

This bombshell not only earned great sums but also enjoyed her money and invested it wisely. She was famous for her glamorous clothes, furs, and fabulous diamond jewelry. She bought real estate, (managing it herself when Jim Timony, who played many roles in her life from lover to financial adviser, died), and parlayed a $16,000 investment in Van Nuys, California, into $5 million. She bought stocks, horses, and ranches, too.

What makes Mae our all-time Queen of Money Awareness, however, was not only her exceptional earning power and intelligent use of money, but the way she achieved balance in her unique lifestyle.

> Hard as I worked, I would be lying to say I neglected all of my emotional side. I'm a girl who likes balance in everything.

At times she turned down lucrative deals because she wanted to cater to spiritual or emotional needs:

> Money is a splendid commodity . . . and everybody should have lots of it. But money to burn does not necessarily produce the flames I need right now.

At other times, the star took on new challenges, not because she needed the money but because she loved her work.

> If I'm not convinced that what I do is great entertainment, I would rather do nothing at all but sit home and polish my diamonds.

Not surprisingly, this extraordinary woman's need for sexual pleasure could not be filled by only one man. Independent, and in charge of her own destiny, she saw no reason to marry, curtail her desire, or fashion a life (which in no way resembled the typical female lifestyle of her time) to suit conventional morality. She satisfied her sexual needs with the same self-reliant assurance with which she took care of herself financially, often to the dismay of her partners, who were asked to call her "Miss West" in public and "Honey" in bed.

> The men who had so far loved me were strong and important citizens who had been attracted to me because they had become aware I was not like the other women they knew. They soon discovered I would not conform to the old-fashioned limits they had set on a woman's freedom of action. Or the myth of a woman's need of male wisdom and protection. This baffled men. Often made them angry, but oddly enough, once they knew they could not change my philosophy or dominate me, none of them left me. My problem was actually how to get rid of them.

Mae did marry once, when she was seventeen, but kept her husband a secret, locking him up in hotel rooms so she could enjoy sex with fellows outside. Much later, he sued her for alimony. The judge ruled in her favor, but Mae felt "a little sorry" for her husband, now toothless and old, and made him a settlement of some blue-chip stocks.

Like modern women with healthy financial identities, Mae enjoyed. She relished the life she had designed to suit her needs, and even in old age worked, loved, and radiated a sense of power, self-control, and youthful vitality.

I got fun out of being a legend and institution.

In only one way was Mae West deprived: She failed to form close, supportive friendships with other women with whom the "legend" (perhaps understandably) did not identify.[2]

Detecting the Healthy, Wealthy, and Wise

The women in our study who were non–Money Phobic bore little resemblance to the inimitable Miss West, yet they conceived their lives as creatively as the thirties star conceived hers. These healthy, wealthy, and wise women, who also led very different lifestyles from one another, came from different kinds of families and parts of the country. All had arrived at their healthy financial identities via different routes; some had been able to separate from their parents' messages about women and money through outright rebellion, or by modifying the script they had been given over time. They had been able to incorporate positive elements of the family message into their adult lives, and, in retrospect, felt grateful to or accepting of their parents—a sign that they saw themselves as separate from them, and were comfortable with their own individuality. All had formed relationships with people who had helped them achieve personal and financial goals, and seized available opportunities to advance their earning power. All had taken risks. Though these non–Money Phobic women were earning better-than-comfortable amounts, none was rich. Every one, however, took pleasure in her financial independence and used money to create harmony in her life. Let us now look into the money mirrors of three successful women who enjoy money, work, and love.

Connie, Who Inherited a Healthy Financial Identity

Connie was fortunate to inherit a positive financial identity directly from her parents. She took what she had learned at home, however, and used the knowledge to create a modern lifestyle that was very different from her family's expectations.

We knew we had uncovered a rare bird when we read Connie's questionnaire. She wrote that her parents had taught her that "Financial planning is important and fun; investing is necessary, and don't be afraid to take a chance, and it is a parental obligation to instruct children about financial matters." We interviewed Connie to learn exactly how these important messages had been transmitted and how she had incorporated them into her life.

Connie was born in Illinois. Her father owned his own lucrative business, and her mother, a housewife, participated in all of the family's financial activities and played an equal role in decision-making.

> My parents would talk in a very disparaging manner about families in which the wife didn't know what was going on financially. They both thought that was really terrible.

Though her parents bickered, they never argued about financial matters.

> I don't remember a fight about money. I saw them as a team.

Early on, her parents taught Connie to be assertive about money. When she was a child they asked her to collect for the Community Chest. "I never had trouble asking for money," she reminisced. She also recalled that her parents neither deprived her, nor used money to control her behavior.

> If I asked for something frivolous—like a certain doll—and talked about it a lot, they would realize it was important to me. I got the doll, but not immediately. It was delayed gratification, but I don't remember feeling resentful about the delay.

Connie was the only student in her high school who had her own checking account, given to her by her parents, who taught her how to balance it. She also earned money of her own by teaching art to neighborhood children for a fee she charged to their parents. In college she worked as a waitress, even though her upper-middle-class parents would have been glad to provide her with discretionary cash.

> I didn't tell my parents at first because I didn't think they would understand. The college situation was so artificial; I had to have a taste of the real world. I liked having my own money. It was freedom. For me, economics is the bottom line.

Having inherited a sense of the value of money, Connie used this sound training to fly away from home. Instead of remaining in Illinois and teaching art, as her parents expected her to do ("a narrower kind of life"), she set off for New York to become an exhibiting sculptor. She taught part-time to support herself as she continued her education.

I got support from my parents to be an artist, but not to leave Illinois. My father was even more upset than my mother. He tried to bribe me to stay by buying me a car. Since he had never before used money to control me, I viewed his offer as a joke. What did I care about a car? When I enrolled in graduate school, it made coming to New York more acceptable to them.

Later, Connie, who had learned how to take financial risks from her parents, bought her own co-op with their ongoing help. When a couple in her building threatened to purchase her unit out from under her, because they did not think a struggling single woman would be able to buy, she called her father for advice.

I said, "Daddy, they're trying to steal my apartment!" He said, "Don't let it bother you. You're worth more than they are." He was talking about his money, not mine. I had a few hundred in my checking account. What he was saying was, "You have my complete support."

When she felt she was not making enough from part-time teaching jobs to have a comfortable lifestyle and finance her art, Connie continued to expand her parents' original script. Positive money messages she had grown up hearing enabled her to take a bold, innovative step: She started her own construction business with another woman.

My father had always talked to me about his business and investments. Once I had my own business, we had more to talk about. He would tell me about estimates and competition.

After a television talk show personality, intrigued by the idea of women in the building trades, invited Connie and her partner to be guests, her business boomed. By now a full-fledged financial adult, Connie invested the profits in land and stocks, consulting her accountant, her brother, an MBA, and friends for advice. She also continued to pursue her dream career in art, as well as her money-making business. In order to have two careers, however, she had to curtail her desire for money, and use what she had to buy herself security and time, instead of material things. She found her salary of between $35,000 and $40,000 a year sufficient.

Sometimes I work for very wealthy people, and I see what it would be like to be rich. I have moments of envy, but they don't last long. It takes a tremendous amount of energy to maintain that lifestyle. Wealthy people tend to be nervous and demanding. I'm glad I'm not obsessed with getting more and more stuff.

Although Connie later married and had a late-life child, at the time we interviewed her, she did not plan to marry. At thirty-nine, she had designed a romantic life that was as untraditional as her dual career; she was dating a number of men. Her love life, and personal feelings of self-esteem, she said, had improved as she had become financially self-assured.

Sometimes I think, "Gosh, who would have ever thought my life would be like this?" For years I had no boyfriends, and now I have five or six men in love with me. To me, that's a miracle. Sometimes I feel like I'm on the fringe of society, but I don't really care. When I do think about settling down with one person, I feel not any one person could give me everything I need.

Though Connie is grateful to her parents for giving her a healthy financial identity, she stresses that her relationship with them was not in every way ideal.

I can feel angry about, "I didn't get this. Or if only they had done that, this would have been different." But money is an area where I can say they did a really good job, and feel great about that.

Priscilla, Who Said "No" to Poverty and Dependence

Most women have not inherited good money messages from their parents, as Connie had, and have to separate from their inherited money messages in order to achieve a healthy financial identity by themselves. Priscilla, forty, born in Savannah, Georgia, was one of our participants who had done that successfully.

Priscilla's mother was a housewife and her father a truck farmer who barely earned enough to support his large family. The second youngest of eight children, Priscilla decided at an early age that she did not want to grow up without any money.

We always had the necessities of life but we never had extras. I didn't want to always be poor!

By the time she was in the eighth grade, she saw economic independence as a way to avoid her mother's subservient life.

I always felt sorry for my mother. She's very religious, and before she went to church my father's meal would be on the table. And when she came back she'd have to clean up the dishes. I never wanted that! And I always felt that the only way you didn't have to behave like that was if you could be independent.

Unusually clear about her financial goals, Priscilla found a family money mentor in her rebellious older sister.

> She's very self-centered. I guess that's one of the reasons why she's been so successful. And she really was a role model. She told me the facts of life and paid a lot of attention to me. I wanted to be like her, not like my mother.

Priscilla's sister encouraged her to get financial aid and go to college. She even paid for a semester in the dormitory so Priscilla could have a taste of independent life away from home. Like many women her age, Priscilla had considered a career in education, but revised her plans when she learned that teachers started at under $10,000 in her state at that time—hardly a ticket out of the poorhouse. She changed her major to accounting, a field few Southern women of her generation braved.

> I got into it for the money. That's the pure reason.

For Priscilla, a satisfying sex life came in the form of one committed relationship. When she was twenty-three, she married a nuclear physicist who had also fought his way free of a family background similar to hers, a man very unlike her father.

> He never put any restraints on me at all. He was always very supportive.

Priscilla and her husband left the South and moved to Westchester, New York, where she worked for the state tax office and he was employed by a large private firm engaged in government research. When the Equal Employment Opportunity Commission began pressuring Priscilla's office to promote more women, she took advantage of the opportunity. Though the EEOC was on her side, Priscilla still had to fight. Evaluations from a sexist manager were not what she thought she deserved, so she requested counseling sessions.

> I said, "So what should I do differently?" And there wasn't anything.

Though Priscilla's husband makes a lot of money and could easily support her, she prefers to work and share financial decisions and goals. She proudly considers herself self-supporting, and knows emotional dependence is not the same as financial dependence.

> Although he is not chauvinistic, I just like the fact that I don't have to depend

on him financially, though we do have a very close relationship. To be self-supporting gives me security, confidence, and lots of positive feelings.

Like many non–Money Phobic women, Priscilla, who earns in the $60,000 range, feels she has enough money. Though she works hard and enjoys her job, she turned down an opportunity to apply for a position with a higher salary because she felt her present job offers her more personal time and flexibility.

> We're not interested in buying an expensive car or a bigger home. We travel once a year, and there's just nothing else we want to do or buy. What we have is adequate, actually more than I ever anticipated.

Priscilla's sense of personal satisfaction has enabled her to make peace with her mother, whose traditional role she rejected.

> For the first time I can really tell my mother that I love her. The distance between us has brought us closer together. Nobody's perfect, and I guess she did give us as much love as she knew how to give.

The same delight with her status quo led Priscilla to question the wisdom of having a baby when she realized her biological clock was ticking. Like other money aware women, she sought balance in her life and rejected the desire to "have it all."

> I knew I would never give up my career. I would put my child in daycare, and I wondered if I would blame myself if it developed problems. I also think I was concerned with altering what I had. I hate to keep saying this, because I guess it sounds artificial, but I'm really happy. Not everything is perfect, but I'm very satisfied. My husband doesn't have a desire to have children, and I wondered if our relationship would deteriorate if I had to take total responsibility for an infant.

Instead of depriving herself of the opportunity to enjoy motherhood or giving birth to a baby, which might have interfered with her job and her marriage, Priscilla continued to rewrite the traditional script. Several years ago she and her husband adopted a seven-year-old girl.

> We felt that with an older child there would be fewer unknowns. And there are so many older children like Cathy in orphanages who don't have homes, that nobody knows about or wants to adopt.

Molly, Who Achieved a Healthy Financial Identity in Time

Both Priscilla and Connie, in different ways, were able to develop the foundations for a healthy financial identity at an early age. For most women developing a healthy financial identity is a slow process of self-discovery that demands recognition of problems and goals, a desire to change, and hard work and perseverance. Molly, our third example of a non–Money Phobic woman, struggled against obstacles that face most of us when we deal with money and earning power, but was able to change. By incorporating money mentors into her life, and gradually recognizing her ambitions and talents, she achieved a healthy financial identity over time.

Molly, now fifty-two, was born in a New York suburb. Her loving and indulgent middle-class Italian parents raised her to be a money denier; they hoped she would marry a high-earning man who could offer her a luxurious life. They sent her to college, mainly because they believed that she might find a rich husband there. Molly, who was not rebellious, tried to fulfill her parents' expectations, but felt stifled.

> I grew up feeling I wanted to have contact with all this stuff out there in the world, and knew if I didn't figure out how to do it, I wasn't going to have it. But I also wanted to be a good girl and I wanted my parents to love me. I wasn't strong enough or rebellious enough to make a break with them and do my own thing.

When she graduated from college, Molly married her high school sweetheart, instead of a handsome prince, and they moved to Manhattan and had two children. After several years of being a mother and a homemaker, however, Molly grew bored and her marriage foundered.

> I wasn't happy because I wanted to go back to work. I knew I had to be doing something, and I don't think that necessarily meant making money. Career was not part of my vocabulary then. I just didn't want to stay at home, taking care of two children and making dinner for my husband. I wanted to do something that was for me. When he couldn't do it for me or with me, I did it myself.

Molly and her husband were divorced, and she slowly began to discover the money-making part of her identity.

> I think I am a very ambitious person, but I don't think I knew or felt that until I was in my mid to late thirties. The process I went through from the time I separated was a slow one.

An inadequate divorce settlement made it imperative for Molly to earn:

If I didn't have children when I got divorced, I could have partied and partied and made barely enough money for myself. I needed more; it was a reality. Having the children made me feel I needed to earn money, and find ways to do it.

Molly quickly learned that she was not afraid of risk and saw starting a business as an exciting adventure. From the first she chose an independent career path, creating jobs for herself that offered the flexibility she needed to work and take care of her children. Intuiting a profitable real estate market in downtown Manhattan loft buildings, she got a salesman's license and convinced a broker to let her set up a "loft desk" in her office. She rented and sold the "trendy" new living spaces, doing business on her bicycle. Next, Molly, who had a bent for fashion, "did flea markets," selling antique jewelry and clothes. When she decided to open a boutique, featuring both antique clothing and her own designs, in the up-and-coming SoHo district, she learned how to negotiate with her father and employ him as a money mentor as well as a financial resource. Her father had already refused to loan her the money she needed to buy a loft of her own.

I told him the part of SoHo where I would be opening the store would soon be booming. "Look at that loft I could have bought for $18,000 that's now worth $100,000," I said. He asked me how much I needed. In my mind I had no idea of money. I spent it, I earned it, I spent it—I didn't even balance my checkbook then. I took a guess and said $10,000. He hesitated, and I reminded him about the money he said he'd put away for my sister and me to have as an inheritance. I asked him if I could have $10,000 of it now, and he said okay. I think that since I was supporting myself, he felt I had some retail talent.

Once Molly demonstrated that she had a financial identity, her father started to treat her like an adult, instead of like a fairy tale princess. When she got "bored" with her store and decided to open her own fashion design company, she was able to ask her father to invest in her again. Unafraid of risk, she was not stopped by lack of knowledge or experience in this new field.

I think when my marriage ended I felt like such a failure that after that taking risks was easy—what did I have to lose? I didn't know anything about the fashion business, how it worked, how to market my designs, write orders, net terms, delivery dates. I knew nothing. But it was a new project and I was very excited. It was a challenge.

To help her realize her goals, Molly took a seminar sponsored by American Women's Economic Development Corporation (AWED), designed to help women start their own businesses, and took on a partner, another woman, whose talents complemented hers.

> The things I do that make our partnership successful are very different from the things Jan does. She examines everything very closely and pays attention to the big picture. But she's always a little bit scared of the next step, and I have to shove her along and convince her.

Molly and her partner also employed an accountant, who helped them negotiate with each other, and with a bank when they needed a loan to move their business to larger quarters in the garment center. Forming this new financial relationship with an institution also expanded Molly's financial identity.

> I never felt so nervous and so grown up as the day we signed the loan.

Her business soon netted Molly a personal salary of $50,000 plus. She had come a long way from the rescued princess her parents wanted her to be and the penniless divorced mother who needed to earn. Like many entrepreneurs, however, she needed to push on to new and more challenging territories in order to feel emotionally satisfied, and soon became restless in her profitable business. When we interviewed her, she was considering ideas to expand and change it. An unfortunate event—her father's death—had enabled her to separate even further from her parents' money message and to contemplate earning more.

> My father had a secure job, but he wasn't aggressive and he didn't make a lot. Something happened to me when he died; it kind of freed me to make more money. I had a strong relationship with him, and wanted his approval. There was a part of me that thought, I can't be more successful than my father, because he's a man.

Like many non–Money Phobic women, Molly has brought the financial awareness she has gained in the marketplace into her personal life. As we reported in preceding chapters, she began to save for retirement and to consider the money messages she was giving her children; she learned how to "negotiate" with her ex-husband for prompt delivery of child-support checks. After many years of single life, Molly became involved with a man whom she at first thought was not her "type." Shortly after our interview with her, she married for the second time. Unlike her first husband, this one takes pleasure in seeing her as an equal and encourages her ambitious goals.

> He's younger than me. And when we met, he told me he was tired of women who felt he should take care of them, and buy them things, and who weren't going to do anything for him but lie there. That's paraphrasing. He likes that I'm independent and have my own business. He's proud of me, and talks about me to a lot of people. He doesn't make me feel that it's not okay to be ambitious and successful, or feel threatened if I make more money than he does. I don't have the feeling I have to give up myself to be with him.

As Molly discovered, an equal relationship that provided support for her financial and personal goals also provided a new kind of sexual chemistry:

> We have an incredibly good sexual relationship. It's never even had a bad day, and this has been going on for two years. We have that!

Finding and Using Money Mentors

What do Connie, Priscilla and Molly have in common? Although the three women arrived at money awareness via different routes, all cultivated money mentors—in their personal and professional lives—who helped them develop fearless and joyful financial styles.

Feminist psychologist Carol Gilligan has observed that women, more than men, define themselves in a context of important human relationships and see themselves as interdependent with other people. For this reason, it may be easier for a woman to change any behavior with the positive influence and help of others than by herself. To vanquish Money Phobia, women need sympathetic friends, lovers, and professionals who can give them information and support.

Chapter Ten

The Money Awareness Program: Tools for Overcoming Money Phobia

The following "Tools" will help women develop money awareness by identifying their dreams, fears, and desires in relation to money. We have found that it is easy for women to talk about money in vague or abstract terms. When you must come up with specific answers to specific questions, and formulate specific money-related plans and tasks, however, you will have a better understanding of what areas of financial behavior you need to change, and how to form long and short-range financial goals. The tools also ask you to look at money in the context of your entire life, the important people in it, and in relation to time—your past, present, and future.

Tool #1: The Money Awareness Questionnaire

The following questions were selected from the questionnaire we used as a data base for our money study. It includes the questions that helped women initiate serious thinking about their financial situation and attitudes. We suggest that the reader either write down or tape record her answers.

Family Attitudes

1. Classify the financial status of the family you grew up in: (a) Lower class, (b) Working class, (c) Middle class, (d) Upper middle class, (e) Upper class
2. Briefly describe your father's attitude toward making and spending money.

3. Briefly describe your mother's attitude toward making and spending money.
4. Briefly describe sibling(s) attitude(s) toward making and spending money.
5. Who managed the money in your family?
6. Describe your parents' attitude toward your current occupation.

Work History

1. When you were a teenager how did you think your financial needs would be taken care of when you reached adulthood?
2. Briefly describe your work history since childhood. (What was your first paying job? How old were you when you got it? How much were you paid? Second job? etc.)
3. How did you choose your present occupation? Did you receive help with this choice? If so, explain.

Present Financial Situation and Goals

1. How much money do you need to live per year? Explain how you arrived at this figure.
2. Are you satisfied with your current income?
3. Would you like to make more money? Explain your answer, giving reasons.
4. What is your "ideal" income? How much of an increase does the "ideal" figure represent over your present income (percentage or dollars)?
5. How could you imagine earning your ideal income? Explain.
6. Can you imagine acquiring your ideal income in any way other than earning it yourself? Explain.
7. Are you currently engaged in any work or activity that might make it possible for you to acquire your ideal income? If yes, explain.
8. If you made more money, what would you do with it? Explain how your lifestyle would change, how you would invest the money, etc.
9. If you could have any job, title, or do any income-producing activity, what would it be?
10. If you could choose any type of work environment, what would it be?
11. Are you currently contemplating a career change?
12. If you don't earn money at the present time, under what circumstances would you begin to earn?
13. What are your individual annual earnings before taxes?
14. If your income varies by more than $5,000 annually, explain why.
15. Do you presently have (a) Money market account, (b) stocks, (c) bonds,

(d) other investments in financial products, (e) real estate, (f) IRA, 401 (k) or other retirement accounts?

16. What is your net worth?

17. Who advises you how to spend or invest your money?

Future Financial Goals

1. Do you expect to continue income-producing activities? Until what age?

2. Where will the money you plan to live on when you are over sixty-five come from?

3. What do you imagine your financial situation will be like in one year? five years? ten years?

Support

1. At what age did your parents stop providing financial support?

2. Do you now support yourself?

3. Do you ever accept money from your parents? Explain.

4. Do you support, or partially support, anyone else (husband, child, relative, or other)?

5. If married, or living with someone, what percentage of household expenses do you supply?

6. Have you ever supported a man/men or helped a man/men financially? If yes, how and for how long? How did you feel about it? How did the man feel about it?

7. If you have been divorced or separated, how did the split affect your attitude toward making and spending money?

8. If you have a child/children, how has being a mother affected your attitude toward making and spending money?

9. Do you plan to have a child or more children? If yes, how do you see your money-making activities changing as a result? Will you manage money in the same way as you do now?

10. Do you like the idea of being supported by someone else? Why or why not?

Spending

1. Do you classify yourself as a "saver" or a "spender"?

2. What do you spend most of your money on?

3. If you have "extra" money, what do you do with it?

4. Are you a compulsive or "binge" shopper? If yes, what do you shop for, and what moods or feelings induce you to shop?

5. Do you have debts (personal, bank loans, or credit card)? Explain.

How do you feel about them?

6. If you have credit cards, how do you use them?
7. Do you have a weekly/monthly budget? If yes, do you stick to it?
8. Do others label you "cheap," "generous," or "extravagant"? How do you label yourself?

Money Issues in Your Relationships

1. If you are married, living with or involved with a man, does he earn more or less than you do? How much more or less? Give percentage or dollars.
2. If there is a difference in your incomes, how do you feel about it? How does he feel about it?
3. How does your present partner feel about the money you make?
4. Is there career/financial competition between you and your present partner? Between you and the men you work with? Describe this competition and how you handle it. How does it make you feel?
5. Have you been married or lived with a man (men) in the past? If yes, for how long?
6. What did the man (men) do for a living? What did you do?
7. Did the man (men) earn more or less than you did? How much more or less (percentage or dollars)? Did the difference in your incomes change during the time you were together?

Dreams, Anxieties, and Risk

1. What is your earliest memory of money?
2. What role does money play in your daydreams and fantasies?
3. If you are, or have been, in psychotherapy or psychoanalysis, have money problems and anxieties been discussed or treated? If so, how?
4. Have you ever made an investment or taken a financial risk? Explain your feelings about doing it and the outcome.
5. Describe any anxieties or problems you now have or have had in the past in relationship to money. (Do you have saving/spending problems that make you uneasy? Do you have earning problems, negotiating or managing problems?)

Tool #2: The Family Money Tree

Every family has its own secret money script and its own financial theme song, whispered or shouted, limiting what we hear—or don't hear—about money. Tracing your family "Money Tree" will help you see which of your relatives' money attitudes you have inherited, and how they affect your financial behavior. Answer the ten following questions about each relative

The Family "Money Tree"

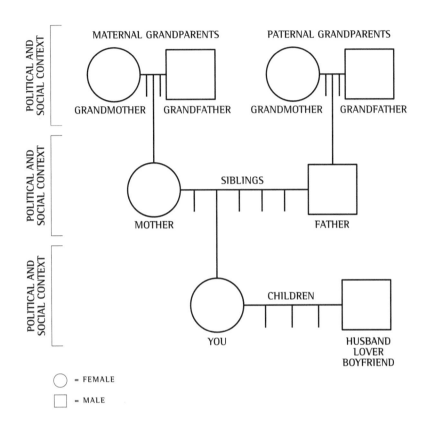

on the tree, then fill in the circles and squares with short phrases which capture that individual's attitude toward money.

1.   What was the social and political climate in which he/she was living?
2.   How much money did he/she earn?
3.   What was his/her lifestyle like? Where and how did he/she live?
4.   What role did he/she have in managing money?
5.   What was his/her attitude toward planning, saving, and investing? Toward risk-taking?
6.   How did he/she set financial goals?
7.   What did he/she spend money on? Were his/her spending patterns consistent?
8.   How did money fit into his/her life? Was money important to him or her?

9. What was his/her greatest success with money? Greatest failure?
10. In what ways are your financial attitudes and behavior similar to or different from this person?

Tool #3: The Financial Identity Checklist

The following questions will help you evaluate your financial identity by defining financial tasks and asking if you do them. You should keep track of the relationship between these tasks, your Family Money Tree, and your future financial goals. The more financial tasks you accomplish, the more highly developed is your financial identity. Answer each question "yes" or "no." The "nos" indicate areas that need work or awareness.

1. Are you able to talk about financial matters with friends and family members openly and comfortably?
2. Do you open, read, and understand all statements and information from financial institutions, like banks, brokerage houses, and insurance companies?
3. Do you participate in all financial decisions involving investments and major purchases instead of allowing someone else to make them for you?
4. Do you have a financial adviser or planner, or someone you turn to for help with financial decisions?
5. Is your name on all assets jointly owned with another person?
6. Do you have a will?
7. If your investments (including real estate and insurance plans) have been purchased by someone else in your family, do you understand the details and the terms?
8. Do you know how much you make and spend in a year?
9. Do you know what your net worth is?
10. Do you understand how your taxes are computed?
11. Have you taken advantage of all legal options for reducing your tax burden?
12. Do you have short-term financial goals? (That is, do you have plans that involve spending, saving, or earning money that you want to accomplish within the next year?)
13. Do you have long-term financial goals? (That is, do you have plans that involve spending, saving, or earning money that you hope to accomplish in the next five to twenty years, such as retiring from your job, reviewing the hours that you work, sending your children to college, or buying a home?)
14. Have you formalized plans to meet both short-and long-term goals yourself, or through a cooperative effort with your partner?

15. If you are single or divorced, have you made plans to live on your own income, or on investments and savings made with your income, in the future?

16. If you are not happy with your present income, have you formulated specific plans about how to increase it yourself?

17. Do you see and investigate opportunities to increase your income, including making profitable investments?

18. Do you take advantage of opportunities to increase your income?

19. Have you formulated a network of people with whom you can discuss your professional interests and goals?

20. Do you save money on a regular basis?

21. Do you know what you are saving money for?

22. Is the money you have saved helping you fulfill your financial goals? (For example, if you are saving for retirement, is the saved money earning dividends or a maximum rate of interest?)

23. Do you always pay your "basic nut," or your regular monthly bills, on time?

24. If you use credit cards to make purchases, do you make monthly payments on time?

25. Do you avoid using a cash advance from one credit company to make a payment to another?

26. When you shop, do you buy only what you went shopping to purchase?

27. When you shop, do you pay the amount you had budgeted for the item, give or take a few dollars?

28. When you shop, do you feel satisfied with your purchases?

29. If you need a loan, do you shop around for the best available rates?

30. Have you shopped for the credit card that charges the lowest rate of interest and/or yearly fee?

31. If you have children, do you know what they do with the spending money you give them and approve of their purchases?

32. Have you taught your children how to negotiate for things they want?

33. If you have children, do you tell them about your family's financial goals, and how they are to be realized?

34. If you have children, do you know how you will pay for their college education?

35. If you have children, do they ever participate in family financial decisions?

36. Have you taught your children how to do basic financial tasks, like balance a checkbook, or read a financial statement?

37. Have you taught your children how to open a savings account, and save for short-range and long-range goals?

38. When faced with a negotiation for pay, do you familiarize yourself with pay scales for your position in your field or for the job you are about to do before you negotiate?

39. Do you discuss the upcoming negotiation with a knowledgeable friend or mentor?

40. When you have to negotiate, do you go into the negotiation with a specific strategy?

41. Do you negotiate with people in your personal life, instead of ignoring money problems that arise? (For example, if you go out for dinner with a friend who asks you to split the check, and the friend's share is more than yours, do you discuss the matter if it bothers you?)

42. Have you devised a system for dividing expenses with your partner that is mutually satisfying?

43. If you are in the process of getting a divorce, are you familiar with the divorce laws in your state?

44. If you are married, are you aware of the value of the financial assets you have contributed to the marriage, and have you made your partner aware of them?

45. Do you give money each year to charitable or philanthropic causes and, if so, how much?

Tool #4: The Money Awareness Blueprint

By asking yourself the following questions and writing down the answers you will have begun to develop the blueprint you need to formulate specific financial goals. To be well-formed a goal needs to be (1) stated positively, (like "be firm and thin" instead of "lose weight"), (2) within one's control, (3) specific, i.e., quantifiable, (4) put in the context of your whole life, (5) ecological, or healthy (a goal that you must work for fifteen hours a day to achieve, for example, is not ecological).

Desired Outcome Questions (Goals)

1. What specifically do I want?

2. How exactly do I want to be?

3. How will I know I'm achieving my outcome? What will I be doing, thinking, feeling? What will I be seeing and hearing?

4. What is the context of my outcome? What areas of my life (when, where, with whom) will be affected? How fast do I want the changes to take place? How much of my life do I want to be affected, including my health?

5. What are the advantages to achieving my outcome? What are the advantages to not achieving my outcome? What is stopping me from

doing and being what I want? Do I have emotional objections stopping me?

Present State Questions

1. What is going on now? What am I doing? What am I getting?
2. When I think about what is going on now, what do I see, hear, and feel?
3. What am I doing in the different contexts of my life? With family, friends, and career?
4. What are the advantages to remaining in my present state?

What's Needed to Change Questions

1. Do I need another resource?
2. Do I need more information, more, or different skills?
3. Do I need to change? Do I need to change the way I think about things? The way I act in the world?
4. What is the first step? What is my timetable for completing it? What is my timetable for achieving my desired outcome?
5. What can I do in one week toward achieving the desired outcome? What can I do in six weeks? What can I do in one year?

Tool #5: The Money Watch

The Money Watch is a money-awareness exercise that helps women detect their spending patterns and the anxieties and other emotions involved in them. Although this tool is especially useful to help overspenders curb their "appetites," it helps all women learn much about where and how they spend, and why. It is best to go on The Money Watch with a money buddy, or with members of a money-awareness group. Because this simple exercise is surprisingly traumatic, it is important to be able to discuss your feelings about it, and your desires to stop money watching, with an encouraging friend.

Step 1. Get a small notebook and make three columns labeled: (1) Amount Spent; (2) On What; and (3) Feelings.

Step 2. For an entire month write down on what every penny is spent, including rent, candy bars, and credit card charges. Emotions about the expenditure should be noted in the final column. If the feelings are complex, describe them in detail in the back of the notebook.

Step 3. At the end of the month, review all expenditures and the feelings they inspired. Money watchers often find their expenses have dropped in the course of the exercise, and that they have become more conscious of when and why they spend.

Tool #6: Forming a Money-Awareness Group

A money-awareness group is a consciousness-raising group devoted to money problems, in which each member formulates and accomplishes specific financial goals. The group should create a comfortable, accepting, uncritical atmosphere where each member can feel free to discuss her fears and failures, as well as her triumphs with money.

Composition of Group

The group should include women who know each other, as well as some strangers. Choose women who are interested in developing money awareness, who are serious about wanting to change. Limit the size of the group to between seven and ten members.

Contract

The group members should agree to commit themselves to a specific number of meetings (at least six to eight), and to decide how often the group should meet. Groups should meet at least once a month, until the agreed-upon cycle of meetings is completed. At this point, the group can negotiate to begin a new cycle of meetings and admit new members. A new member should not be admitted in the middle of a cycle. Each meeting lasts three hours, with a fifteen-minute coffee break.

Group Rules

Members should promise to keep group confidences. All members should participate equally. To make sure talking time is equally divided, the group may want to set time limits on how long any one person may speak at one time. Members should agree to support and share, and refrain from giving advice, unless the advice is asked for, or is about specific financial matters— for example, how to close on a real-estate purchase.

Group Leader

Each session should have a leader and a timekeeper. These roles should be shared by group members. Because the subject of money is anxiety producing, members may tend to stray off the subject. The leader's job is to bring the discussion back to the topic of money, and to encourage members to share their feelings of discomfort about discussing it. The timekeeper makes certain that the group sticks to its three-hour limit, and that no one member "hogs" the discussion. If the group has set limits on talking time, the timekeeper will be in charge of noting when the limit has been reached.

Format

FIRST SESSION

1st hour

- Clarification and adoption of contract and rules
- Initial go-round (five to ten minutes), with each member introducing herself and describing the role money has played in her life—that is, the money messages she got from her parents, and how they affected her own concept of money in her career, lifestyle, and relationships with men and women. The Questionnaire (Tool #1) and the Family "Money Tree" (Tool #2), which group members might want to complete before the first session, provide a good basis for this discussion.

2nd hour

Open discussion on a selected topic:

- How much money do you need?
- Shopping: the emotions that induce me to spend
- Money and men
- Negotiating in the workplace and at home
- Financial risk-taking
- Sharing financial information on investments, tax planning, etc.
- The Seven Symptoms of Money Phobia, as we have defined them in this book, also provide good discussion topics. Members can be asked to relate their own experience to our definition of money squeamishness, money denial, etc.

For each topic members should also attempt to relate their individual experiences to larger cultural and political issues. This helps remove inappropriate guilt for problems they cannot totally change.

Coffee Break

3rd hour

Formulate personal financial goals and ways to implement them. Each member should select a short-term goal—which she will accomplish before the next meeting of the group—and a long-term goal, which she will accomplish in about six weeks, before the group concludes its meetings. Each member should describe her goals, how she has selected them, and the meaning they have for her. For example, if her short-term goal is to balance her checkbook, she may discuss the feelings that have kept her from doing so in the past, and why she now wants to accomplish this task. If her long-term goal is to make a legal will, she may talk about how this task raises questions about her relationship to important people in her life. The leader should write down each member's goals.

SUBSEQUENT SESSIONS

1st hour

Update on the goals. Each member describes her experience of accomplishing, or failing to accomplish, the short-term goal she selected at the last session.

2nd hour

Open discussion or continue to discuss topics suggested for first session.

Break

3rd hour

Select new goals. If group help is needed to accomplish a goal, the member should ask for and describe it.

LAST SESSION

Members discuss how and why they accomplished, or failed to accomplish, their long-term goals. Evaluation of individual and group progress. What was helpful? What needs to be changed?

Notes

Introduction

1. John Kenneth Galbraith, *Money: Whence It Came, Where It Went* (New York: Bantam, 1976), p. 6.

Chapter 1

1. Gloria Steinem, in *Revolution from Within* (Boston: Little Brown and Company, 1992).
2. Robert Seidenberg, "The Trauma of Eventlessness," in *Psychoanalysis and Women*, ed. Jean Baker Miller, M.D. (Middlesex, England: Penguin Books, 1973).
3. Joyce Jacobsen, *The Economics of Gender* (Cambridge: Blackwell Publ., 1994), introduction.
4. Patricia O'Toole, "Redefining Success," *Working Woman*, November 1993.
5. Pepper Schwartz, "Me Stressed? No, Blessed," *The New York Times*, November 17, 1994.
6. Sam Roberts, "Women's Work: What's New, What Isn't," *The New York Times*, April 27, 1995.
7. Maggie Mahar, "The Truth about Women's Pay," *Working Woman*, April 1993.
8. Patricia O'Toole, "Redefining Success," *Working Woman*, November 1993.
9. Amanda Bennett, "More and More Women Are Staying on the Job Later in Life Than Men," *The Wall Street Journal*, September l, 1994.
10. "The Shower of Gold," in *The Complete Brothers Grimm Fairy Tales*, ed. Lily Owns (New York: Avenal, 1981).
11. Gloria Steinem, "Revaluing Economics," in *Moving Beyond Words* (New York, Simon & Schuster, 1994), p. 204.

Chapter 2

1. The quotations and information in the Doris Day case history are from A.E. Hotchner, *Doris Day: Her Own Story* (New York: William Morrow, 1976). The story has a somewhat happier ending. Eventually Day recovered some of the money Melcher had invested through legal proceedings.

Chapter 3

1. Marilyn Elias, "Short-Changing Girls in Teaching Money Matters," *USA Today*, October 19, 1993. One of the authors of the study we have referred to, Jerome Rabow, also wrote an interesting paper on women and their relationship to money, "Women and Money: Identities in Flux" in *Humanity & Society* (Volume 15, Number 3, 1991).
2. Sigmund Freud, "On Beginning Treatment (Further Recommendations on the Technique of Psychoanalysis)," in *Standard Edition of the Complete Psychological Works of Sigmund Freud*, Vol. 12, ed. and trans. James Strachey (London: Hogarth Press, 1958), p. 131.
3. Nancy Woloch, *Women and the American Experience* (New York: Alfred A. Knopf, 1984), p. 101.
4. A. E. Hotchner, *Doris Day: Her Own Story* (New York: William Morrow, 1976).
5. The quotations in this section are from Terry Garrity with John Garrity, *The Story of "J": The Author of The Sensuous Woman Tells the Bitter Price of Her Crazy Success* (New York: William Morrow, 1984).

Chapter 4

1. We are indebted to Ruth Sidel's portrait of "The New American Dreamers" in *On Her Own: Growing Up in the Shadow of the American Dream* (New York: Viking, 1990) for some aspects of our portrayal of the "New Money Denier."
2. Susan Faludi, *Backlash: The Undeclared War Against American Women* (New York: Crown Publishers, Inc. 1991), p. 25.

Chapter 5

1. Maggie Mahar, "The Truth About Women's Pay," *Working Woman*, April 1993.
2. Sam Roberts, "Women's Work: What's New; What Isn't," *The New York Times*, April 27, 1995.
3. *Ibid.*
4. For the discussion about the twenties and thirties we are indebted to Julie A. Matthaei, *An Economic History of Women in America* (New York: Schocken, 1982) and Carol Hymowitz and Michaele Weissman, *A History of Women in America* (New York: Bantam, 1978).
5. Susan Ware, *Holding Their Own: American Women in the Thirties* (Boston: Twayne, 1982), p. 27.

6. Eleanor Roosevelt, *It's Up to the Women* (New York: Frederic A. Stokes, 1933), p. 148.
7. Joyce Jacobsen, *The Economics of Gender* (Cambridge: Blackwell Publishers, 1994), introduction.
8. *Ibid.*
9. "From Pin Money to Paychecks—Women as the 'New Providers,'" *The Christian Science Monitor*, May 11, 1995.
10. Elizabeth Kolbert, "Judith Resnick," *The New York Times*, February 9, 1986.

Chapter 6

1. Diane Harris, "Solving Marcia Clark's Money Trials," *Working Woman*, May 1995.
2. Caroline Arthur, "15 Million Americans are Shopping Addicts," *American Demographers*, March 1992.
3. Ellen E. Schultz, "Frittered Away: Offered a Lump Sum, Many Retirees Blow It and Risk Their Future," *The Wall Street Journal*, July 31, 1995.
4. Our information about the life of Barbara Hutton comes from C. David Heymann, *Poor Little Rich Girl: The Life and Legend of Barbara Hutton* (New York: Random House, 1983).
5. Gloria Steinem, "The Masculinization of Wealth," in *Moving Beyond Words* (New York: Simon & Schuster, 1994).
6. Hans Christian Andersen, "The Little Match Girl," in *Andersen's Fairy Tales*, trans. Mrs. E. V. Lucas and Mrs. H. B. Paul (New York: Grosset & Dunlap, 1945).

Chapter 7

1. Bonnie Siverd, "Love and Money in the 1980s," *Working Woman*, November 1985.
2. Regina O'Grady Le Shane, "Older Women and Poverty," *Social Work*, September 1990, and "A Woman's Special Dilemma," *U.S. News & World Report*, June 13, 1994.
3. Our information about Hetty Green comes from Arthur H. Lewis, *The Day They Shook the Plum Tree* (New York: Harcourt, Brace & World, 1963).

Chapter 8

1. Susan Faludi, *Backlash: The Undeclared War Against American Women* (New York: Crown Publishers, 1991), p. xiv.
2. Ronni Sandroff, "When Women Make More than Men," *Working Woman*, January 1994.
3. Galbraith is quoted by Gloria Steinem in "Revaluing Economics" in *Moving Beyond Words* (New York: Simon & Schuster, 1994), p. 214.
4. The story of Meredith Vieira is told by Elsa Walsh in *Divided Lives: The Public*

and Private Struggles of 3 Accomplished Women (New York: Simon & Schuster, 1995).

5. Susan Faludi, *Backlash*, p. 364.
6. Maggie Mahar, "The Truth about Women's Pay," *Working Woman*, April 1993.
7. Susan Faludi, *Backlash*, p. xvi.
8. Sam Roberts, "Women's Work: What's New, What Isn't," *The New York Times*, April 27, 1995.
9. The story of Alison Estabrook is told by Elsa Walsh in *Divided Lives: The Public and Private Struggles of 3 Accomplished Women*.
10. Philip Blumstein and Pepper Schwartz, "The Dow Jones Emotionals," *Playboy*, August 1984.
11. Susan Faludi, *Backlash*, p. 25.
12. Laura Mansnerus, "The Divorce Backlash," *Working Woman*, February 1995.

Chapter 9

1. Ronni Sandroff, "When Women Make More Than Men," *Working Woman*, January 1994.
2. Our information about Mae West comes from her autobiography, *Goodness Had Nothing to Do With It* (New York: Belvedere Publishers, 1959) and from George Eells and Stanley Musgrove, *Mae West* (New York: William Morrow, 1982).

Bibliography of Recommended Reading

Historical and Political Background

Faludi, Susan. *Backlash: The Undeclared War Against American Women.* New York: Crown Publishers, Inc., 1991. A controversial and astute analysis of the way feminism has been blamed for social, political, and economic injustices against women.

Friedan, Betty. *The Feminine Mystique.* New York: W. W. Norton, 1963; Revised edition, 1983.

Weitzman, Leonore J. *The Divorce Revolution.* New York: Free Press, 1985. An important discussion of what no-fault divorce means to modern women.

Woloch, Nancy. *Women and the American Experience.* New York: Alfred A. Knopf, 1984. History from the female viewpoint.

Women and Work

Gilman, Charlotte Perkins. *Women and Economics: A Study of the Economic Relations Between Men and Women as a Factor in Sexual Evolution.* Edited by Carl N. Degler. New York: Harper Torchbooks, 1966. While other feminists were fighting for the vote, Perkins Gilman questioned the destiny of women in a modern industrial society. Originally published in 1898.

Jacobsen, Joyce. *The Economics of Gender.* Cambridge: Blackwell, 1994. A clear and multi-dimensional textbook approach to the subject, with graphs, charts, and current studies cited.

Kessler-Harris, Alice. *Out to Work: A History of Wage-Earning Women in the United States.* New York: Oxford University Press, 1982. Explores the transformation of women's work into wage labor and the social repercussion.

Sidel, Ruth. *On Her Own: Growing Up in the Shadow of the American Dream.* New York: Viking, 1990. An expert on women and work issues examines the American Dream in relation to real working conditions for women.

Steinem, Gloria. *Moving Beyond Words.* New York: Simon & Schuster, 1994. The former editor of *Ms.* magazine writes about rich women, economics, and her experience with "Sex, Lies, and Advertising."

Walsh, Elsa. *Divided Lives: The Public and Private Struggles of 3 Accomplished Women.* New York: Simon & Schuster, 1995. A journalist's detailed investigation into the way three career-oriented women balance work with personal priorities.

Working Woman Magazine. The latest news on the pay gap, issues of interest to corporate women, and divorce from the economic standpoint.

Women's Psychological Development

Eicbenbaurn, Luise, and Susie Orbach. *Understanding Women: A Feminist Psychoanalytic Approach.* New York: Basic Books, 1983.

——. *What Do Women Want?: Exploding the Myth of Dependency.* New York: Berkley Books, 1985. Both books provide major insights into women's psychological development from a clinical perspective.

Gilligan, Carol. *In a Different Voice: Psychological Theory and Women's Development.* Cambridge, Mass.: Harvard University Press, 1982. A groundbreaking examination of theories of moral development and how they have distorted the psychological understanding of women.

Miller, Jean Baker, M.D. *Toward a New Psychology of Women.* Boston: Beacon Press, 1976. Examines the psychological consequences of sexual inequality.

Psychoanalysis and Women. Middlesex, England: Penguin Books, 1973. A collection of papers by analysts appraising and defining the psychology of women, including Robert Seidenberg's "The Trauma of Eventlessness."

The Psychology and Sociology of Money

Borneman, Ernest. *The Psychoanalysis of Money.* New York: Urizen Books, 1976. Collection of the major works in the psychoanalytic literature on the origin and nature of money.

Brown, Norman. *Life Against Death: The Psychoanalytic Meaning of History.* New York: Vintage Books, 1959. Chapter "Filthy Lucre" describes money as a manifestation of the death instinct.

Crawford, Tad. *The Secret Life of Money: How Money Can Be Food for the Soul.* New York: Allworth Press, 1996. An exploration of cultural lore.

Simmel, Georg. *The Philosophy of Money.* Boston: Routledge & Kegan Paul, 1982. Provides a wide-ranging discussion of the social, psychological, and philosophical aspects of money.

Mellan, Olivia. *Money Harmony: Resolving Money Conflicts in Your Life and Relationships.* New York: Walker & Co., 1994. Couples and money.

Books That Demystify Money and Its Institutions

Berg, Adriane. *Your Wealth-Building Years.* New York: Newmarket Press, 1987. Excellent primer and reference tool.

Hill, Napoleon. *Think and Grow Rich.* New York: Fawcett Crest, 1960. The granddaddy of how-to books on achieving financial independence through the power of positive thinking and organized planning. Still our favorite.

Milano, Carol. *Hers: The Wise Woman's Guide to Starting a Business on $2000 or Less.* New York: Allworth Press, 1991. A step-by-step approach.

Mundis, Jerrold. *How to Get out of Debt, Stay out of Debt, and Live Prosperously.* New York: Bantam, 1990. The "Bible" of living debt-free.

Patterson, Martha Priddy. *The Working Woman's Guide to Retirement Planning.* Prentice Hall, 1994. The author is Director of Employee Benefits Policy and Analysis for KPMG Peat Marwick's Consulting Practice.

Weinstein, Grace W. *Children and Money: A Parent's Guide.* Rev. ed. New York: Plume, 1985. How to give your children positive money messages.

Books on Money and Spiritual Growth

Cameron, Julia. *The Artist's Way: A Spiritual Path to Higher Creativity.* New York: Jeremy P. Tarcher/Putnam Book, 1992. Money and creativity, including a chapter on "abundance."

Fields, Rick, et al. *Chop Wood, Carry Water; A Guide to Finding Spiritual Fulfillment in Everyday Life.* New York: Jeremy P. Tarcher/Perigee, 1984. A zen approach with a chapter on money.

Literary Works and Biographies with Financial Themes

Brookner, Anita. *Hotel Du Lac.* New York: E. P. Dutton, 1986. "Earning is what you do when you're an adult," says Brookner's heroine, a romance novelist who refuses to marry for money.

Colette. *The Vagabond.* New York: Farrar, Straus & Giroux, 1955. One of the first feminist novels, recounting the adventures of a divorcee who supports herself as a music hall artist and rejects the comforts of marriage to a well-off man who does not respect her independence.

Heilbrun, Carolyn. *Writing a Woman's Life.* New York: Norton, 1988. The feminist author of the Amanda Cross mystery series tells women of the importance of avoiding "closure" and writing their own scripts.

Rose, Phyllis. *Parallel Lives: Five Victorian Marriages.* New York: Alfred A. Knopf, 1984. Famous Victorian marriages and the role money played in them. Includes money mentorship of George Eliot by George Henry Lewes.

Woolf, Virginia. *A Room of One's Own.* New York: Harcourt, Brace, 1929. The time-honored discussion of the importance of financial independence to creative women.

Index

About the Authors

ANNETTE LIEBERMAN, C.S.W., is a psychotherapist in private practice, business consultant, and workshop leader in New York City, who has specialized in working with women for over twenty-five years. Her workshop clients have included the MS. Foundation, American Women's Economic Development Corporation, Actors' Equity, YWCA, and Financial Women of America. She has appeared on dozens of TV and radio shows including "Donahue" and "Oprah," and has been interviewed in the *New York Daily News, Redbook, Cosmopolitan, Harper's Bazaar, Self,* and *Glamour.* She is the creator of M.A.P.–The Money Awareness Program.

VICKI LINDNER is a fiction writer, essayist, and journalist. She is the author of a novel, *Outlaw Games*; her short stories and non-fiction pieces have appeared in many popular and literary magazines from *Cosmopolitan* to the *Kenyon Review.* She is an Associate Professor of English at the University of Wyoming.

Allworth Books

Allworth Press publishes quality books to help individuals and small businesses. Titles include:

The Secret Life of Money: How Money Can Be Food for the Soul
by Tad Crawford (softcover, 6 × 9, 288 pages, $16.95)

Old Money: The Mythology of Wealth in America
by Nelson W. Aldrich, Jr. (softcover, 6 × 9, 336 pages, $16.95)

Hers: A Wise Woman's Guide to Starting a Business on $2000 or Less
by Carol Milano (softcover, 6 × 9, 208 pages, $14.95)

Smart Maneuvers: Taking Control of Your Career and Personal Success in the Information Age by Carl W. Battle (softcover, 6 × 9, 224 pages, $12.95)

Legal-Wise: Self-Help Forms for Everyone by Carl W. Battle
(softcover, 8$^1/_2$ × 11, 208 pages, $16.95)

Senior Counsel: Legal and Financial Strategies for Age 50 and Beyond
by Carl W. Battle (softcover, 6$^3/_4$ × 10, 256 pages, $16.95)

Retire Smart by David and Virginia Cleary
(softcover, 6 × 9, 224 pages, $12.95)

The Family Legal Companion by Thomas Hauser
(softcover, 6 × 9, 256 pages, $16.95)

Your Living Trust and Estate Plan by Harvey J. Platt
(softcover, 6 × 9, 256 pages, $14.95)

Immigration Questions and Answers by Carl Baldwin
(softcover, 6 × 9, 176 pages, $14.95)

The Writer's Legal Guide by Tad Crawford and Tony Lyons
(softcover, 6 × 9, 304 pages, $19.95)

The Business of Being and Artist, Revised Edition by Daniel Grant
(softcover, 6 × 9, 272 pages, $18.95)

Please write to request our free catalog. If you wish to order a book, send your check or money order to Allworth Press, 10 East 23rd Street, Suite 400, New York, NY 10010. Include $5 for shipping and handling for the first book ordered and $1 for each additional book. Ten dollars plus $1 for each additional book if ordering from Canada. New York State residents must add sales tax.

If you wish to see our catalog on the World Wide Web, you can find us at Millennium Production's Art and Technology Web site:
http://www.arts-online.com/allworth/home.html
or at http://www.interport.net/~allworth